OPEN MARRIAGE
A New Life Style for Couples

OPEN

A New Life Style

MARRIAGE

for Couples

by Nena O'Neill & George O'Neill

M. Evans and Company, Inc., New York

To each other

ISBN: 978-0-87131-438-3
ISBN 0-87131-438-X Paperbound
Library of Congress Catalog Card Number: 75–164550

M. Evans and Company, Inc.
216 East 49 Street
New York, New York 10017

Design by Paula Wiener

Manufactured in the United States of America

9 8 7

Contents

Foreword

Open Marriage was a runaway best-seller in 1972 because it developed a refreshing, unique perspective on the intimate potential of an egalitarian partnership. The book stayed in print for twelve years and was translated into fourteen languages because it offered reasonable hope for a more sensitive, intimate, and exciting view of marriage.

Nena and George O'Neill interviewed couples and reflected on their reservoir of knowledge about intimate relationships from a perspective that used their collective awareness of psychology, anthropology, and sociology. The result is a prophetic conceptualization of what egalitarian, growth-oriented marriage can be in spite of our highly competitive, work-obsessed society.

Not since Bertrand Russell's *Marriage and Morals* in 1929 has there been such an original treatise on the changing nature of modern marriage. Studies come and go, but this qualitative analysis of the role definitions and communication patterns that we can learn to integrate in our own partnerships represents a new view of marriage. By complementing and extending beyond Judge Ben Lindsay and Ernest Burgess's companionate marriage theories and by incorporating "vital marriage" as researched by John Cuber and Peggy Harroff, the O'Neills have taken a giant step toward what it means to be both modern and married. Open marriage is contrasted with the prison image of closed marriage—where the goal is to fit people prescribed role patterns in the name of "love."

Not everyone is suited to an open marriage. The O'Neills do not force us into their view of marriage. But it is to their credit that the core of their book has increasingly come to define marriage. Specifically, the individual strengths of partners, the freedom and the privacy each needs to continue to grow as a unique person, the honesty and open communication that are required for deepening intimacy and meaningful commitment without destructive jealousy, and the excitement of living in the present are often-held goals in both new and more seasoned marriages.

Open Marriage has been misinterpreted and blamed as an unqualified license to engage in free sex by those who have failed to read it carefully. To their credit, the O'Neills were precise and balanced about the possibility of mutually agreeing to sex with others. The publication of *Open Marriage* has ushered in an age where illicit affairs and prudish "arrangements" are no longer the only choices for those desiring freedom with honesty and responsibility. The O'Neills' synergistic model is based on mutually agreed-upon guidelines which ensure that personal freedom leads to personal and relational growth and that intimate friendships with others are equally responsible, sensitive, and honest.

An open marriage is more than armchair theory. Today's middle class has developed a genre of marriage that is companionate—open in some areas and closed in others. Thus, most marriages are not either entirely open or entirely closed, but usually include a blend of guidelines that are constantly subject to change. The O'Neills have identified the processual nature of modern marriage, leaving the static, institutional view to those who still wish a traditional marriage with a husband and father who dominates his wife and children.

All of this is not to say that everyone with an open marriage has an open agreement to sex with others. But sexually open marriages are far from figments of our imaginations. A recent national survey found that 15 percent of a mostly upper-middle-class sample of married couples (with both spouses agreeing) reported they had a sexually open marriage.

Nena and George O'Neill's book has profoundly and irrevocably affected our culture. There can be no turning back to a no-choice view of traditional marriage. *Open Marriage* is one of the first watershed events that has led to better communication and commitment based on real choice, resulting in more creative partnerships. The book has both reflected and affected modern marriage. It has been highly influential with the young, who are now approaching or are in the midst of middle age.

The women's movement has supported and been supported by *Open Marriage*. The term *open marriage* is now in major dictionaries, many social scientists do research about various aspects of open marriage, and no comprehensive marriage and family textbook can afford to leave out a full discussion of open relationships.

This reissuing of *Open Marriage* will enhance the social visionary status of Nena and George O'Neill, and it will reemphasize the importance of their synergistic view of love and marriage. George O'Neill would be very proud of the immense staying power of *Open Marriage*. His untimely death a few years ago made many of us more aware of the incredible contribution of his collaborative effort with Nena O'Neill. George's insights live on in this new edition, and

Nena O'Neill can be counted on to continue to develop original insights about egalitarian partnerships.

Bertrand Russell would have enjoyed *Open Marriage*. May laypeople and scholars continue to profit from the many insights in this ground-breaking book.

January 1984

ROGER W. LIBBY, PH.D.
Center for the Family
University of Massachusetts
Amherst, Massachusetts

Update

During the ferment of the sixties, all segments of society experienced an awareness of new possibilities. *Open* was the catchword of the day: open society, open classroom, open systems, open climate. It is not difficult to understand why George and I called our marriage model an open marriage. The juxtaposition of such apparently contradictory terms was both intriguing and disturbing, and yet perfectly represented our concept.

We wanted to jar people into a recognition that marriage did not have to be a monolithic structure but could be adapted to changing needs by the persons involved in it. In giving a name to the type of relationship we saw evolving, we hardly anticipated the enormous impact and instant misinterpretation of the term. It is helpful at this point to distinguish between the terms *open marriage* and *sexually open marriage* (SOM). Open marriage as we conceived it refers specifically to the central concept and main content of the book, describing a relationship of commitment and equality where each partner's individual growth contributes synergically to the marriage bond. SOM refers specifically and only to the explicit agreement, entirely optional, that each partner can have a separate relationship outside the marriage, which might, under certain conditions, include sex.

What has happened to open marriage in the twelve years since publication? Almost everything that we suggested as guidelines for growth in marriage has become an accepted and desired expectation for contemporary middle- and upper-class marriage: companionship, heightened intimacy, effective communication, shared roles, equality, and trust and privacy are all desired qualities. The one notable exception is the sexually open aspect. Today, a majority of couples still prefer sexual exclusivity. If they fall short of this ideal, and over one-half of marrieds do, they still prefer the hidden affair to any alternative open arrangement.

Considering the major impact the concept of open marriage has had, it is ironic that the term *open marriage* has become a household word synonymous with a marriage of noncommitment. It has become a generic term meaning exactly the opposite of what the whole book is about—a lifestyle of intimacy and commitment designed to keep couples together.

This misinterpretation is not surprising in light of the initial reaction to the book: astonishment, prurient interest, relief, and moral indignation not only about the equality of roles and "free" sex but also about the suggestion that couples, and especially the wife, could make choices for themselves. Like a Rorschach test, *Open Marriage* mirrored the reader's perceptions, to say nothing of the perceptions of those who did not read it but felt they knew what it was all about anyway. In particular the concept was threatening to many.

The major reaction to the book, however, was excitement

and revelation. In large part the book's popularity was due
to the fact that the concept confirmed people's emerging
beliefs and hopes for marriage. The typical response was
"You've put into words exactly what I've been thinking."
Since it spoke to a felt need, the book gave people the courage to break with tradition and try new behaviors in marriage.

The major benefit of open marriage was to give individuals new insights about partnership and a different way of
looking at marriage. *Open Marriage* provided a practical
platform for liberation and equality in marriage, and along
with the pioneering foundation work of the women's movement and the libertarian climate it radically altered our
thinking about husband and wife roles. As one woman said,
it gave her the "freedom and courage to break with tradition and carry out what I have been thinking of doing anyway." For those who were already experimenting with open
relationships (nonsexual as well as sexual) before we gave
this relationship a name, open marriage confirmed their con-
victions and provided a philosophical base for their actions.

In light of these changes it is revealing to look at some of
the suggestions we made twelve years ago. Dual-career marriages are now commonplace; child care is shared. The fact
that most working wives still do most of the housework
attests to the tenacity of role patterns, but on the other hand
women now share more fully in decision making and money
management. Younger couples are more honest and open
with each other. There is a definite trend toward couples
taking separate vacations and attending some social events
alone and others with friends of either sex. More couples
have long-distance and part-time marriages. We strongly
argued against too much togetherness, but today with both
partners working the problem is exactly the reverse: how
do we get *any* time together? As anything other than a clari-
fying device, a written contract has not won wide acceptance. A child is no longer a necessary adjunct to marriage.
Couples no longer lean so heavily on each other, nor do they

expect all of their needs to be fulfilled within the marriage. Sexual exclusivity is now a choice instead of an enforced rule.

The former popularity of sexually open marriage was due to a particular confluence of circumstances and the open climate of the times. We were on the verge of a new era, and SOM was used as a bridge between the old and the new. The big new freedom was sex, and since divorce was not yet the common solution for troubled relationships, open marriage with its implied freedoms yet promise of stability seemed to trigger the possibility of married couples having it all. In the midst of sexual and social change, people latched on to SOM to allay their fears of change. In an oddly beneficial way, the contemplation of SOM siphoned off anxiety, stalled off the unknown, and helped many during this transition period. A common response from those who, knowing themselves well, rejected SOM, was, "I can understand it and even want it intellectually, but emotionally I just can't handle it."

How did some people handle it? A few persons used SOM to justify what they were already doing, others to be in vogue or simply to satisfy curiosity. Many couples tried it in an unsuccessful attempt to save already failing marriages. Others used it to avoid facing problems in their relationship. Some were deliberately experimenting. For the majority, SOM became a time-limited phase in their marriage. Afterward they returned to sexual exclusivity, either satisfied that SOM was not for them or prepared to finally deal with their marital problems. For a very few, SOM is still a permanent life-style; for others, it is a recurring phase in their married lives. Some newly marrieds, fiercely determined to put principles into practice, found SOM difficult because they had not yet had time to form a sufficiently strong primary bond.

For the majority it proved neither a panacea nor a viable life-style. Jealousy and honesty proved to be the most formidable impediments, and so habit and cultural conditioning won out over intellectual theory and philosophy. Couples did not know how to deal with jealousy or when and how to communicate honestly with sensitivity. Jealousy, a most tenacious and deep-seated emotion, deserved more attention than we gave it in the book. Far from eradicating it, we are only beginning to understand its function and know how to diminish it. These ordinary jealousies were more than most couples cared to experience. In addition, the lack of social supports and the fundamental complexities of this type of relationship discouraged many couples. And so, finally, "Better an affair," they said, most preferring not to know about extramarital sex if it occurred.

Nevertheless, research has found that those who were committed to sexually open marriage cited numerous benefits, such as reduced role-playing, better marital sex and communication, higher self-esteem, and greater fulfillment of personal needs. Despite the complications and difficulties, new insights and values emerged in their relationships. All of these trials with sexual freedom were not easy. So the strong motivations that impelled couples, suited and unsuited by temperament, to risk new behavior in such an incendiary and vulnerable area should be taken into account.

In sharp contrast to a decade ago, numerous contributing factors can be cited for sexually open marriage's current lack of popularity. First, the experimental climate of the humanistic movement has given way to economic concerns. Ambition has replaced a preoccupation with self and personal growth. There seems to be more concern over economic survival than intimate relationships. Second, after an era of unprecedented attention to matters sexual, sex has finally settled down to a more balanced position in our relationships. Third, prior to the sixties, premarital sex was forbidden; so for some people, anything construed as license for sexual variety after marriage seemed inviting. With premarital sex now an accepted experience and with innumerable occasions for different sexual partners in between divorce and remarriage, sexual variety is more commonplace and no longer a novelty. Fourth, in the old days women were expected to accept the traditional sexual double standard in marriage. Today women command a more powerful position in marriage. A woman can now support herself economically, walk out of a double-standard marriage, have her own affair too, or insist that the topic of extramarital sex be discussed openly and dealt with. Fifth, when SOM was popular, being single was not yet a desired state. One was expected to marry and have one sexual partner for life. Today being single is an accepted life-style, along with whatever sexual freedom or commitment the person wishes to practice.

While it may no longer be popular, sexually open marriage is still an option today. A small percentage of couples have always had this type of relationship in the past and will continue to do so, no matter what the prevailing pattern may be. This year, a major study of over three thousand couples found fifteen percent of the sample claiming to have a sexually open marriage, a much higher percentage than most might have expected, even for this largely middle-class sample, and far beyond estimates for the general population. No statistics exist for how many couples in our society have tried SOM or still have one.

What has happened to those couples who were sexually open? Were their marriages any different from sexually exclusive ones? The twelve research studies carried out so far show few appreciable differences. A recently completed longitudinal study found no difference in the rate of separation or divorce between those in an SOM and those in a sexually exclusive marriage. The studies show a preponderance of firstborns involved, neither more nor less neuroticism, and the same degree of marital adjustment as sexually exclusives on measures of satisfaction, cohesion, consensus and affectional expression. The most intriguing finding suggests some difference does exist in the personality configuration of those involved in SOM. These individuals tended to be risk takers, nonconformist, creative, imaginative, future-oriented, stimulated by complexity, and socially innovative. Thus, a certain personality type seems to be attracted to

SOM and better able to manage this complex life-style. Other topics of research included defining the ground rules for reducing potential threats to the marriage and psychotherapists' attitudes toward SOM clients. Only one study explored nonsexual aspects of an open marriage and developed a method for measuring spousal openness and its relationship to marital satisfaction. Much more data needs to be collected, and I am hopeful that the future will bring more sensitive research designs to test the validity of specific aspects of our concept. The whole issue of nonexclusivity and the degree and variety of patterns couples are using today needs more attention and research.

Although our cultural ideal is still sexual exclusivity, the fact is that extramarital sex happens, and in ever-increasing numbers. We presented sexually open marriage as a civilized, aboveboard way of dealing with it. Perhaps in the future, given certain conditions, some less difficult way of dealing with this universal cultural behavior will emerge as viable and popular. In the meantime, extramarital sex (hidden or tacitly accepted) and frequent divorce appear to be the most common pattern.

It would be an error to assume that this change means we have returned to conservatism in marriage. Cultural change is not linear but a rising spiral. Some old items are dropped, a few new ones assimilated, and some are transformed, always on a different level. While this transition is characterized by ambivalence and confusion between men and women over commitment, sexual choices, and future goals, we should not underestimate the real advances. Equality and the steadily increasing degree of openness between partners quietly move forward, and are sometimes even taken for granted. A variety of options can be chosen, and through information and research we understand more of the chemistry and artistry of caring relationships between men and women. We may not yet know how to use this information but it is there.

In every marriage there are pairs of conflicting and quite

paradoxical needs: security and freedom, stability and excitement, dependence and independence, attachment and autonomy. George and I hoped our model would provide a way of living with this paradox and benefiting from it in a truly synergistic way. By loving, supporting, and sharing each other's growth, couples can discover each other anew while nurturing the intimate bond that is so necessary to a long-term and joyful married life.

That couples can now enjoy many varieties of marital experience—including a traditional one—and can adapt their own marriage rules to their changing needs is the best testament I could have wished for the endurance of an equal and open marriage as we first envisioned it.

January 1984

NENA O'NEILL

Preface and Acknowledgments

Without a belief in man's potential, creativity, curiosity, and an optimistic outlook on the future of marriage, we would not have been interested in researching the topic and could not have written this book. Our observations on how changing conditions in our society were affecting marriage, and our abiding interest in people and the forces that shape human behavior provided the main impetus for our research.

In 1967 we began to explore contemporary marriage and the innovations and new life styles people were creating in urban and suburban middle-class settings. We talked to people living together in a variety of arrangements from non-marriage through group marriage. As our research progressed we found that people were seeking alternatives not only because they were dissatisfied with traditional marriage but because they needed room to grow. We began to synthesize and delineate those qualities and conditions that seemed most necessary for growth for a man and woman living together in today's world. In writing a preliminary draft on the subject in 1968, we defined such a relationship as *open marriage.*

Our book would not be complete without mention of those individuals whose work and thinking have influenced us in many ways: the anthropologist, Dr. Ruth Benedict, and the psychologist, Dr. Abraham Maslow, whose pioneering work in their respective fields has deepened our perspective; the body of researchers in the field of humanistic psychology who have developed valuable insights and innovative methods for better human relations; and Dr. David Kahn, clinical psychologist and friend, who first introduced us to this third force in psychology.

More immediately, we are especially indebted to John Malone, our project editor, whose skills, cooperation, endless patience, understanding and friendship saw us through the challenge, excitement and labor of completing this book. We appreciate the encouragement of our editor, Herb Katz, and our agent, Mary Yost, who believed in us and our concept. We extend a special thanks to Edward Brecher, writer and friend, whose help in numerous ways throughout the past years has been important to us; and to the following persons who have been helpful in one way or another, perhaps in ways they themselves may not even recognize: Michael and Anne O'Neill, Brian O'Neill, Robert C. Snyder, Elaine Kashins, René Champion, Hertha Champion, Carmen Cook de Leonard, Roz Heller, Helen Anderson, Harry A. Royson, Betty and Bill Dick, Ellie Bragar, Martin and Jan James and many who must go unnamed.

And, finally, we owe a special debt of gratitude to the many people we interviewed and questioned endlessly, who gave of their time, energy and trust along with their enthusiasm, and who so willingly opened up their lives and hearts to us, revealing their hopes, dreams and the sometimes painful realities that structured their lives.

Two consistent threads ran through all our interviews: one was the desire for freedom, and the other, a longing for relatedness to another—a search for a deeply personal and mutual commitment in a relationship that would not bind or constrict growth. We hope that the concept of open marriage will help couples to realize that there *can* be both relatedness and freedom in marriage, and that freedom, with the growth and responsibility it entails, can be the basis for intimacy and love.

August, 1971

NENA O'NEILL
GEORGE O'NEILL

1 Why Save Marriage at All?

The Case against It

"Marriage: a community consisting of a master, a mistress, and two slaves, making in all, two." This sardonic definition of marriage was made by Ambrose Bierce around the turn of the century. Acid commentaries on marriage are nothing new. Wits have been founding their reputations upon them for centuries. But in the last two decades, this most venerable of human institutions has been on the receiving end of an increasing number of hard knocks, and not just from literary types exercising their professional scorn. The shortcomings of marriage are now being spelled out by an ever-growing legion of the divorced, the unhappily married, and young people who, in the somber light of their elders' bitter experiences, have become exceedingly wary about making any commitment to such a disaster themselves. What's more, many in the ranks of the disillusioned not only rail against marriage but would go further and deny its necessity. The already divorced often swear never to marry again, the unhappily married search despairingly for companionship outside the bondage of their union, and the young simply throw their toothbrushes together and put both names on the mailbox. An additional multitude of married couples give up in boredom and succumb to a marriage of mere convenience and a life style of alienation.

Those who doubt the necessity of marriage do have some powerful arguments on their side. Married bliss now seems a mirage in the distance, ever more elusive, receding further and further beyond our grasp. Nearly one in three marriages ends in divorce, and some researchers contend that at least 75 percent of our marriages are ailing. Many people, faced with such statistics, begin to wonder why they should take a chance themselves. Why, in a world of instant and carefree sex, liberalized moral codes and situational ethics, get married at all? Why not just live together, or—as some suggest—together with many?

Young people experiment with group marriage, married couples swap partners for the evening, and movie stars frankly discuss their once secret liaisons in public interviews. There are communes, in all shapes and sizes, utopian and utilitarian, some permitting free sex, others attempting to preserve monogamy even if not marriage. Young women, increasingly dissatisfied with marital constrictions, refuse to marry at all. Some, as bachelor mothers, courageously choose to raise their young alone. In fact, you can now adopt children even if you've never been married; your maiden Aunt Mamie, who long ago made the choice to remain single, can nevertheless give a child a loving home.

Others are looking for the answer in polygamy. The threesome is currently in as a living arrangement. Even those who ostensibly prefer monogamy actually practice serial—

or sequential—monogamy through constant divorce and re-marriage—which can give you over the years as many wives (or husbands) as a polygamist. An increasing number of men and women refuse to legalize any union whatsoever and choose to live in a variety of non-marriage arrangements. The only people, indeed, for whom the old-fashioned marriage seems to hold a real mystique are homosexuals, who for the first time are able to find clergymen willing to marry two partners of the same sex.

Psychologists and sociologists, confronted by these many manifestations of a disintegrating institution, have suggested numerous dramatic and imaginative—if not always practical—alternatives to traditional marriage. Robert Rimmer suggests that two couples with their children join together in a corporate marriage, pooling all their resources, sexual, emotional and economic, in a kind of double-the-pleasure togetherness. Swedish experiments have the husbands staying home to mind the baby while the wife goes out to stalk the prey and bring home the bacon. Extended family networks have been proposed, as well as state and day care nurseries for raising children; the first would provide group support and companionship and spread the responsibility for child-rearing, the second would free mothers (and fathers) from the rigors of daily child care. There are suggestions for marriage in stages, according to age and maturity, moving from childlessness to child-bearing. Others go further and suggest compulsory birth control and stiff prerequisites for obtaining a marriage license. Even term contracts in marriage, lasting anywhere from five to twenty years with options for renewal, have been proposed.

The permutations, in fact, are almost endless and have the eventual effect of creating general confusion. Obviously a given proposal might enhance the relationship of one couple, but prove destructive to another. Faced with such a contradictory array of hypothetical solutions, many people might feel that marriage as we know it now at least provides the assurance of the known. But can we find other virtues in marriage aside from the fact that most alternatives seem even chancier? Is marriage in fact worth preserving?

Shall I Wear My Mother's Wedding Dress?

First, of course, there's the matter of tradition. Men and women have been getting married since the dawn of history, and even the particular traditions of the Judeo-Christian marriage go back for many centuries. Granted that many of the customs associated with Western marriage have already disappeared and that orange blossoms and Lohengrin can be expected to follow the dowry and the hope chest into oblivion, the tradition of marriage permeates our culture too thoroughly for its hold to be diminished much by the loss of a few external trappings. Daughter Judy may want to get married in mauve bluejeans instead of her mother's wedding dress, but she does want to get married. After all, that's what you do in life, isn't it, unless you're a loser?

Still, Judy is a conventional girl, even in jeans. But there are many unconventional girls around, to whom the fact that everybody gets married is the best reason in the world *not* to do it themselves. In a time in which the only constant is change, tradition in and of itself is a bankrupt argument for the preservation of anything. Customs and conventions are being impatiently discarded like the superfluous plastic wrappings we rip off packages. Our young adults in particular resist the arguments of tradition. "Tradition, perdition, that's what I think of marriage," said the bearded cab driver/writer talking to us about his current relationship with Janey, a dancer. "Do you think that a piece of paper will make us feel any better? We live and love and I don't need any rules to tell us how to do it. *If* I ever get married, I want to know where my head is at first, and meantime Janey and I are trying it out for size."

Such couples, by living together, are exercising their right to a full sex life and meaningful relationship without marriage and without children. Even when children are involved, however, tradition is losing ground. A film star is photographed with her lovely child born out of wedlock. In an accompanying article, she says, "A child brings you back to natural and simple things . . . and I don't care about marriage. I'm not for or against it, I just don't care about it. It's not necessary anymore." This may be shocking to some, but clearly the majority of the public, although they may not actively approve, don't care enough to stay away from an actress' movies because she lives or talks like that. Not anymore.

But tradition in the abstract is easier to disregard than it is in the form of constant and insidious social pressure. Mother may not give a damn what Mia Farrow or Vanessa Redgrave gets up to, but when it comes to her own daughter, that's a little different. On a visit to New York, Uncle Jason takes his twenty-seven-year-old niece Sally out to dinner and, cued by Sally's mother back in Cincinnati, asks, "So why aren't you married already?" Sally, who is too fond of Uncle Jason to be angry, blushes instead and says, "I guess I just haven't found the right guy." But in fact she has, and has been living with him for two years. The telephone number she gives her parents is that of a girl friend, who pretends that Sally lives with her. Some day, of course, Mother and Dad will come to New York and will want to see where she lives, but she'll cross that bridge when she comes to it.

The unmarried man gets it, too, with a slightly different slant. A footloose bachelor of forty finds himself the object of suspicious inquiry. "Did you say you were *never* married?" asks the new business acquaintance at lunch, and the bachelor finds himself forced to comment, not too soon but before lunch is over, on the nice pair of legs on the waitress.

Then there are the more subtle, institutionalized pressures—all those advertisements for the good life (which simply assume you're married), the fantasies of the television situation comedies (even they seem to have found out something's wrong, though, and have started making widows and widowers of their central characters), and the parties you don't get invited to any more as your friends get married and you remain single (unless of course Jack and Jill have a little matchmaking in mind). America is organized around the couple, from the barbecue pit to the ocean cruise, and if you won't join you'd better be prepared to fight. Unfortunately (and to their inevitable regret) many people frantically scrounge around for any partner who will have them and rush into marriage just to acquire that badge of identification: Us—A Couple.

In reaction, singles have begun throwing up bastions of their own. The cooperative apartment building for singles only and the swinging vacation tour of the West Indies with the Sun Club are ways of saying to the married couples, "You can have your blessed unions, we'll take the fun." It is the married couples themselves, of course, who provide the singles with the best possible reason for *not* getting married—they get divorced, in ever-increasing numbers. The bitterness of the under-thirty woman with two children and an ex-husband, the fury of that husband as he signs the alimony check, are powerful arguments against getting married in the first place, and certainly against getting married again.

The cost of divorce, both emotionally and financially, can be devastating. Michael, a middle-aged editor, ranted to us about his alimony payments. "They won't get me again! I can just manage to keep that Sword of Damocles off my neck. One alimony is enough, how can I afford another?" This man's divorce was amicable, but the alimony payments are heavy. Now, for more than a year he has been settled into a relationship with a young woman under thirty. He speaks warmly of her: "My relationship with Maria is solider and tighter than my marriage ever was. Why? Because every morning when I wake up and look at her lying there next to me, I know she totally wants to be there, not because of some ink on a piece of paper. This time I won't let that document get between me and a good relationship."

Yet that lack of ink causes other problems. He notes with compassion his companion's desire for some kind of status, some kind of designation that will convey to the larger world the essence of their relationship. But we have no acceptable word (even "lover" retains overtones of the illicit) for a man or woman in a relationship not sanctified by marriage. The lack of such a word to give her a feeling of identity and place is a recurring unhappiness for the young woman, as is the inevitable if subtle disapproval of her parents. "Why don't you settle down, Maria?" they say, meaning, actually, "Why don't you dump this man, he's never going to marry you."

And so we are brought full circle, back to the pressure of convention. That pressure can be denied, unquestionably, but it takes real determination to carry it off. If the marriage statistics are any guide, there aren't all that many determined people around. In an era in which the institution of marriage is being criticized as never before, more and more people are, paradoxically, getting married. More of them are getting divorced, too, but the majority of these remarry. What is this urge to form couples within a legalized union? There must be more than just social pressure and historical tradition at work.

Man and Structure

One of the simplest explanations for the persistence of marriage, in spite of the widespread disillusionment with the institution as it stands, lies in man's innate need for structure. Structure and form are the essence of all existence and the molders of all creativity. Structure is also necessary to the convenience of living and to the ordering of our experience out of chaos into meaningful units. Structure is knowing that traffic lights go on and off, that night follows day, that spring follows winter and that the rent is due at the end of the month. Addresses and adding machines, bills and banks, clocks and calendars—the list of structural supports for modern life is endless. And as society becomes more complex, as the population continues to grow, more and more—and different—structural forms become necessary.

Institutions are merely our way of formalizing some of the structures underlying human behavior. The institutions of marriage and the family, no matter how diverse in style and configuration they may be, are fundamental to every society. Each marriage institution operates within a specific cultural context of interlocking, interdependent institutions of other kinds—kinship, social, political and economic. This close intermeshing of institutions means that as our society is impelled toward change, each institution will tend to readjust or realign itself in conjunction with the others. Marriage, because of its very personal nature, has been slower to adapt itself to change than other institutions; but it, too, must and will change.

The patriarchal marriage system of the Judeo-Christian tradition, based on an agrarian economy, is simply outmoded today. In the old days back on the farm, Ma and Pa literally pulled the yoke together, forming a cooperative unit for survival. The economic and psychological interdependence of this marital unit occurred in a setting where social sanctions and the entire matrix of society encouraged it to perpetuate itself. Marriage structure matched marriage function. But times have changed.

We live today in a high-speed technological world that knows only flux and change, and it is obvious that what served as a marriage format in the past is no longer adequate to the task. New and complex life styles call for a new marriage format. Conditioned to obsolescence, we may be tempted to pitch marriage out altogether. But patriarchal marriage is just *one* particular format among many alternative formats—or ways of fulfilling an underlying structural impulse.

That we need some structure in our chaotic times should be as obvious as the fact that our old marriage style no longer works. Can the old one be changed? How much of the accumulated tradition can be stripped away? What, obscured beneath the tangled cultural debris of centuries, *is* the basic ingredient of marriage?

The One-to-One Relationship

Marriage didn't just happen. It was created by man to serve his needs. But where and how did it begin? Much as some males might like to believe it, the cartoon of the cave man clobbering his bride and dragging her off by the hair to his cave is not the way marriage began. Other romantic armchair enthusiasts may speculate that man started out in loosely knit bands, promiscuously sharing sex, mates and children along with their grubs and clubs. But while this view of grab-bag communal living is intriguing, contemporary anthropologists find no evidence to support these ideas advanced by early anthropological and philosophical theorists. Even our closest relatives among the primates do not live in promiscuous bands—they may be more eclectic in their sexual life than we like to think we are, but they too follow certain mating patterns.

We simply do not know what man's first patterns in marriage were, even though Desmond Morris in *The Naked Ape* speculates that the pair-bond was the fundamental unit for man in his early stages of human development. But this is only a theory, and as human history and anthropological research show us, man's bonding pattern in marriage has been amazingly diverse, ranging from monogamy through polygamy and group marriage. But even in those societies where other forms of marriage are preferred, monogamy also exists—it is a universal in all societies throughout the world. This type of union of man and woman may not be sexually exclusive or last for a lifetime, but its presence everywhere supports the fact that the one-to-one relationship is a basic human pattern. Some anthropologists, such as Bronislaw Malinowski, have argued that even where marriages are plural, they are composed of a series of individual arrangements or one-to-one relationships.

The one-to-one relationship, whether it is realized through monogamy or within other forms of marriage, fulfills man's profoundly human needs—those developmental and psychological needs for intimacy, trust, affection, affiliation and the validation of experience. It need not be permanent, exclusive or dependent, but the relationship of two people to each other allows a closeness and psychological intimacy that no other kind of relationship offers.

Playing with the Full Deck

Theoretically, marriage should not be necessary to have a full one-to-one relationship. You should not even need marriage to legitimize a child, for that matter. In a world of true human understanding, a child should be legitimate just because he is born. All the requirements for succoring the young—maternal care, assuring interdependency and cooperation with others, as well as psychological intimacy—can theoretically be met without legal marriage. The love and companionship existing between a couple does not need a piece of paper, a marriage document, to make it work, to assure its existence or its perpetuation. Or does it?

Commitment to another cannot be legislated. True commitment comes from within, not from outside a relationship. The signing of a contract cannot guarantee you another's commitment in the emotional sense; why should the absence of such a contract mean a lack of commitment? It shouldn't, of course. But unfortunately, it often does, often enough to make even those who are sure of their partner's commitment think twice. We would not need the marriage contract in actuality if all of us had reached a stage of human development that assured mutual responsibility and trust between all people. Unfortunately, this utopian brotherhood is far short of achievement. In our all too real world, the ultimate step in the establishment of trust between man and woman is still the marriage contract. With this final step each says to the other: here's my deck of cards, the full deck, all of them open on the table, nothing held back.

In regard to this ultimate commitment, a perturbed thirty-five-year-old divorcée said to us, "I don't know where I stand. Marriage for me was too confining, and I don't know if I can make the commitment again, marriage has such a final, sealing sound." She was thoughtful for a moment. "Facing the legal commitment is a much braver thing to do—it is not, after all, the end of the world to break up a marriage if it doesn't work. For after all, in a legal commitment, once having made it, you move faster. Finally, I suppose, I will say yes to some one person, yes, I will build my life with you. At least with legal marriage you have tried to achieve a *total*. If you don't try, all you will have is little bits and pieces."

Those who prefer to form long-term extralegal arrangements or living-in relationships, who refuse to legalize a marriage, are in actuality not ready for this commitment to another. For one of many possible reasons—and our present concept of marriage is largely to blame—they are unwilling to test out their commitment. Given the existing marriage format, which *is* untenable, *is* antiquated, *is* obsolete, it is difficult to chide them for their unwillingness. The old marriage contract *is* unrealistic and its archaic clauses demand unreasonable commitments. But marriage should not be discarded like a disposable tissue. The psychological and structural imperatives for marriage are strong. The real task is to strip marriage of its antiquated ideals and romantic tinsel and find ways to make it truly contemporary, in line with other changes that have taken place in our society.

Now Is Not Then

In the long run it may be that marriage will die out com pletely. Some futurists predict, seriously, a world out of *Amazing Stories,* dominated by females, with men playing the part of drones, a kind of ultimate revenge by Women's Liberation. Less unsettling to twentieth-century males is the concept of loose informal tribes supplanting our nuclear family and providing a kind of support akin to the extended family structure once practiced by some American Indian cultures. From tribes we could merge into one total unifamily. Or we could have, heaven forbid, some stainless-steel biochemical future in which marriage is only a memory and babies are produced in test tubes according to the coded instructions of computers.

But these developments are a long way ahead of us. We live in the here and now. And man is finding in this world of rapid and fluctuating change that he must turn increasingly inward to his personal relationships to supply him with meaning for his life. Our needs for affiliation cloak a more profound need. Only through knowing another in significant and authentic dimensions can we love, explore the potential of ourselves and others, and fight off the alienation of our time. And marriage, in some form or another, still provides the only framework in which people can find the stability in which to experience the full intimacy of a one-to-one relationship. Strikingly reaffirming this need for commitment are the statements of a now happily married woman who until thirty-four had resisted marriage and by her own admission suffered great anxiety and anguish at getting married. Evelyn said, "Without marrying I had lots of intimate long-term relationships, but I never really committed myself. Now I find after marriage that I couldn't have accomplished growth any other way. There is growth in marriage in terms of taking on something, and casting something off. Growth is a process, something you have to enter into. What was it I left behind?" she asked. "What did I cast off? I suppose I left behind my own shell, and took on the ability to open up myself. That is commitment, to completely open up to another." Only through finally committing ourselves to a relationship can we really find out about ourselves or our capacity to grow.

Every indication suggests that, in the here and now, marriage is still the choice of the majority for formalizing our most intimate one-to-one relationships and achieving growth through commitment, and that it probably will remain so for several generations. Rather than wishing marriage off into beanstalk land, as some people would apparently like to do, our efforts should be directed toward realistic changes in the institution. How can we individualize the institution of marriage so that each couple can adjust it to fit their particular needs? You shouldn't have to buy marriage off the rack; like a tailor-made suit or dress it should conform exactly to the contours of those who chose to clothe themselves in it. Since marriage is obviously with us for some time to come, rather than being merely a necessity, it should be a positive affirmation of our desire to grow and expand our love and identity through, with, and to others.

The Legacy of Victorianism

If marriage is to be saved it must become open and free rather than closed and restrictive. Over the past fifty years we have moved at least part way toward a new understanding of marriage: the woman's right to her own sexuality, which was totally denied in the Victorian age, has gradually become an accepted fact. But even as women struggled to gain recognition that they too, like men, had sexual needs, the Victorian marital legacy continued to affect, in other ways, their standing within the marriage. Even now that restrictive legacy determines in innumerable subtle ways the relationships between contemporary husbands and wives.

One of the first explicit challenges to the assumptions underlying Victorian marriage ideals was the publication, in 1927, of a book called *The Companionate Marriage* by Judge Ben B. Lindsey. For daring to suggest that men and women could marry solely for the purpose of enjoying companionship and sex, without producing children, Judge Lindsey became the target of intense vilification. He had proposed two types of marriage, one for procreation and one for companionship. Well-structured, moral and responsible, Lindsey's two-stage plan included ideas—about education for marriage and parenthood, birth control, simple divorce and non-abusive alimony and support arrangements —that were decades ahead of their time.

Lindsey fought for a humane legislation of what he saw as already a fact—men and women living together in non-legal relationships that had every right to be accorded the dignity their spiritual and sexual union deserved. But like most social visionaries, he was too much for the conservatives of his day. Vituperation came from all sides, with howls of "moral decay" and "orgy of free love." One minister, in a tirade typical of the backlash assaulting Lindsey, said:

> Marriage is, after a fashion, a trades union of women for their own protection. The prostitute and the vamp are the scabs who underbid the union wage . . . Married women will do well to reserve their union cards, and keep their dues well paid, and also keep up the high quality of their goods. They have competition.

Please note the central message of this tirade: sex is a device a woman should use to protect her marriage. It will be a recurring theme. There is a great difference between being told what your marriage *should* be and what it *can* be. Judge Lindsey was telling his readers what their marriages could be. But this new, compassionate form of advice was to be the exception rather than the rule. Most marriage "experts" continued to be anxious to advise readers on what their marriages should be.

The debate as to what forms marriage might take was dampened by the drabness of the depression years. But then the coming of World War II served to advance feminine freedom in marriage and in other areas. Wives found they could very well manage alone with husbands off to war. In the war factories they welded and calculated alongside men, demonstrating their practical equality. Through all the states, as well as overseas, they followed their men, adjusting to constant change. Some women served actively in the armed forces. Mobility and the heightened sense of the moment ("Live for today for tomorrow we die") both helped to loosen up a restrictive sex ethic. Condemnation of women who had sex without marriage was temporarily muted, and many marriages survived "infidelities" on both sides that would have destroyed them under ordinary circumstances.

Such heady freedoms, however, were soon to be squelched in the postwar years. Returning soldiers flooded the labor market and women were once again enticed to return to their homes to succor their mates and provide the homely pleasures so threatened by war. And a veritable avalanche of advice was unleashed on the American woman, telling her in no uncertain terms what her marriage *should* be. What she was told served to bind her to the house as completely as any Victorian wife. There was one large difference: she was allowed to have and enjoy sex. Yet even this advance was to bring as much unhappiness as happiness.

In *The Feminine Mystique*, Betty Friedan brilliantly catalogued the societal pressures of the '50s, the pressures which, aided and abetted by the burgeoning media giants, created the togetherness syndrome. Advertising, in intimate association with the women's magazines, brainwashed women into believing that their destiny lay in the kitchen, merrily scouring pots; in the dining room, waxing the table and arranging daffodils; and in the children's room, running up new curtains in anticipation of baby number two. Marriage and motherhood were glorified from all sides; the hard-sell inducements streamed forth endlessly. Absolutely everything, the American woman was told, that she could possibly desire from life could be found in her home, her husband and her children. The Good Housekeeping Seal of Approval Marriage deprived women of identity. Their individualism thus squashed, women experienced frustration and the ache of vague but constant discontent, even exhibiting at times symptoms of malaise similar to those noted in prisoner-of-war camps, such as extreme apathy, childishness and fear of loss of their sexual potency. But the slick magazines ignored any signs of trouble as they sang and burbled their theme—all any woman needs to be normal is *togetherness*.

Sex was intertwined with togetherness in loving embrace. It could hardly be ignored any more. For one thing, those soldiers returning from the war, and especially from stints in the armies of occupation following the war, brought back with them a far wider experience of sex and sexual attitudes than had been available to American men of any previous generation. Wives found themselves competing with memories of fervent fräuleins and geishas, whether the husbands admitted it or not. Competition invariably leads to experimentation. Besides, as you could find out by reading the Kinsey reports (on *Sexual Behavior in the Human Male* in 1948 and on the *Human Female* in 1953) everybody else was apparently already doing it. What really went on in the sexual life of America had at last been made public through rigorous scientific research. Inhibitions began to look plain silly. Now husband and wife could turn to the proliferating marriage and sex manuals to find out how they should best endeavor to bolster their togetherness in bed. And if the wife had any doubts, the message in her weekly or monthly woman's magazine was clear as glass: if you want to keep your husband at home and happy, you'd better learn everything you can about sex. Sex, too, could now be added to the lengthening list of accomplishments expected of the happy Hoovering homemaker.

The Four-Burner Wife

With the addition of sex to her list, the four-burner wife became as thoroughly rooted to her home as the kitchen stove. In addition to being wife, mother, and teacher, she must now also be mistress—the better to insure that her husband didn't have one outside his house. With this last burner at the sizzle, the wife could be assured (so the magazines claimed) that hubby would stick around to keep the home fires blazing.

Not that togetherness was totally a feminine-oriented concept in this most utilitarian of American marriage ideals. Both Gwendolyn *and* Richard, as husband and wife, were led to believe that each could be *all* to the other, that every gratification could be supplied by the one for the other. But the largest burden fell to the wife. After all, she didn't have a career or any intellectual activities to burden her light heart and dimwitted brain. Why shouldn't she spend her time learning how to be the eighth wonder of the world?

"A wife who is emotionally mature, in order to make her marriage a success, must become an actress in a repertory theater and be able to play perhaps . . . twenty-five roles, switching parts at a moment's notice." So wrote George Lawton in a 1956 article called "Emotional Maturity in Wives," one of the most hysterical (in several senses of the word) documents of the togetherness era. Dr. Lawton listed a few of the roles:

She has to be a chaste creature learning from her husband, with appropriate wonderment, the facts of life. She has to be a seductive, glamorous female competitive with other women, and when necessary capable of aggressive behavior. She has to be a sexual partner, skilled, patient, and when necessary sympathetic. She has to be a practical business partner and when necessary provide family income. When her earnings are unnecessary, she must appear completely ignorant of business and money-making. She has to be a co-parent and in an emergency the only parent, and emergencies can come often. She has to be an expert interior decorator, a roommate, a housekeeper, a restaurant keeper, cook, waitress and bus boy all in one . . . she has to be a member of a home discussion group or domestic debating society, managing to be always on the receiving end, an audience of one, asking only those questions which the lecturer can intelligently answer. She has to be a practical nurse and psychiatric social worker, a psychotherapist, a mind reader, an ambassadress and a master diplomat. She has to be a dancing partner and a capable, but not too capable, bridge partner . . . she has to be an intimate friend, confidante, playmate, hostess, and grand-mistress of the art of canapé-making.

After unfolding this herculean list, Dr. Lawton states, with a perfectly straight face: "It's an odd thing, when a young girl is out with her boy friend, neither one realizes how important it will be one day for her to know how to prepare unusual and even exotic canapés." So there you are, modern woman, tossing off a few exotic canapés in addition to (and perhaps in the midst of) performing sublimely in bed.

Is it any wonder that the divorce rate began to climb? Who could meet these expectations? Certainly not Gwendolyn, who found even a game of checkers too demanding after a day of waxing floors, bleaching diapers and contending with a leaky pastry gun. Certainly not most women, for that matter. And even if Richard *could* find such a woman, would he actually want her? This 1950s incarnation of the wife as paragon was more like a gorgon, if you look twice. Perhaps Ashley Montagu is right in his theories on the natural superiority of women. Otherwise she ought to have become extinct in the '50s, perishing from exhaustion at trying to fulfill these multitudinous roles society dictated for her.

What Dr. Lawton has described for us above is a *closed marriage*. It is funny to read about, when presented in this ludicrous way. But the closed marriage is not funny to live. The fact that it is closed is the primary cause, we believe, of the widespread disillusionment with marriage that exists today. Closed marriage is a cultural ideal subtly inculcated by training from childhood; it is formalized by church and state and reinforced by social pressure. It is not until we actually find ourselves in a marriage, and have discovered some of its flaws, that we realize the extent to which we have been duped, that we have been sadly misled by the belief that such a marriage can satisfy all of our dreams. The clauses of the closed marriage contract dictate that Gwendolyn and Richard must always appear together as a couple, must share the same friends and forsake those the other can't tolerate, must always share vacations and most hobbies, must always be available for each other's whim and loneliness, must both put their moneys into a conjugal financial pot and must never feel attraction to anyone else of the opposite sex.

Oh, sure, you, Gwendolyn, can play mahjong with your neighboring housewives, you can go to the ballet with an old college chum (female), and you can exchange recipes and gynecological ailments with other women (they don't even have to be other wives). But male companionship is not allowed. And you, Richard, can go to baseball games with a friend (male), attend a hardware convention with business associates (all male), and play poker with other men. But God forbid you should take another woman to see the Knicks in Madison Square Garden, even if your wife hates basketball.

The Fidelity Trap

During the 1950s the closed marriage was developed to its fullest. But it carried the seeds of its own destruction, particularly in the double standard of sexuality that it promoted. Women had been allowed to discover the importance of sex. Men, of course, have always known how important it was; that was one reason why they had always been excused their occasional fling at infidelity (men will be boys, won't they?). Now that sex was important for women, too, did that mean that women also would be excused that occasional fling? Not a bit of it. A rationale was discovered for persuading women to direct their sexual attentions solely toward the husband. Sex was to be the device by which women were to keep a firm clasp on their husbands; it was the bait in the fidelity trap.

Since sex was a device for trapping the male, since sex was bait, it necessarily followed that women should understand how to make the lure as attractive as possible. The question of sexual fulfillment for themselves was beside the point; they were instructed on how best to fulfill the husband's needs. These instructions, endlessly repeated in the women's magazines of the '50s, were firmly based on Freudian interpretations of feminine sexuality. Two of the best-known proselytizers for this view were the female analysts, Dr. Helene Deutsch and Dr. Marynia Farnham, who elaborated the Freudian doctrine of feminine deficiency into a positive rationale for passivity and dependency. But a new note was added, demonstrated by Dr. Farnham's statements (made together with her sociologist collaborator, Ferdinand Lundberg) that the "traits necessary to the attainment of sexual pleasure" for a woman were "receptivity and passiveness, a willingness to accept dependence without fear or resentment, with a deep inwardness and readiness for the final goal of the sexual life—impregnation." Thus the myth of motherhood as the ultimate feminine destiny served to entrap the woman as well as the man.

Freud's contributions to man's knowledge of himself are of course enormous. But, genius though he was, Freud was still a prisoner of the repressive Victorian society in which he had grown to adulthood, and of the patriarchal traditions of his cultural heritage. These two traditions affected him most distinctly in his theories concerning the biological and intellectual inferiority of women. He created a male-centered developmental framework which we have inherited along with the extraordinary benefits of his work on the unconscious, dreams and ego-defense mechanisms. Woman, to Freud, was only an incomplete man, abnormal, inferior, forever destined by the very makeup of her anatomy to wander the face of the earth lamenting her incompleteness and searching for that which made man complete, a penis. It was not enough to deny her mental powers equal to man's; she was also relegated to a half life of sexuality, for out of the work of Freud and his followers the myth of the superiority of the vaginal orgasm was born. It was a myth that was to survive well into the 1960s. Indeed the 1950s were the years of its greatest ascendancy.

Even though there was an increased openness about sex and more knowledge about its details, sex in marriage was still so hedged about with illusions (as to the nature of female sexuality) and fantasy (the romance of togetherness) as to make genuine, open communication between husband and wife virtually impossible, in or out of bed. The divorce rates continued to climb. But if the American woman had any doubts about her roles as passive bedmate and frenetic housekeeper, there was always another expert to reprove her.

The Power of Sexual Surrender by Dr. Marie Robinson was published in 1959 and has sold more than a million copies in all editions. It is an incredible document, in which the blame for problems in marriage and sex is placed squarely in the lap of women. "Man," she says, "is rarely responsible for his wife's frigidity." In page after page of cliches strung together by prepositions, Dr. Robinson denounces the woman with clitoral orgasm as frigid, rebukes her for autonomy, and harangues her that the only real path to love lies in surrender. A sensitive and sensual woman, who took this book seriously some years ago, remembers that it threw her into a complete tailspin of self-doubt and recrimination. "I found that book extremely threatening," she says.

And no wonder. For Dr. Robinson commands not only physical surrender but psychic surrender.

But there is even more to the psychic state necessary for orgasm than faith in one's partner and readiness to surrender . . . in the woman's orgasm the *excitement comes from the act of surrender* [Dr. Robinson's italics]. There is a tremendous surging physical ecstasy in the yielding itself, in the feeling of being the passive instrument of another person, of being stretched out supinely beneath him, taken up will-lessly by his passion as leaves are swept up before the wind.

Slapstick though her edicts may seem today, the results of this kind of advice were extremely damaging. Women had first been considered sexless, and had had to cope with the guilt of finding that they were not. Then they had been told that only the vaginal orgasm was legitimate, creating a further sense of guilt and forcing them to try to tailor their biology to fit the myth. Now, in addition, they were being told that they must achieve both physical and psychic surrender. All of these demands were in some way false, false to the nature of women, and false to the relationships between men and women.

For it was not just the women who suffered. The "experts" were not only forcing women to bear a false sense of guilt, they were undermining the psycho-sexual life of men—and of course, having achieved these two negative ends, were defeating the institution of marriage itself. The emphasis on female orgasm led men to believe that their masculinity and sexual powers must be judged in terms of their ability to bring their wives to orgasm. "Did you come?" Richard urgently whispers to Gwendolyn. And in this atmosphere of tension Gwendolyn feels a compulsion to perform, leading her to fake her responses. If you add on to this double burden (for the woman to have an orgasm and for the man to bring her to it—every time, of course) the additional goal of simultaneous orgasm, you have a prescription for disaster in the marital bed. Under these conditions neither man nor woman could ever hope to understand the other's true needs and feelings. Instead of being a unifying bond and an expression of love, marital sex became another hurdle that had to be cleared.

Is Sex All There Is?

The 1960s brought relief to the sexual tensions caused by unrealistic expectations. In *Human Sexual Response* (1966) and *Human Sexual Inadequacy* (1970) Masters and Johnson exploded the myth of the primacy of vaginal orgasm once and for all, and through their development of conjoint or couple therapy, replaced the responsibility for sexual fulfillment where it belonged, on both partners, rather than on the female alone. At the same time, the advent of the pill provided the woman, for the first time in history, with absolute birth control and a possible release from former sexual inhibitions. Women could now indulge in sex without premeditation; men's biological prerogative of freedom from impregnation was now women's. Even though the pill had drawbacks, it served to introduce women to this freedom necessary to equality. With the on-going development of safer absolute contraceptives, the sexual equality of women has become, after a century of struggle, an achieved fact.

But this new sexual equality, however much it lessened the tensions of many marriages by freeing them from false sexual expectations, did not seem to be the whole answer.

Gwendolyn and Richard no longer felt impelled to force their sex life into prearranged patterns dictated to them by some best-selling marriage manual, but other kinds of unrealistic expectations remained. People began to wake up to the realization that other aspects of the marriage contract presented problems as serious and as complex as the sexual one.

The rigid role behavior dictated by fiat in the closed marriage can be just as destructive, just as inhibiting, as the demands of sexual surrender and mutual orgasm. Richard has invited some business associates to dinner, for example. Before his marriage to Gwendolyn, Richard spent two years working for the Paris branch of an American firm, and learned to cook a few French specialities. He would like to serve *coq au vin* to his friends. But Gwendolyn wails, "How will that make me look, with *you* cooking dinner?" Convention wins. Richard's creativity is squelched but Gwendolyn's image is preserved, and the guests get roast lamb.

The rules say that the wife must be the cook, housekeeper, duster, washer of dishes and mender of skinned knees. She must always think of home and family first, and be caretaker and supporter of her husband's ego to the exclusion of her own identity and growth. The man must go out and earn a living, hold commerce with the world and be the rock of Gibraltar. He makes the major decisions, puts away the storm windows, cuts the grass and empties the garbage. Authoritarian control and domination by the husband are central themes in closed marriage. The American male, constantly on trial to live up to this role, perceives any autonomous action on the part of the wife as a threat. And Gwendolyn, dissatisfied with her imprisonment, unable to express her disappointments or the longings that are so at variance with the image of wife and mother, turns to nagging and bitter complaints, and her distrust of her own feelings leads to self-disgust.

The price one must pay for sustaining the neurotic rigidities and dependencies that this enforced role-playing and excessive togetherness create were described by Ann, married ten years to an advertising art director who found few interests outside his job. In no uncertain terms she denounced the barriers these ideals and images put up between them. "The old concept of marriage doesn't allow us to have different ideas, it limits the goals for each. All our values can't be the same. Look at what happened with me and my singing lessons. He was really disapproving of my self-growth when you come down to it. Because Fred couldn't stand to hear me practice, I was always self-conscious about singing. He complained all the time—and I think he would have complained even if I had sung like Leontyne Price. Not only that, but he objected to my evenings rehearsing with the little-theater group. Why? He thought that as a wife I should be home with him all the time. He didn't like to be alone. Well, I can tell you it was certainly *complimentary* to me, that he should want me around all the time. But how many compliments do I need? I can't grow on them."

In spite of (or perhaps because of) all this togetherness, deeper emotional feelings, honest and open revelations, are seldom shared by husband and wife. By cutting themselves off from all possibilities of growth, they cut themselves off from their own potential selves and finally from one another. Each censors his or her communications with the mate according to his restrictive idealized images of what husband and wife are supposed to be. Since husband and wife seldom communicate openly, and feel they must live up to role expectations, neither can emerge as a person with his own identity in a closed marriage. How then can liking and respect, which are the prerequisites of love, exist between them?

But are *all* the expectations with which we enter marriage unrealistic? How thoroughly have we been duped?

How deeply have we been victimized by our own idealism? While many things we expect of marriage are unrealistic, we surely are not asking too much when we hope that the relationship with another in marriage will bring us companionship, warmth, understanding, and growth. It is not too much to hope that there should be another with whom we can share our deepest intimacy, to whom we can give our trust and receive trust in return. These expectations as ends are not unjustified. It is the expectation that the traditional (which is to say outmoded) closed marriage can be the *means* by which we achieve these ends that is unrealistic. The theory is right, but the method is wrong. The vital distinction to be made is between realistic expectations of a fruitful *relationship* and an unrealistic *method* of achieving it. A closed, restrictive marriage system actually limits, proscribes and sabotages the attainment of these objectives.

Plant a flower in a pot and its growth is limited to the size of the container; in fact, the container may stunt the growth of the flower. But plant it in a field and something different happens. Open to the sunlight and air, with space to expand, it can grow to the extent of its inherent capacity for growth. The rules and regulations of our traditional, monolithic marriage structure have had a constraining influence on the development of those qualities of growth and interaction we can realistically expect of marriage; what we need to do is to get marriage into a more open context, one in which natural growth can take place. The sexual repression of the Victorian era has lifted, and the subsequent myths that forced men and women to seek sexual fulfillment within a false, predetermined framework have been dispelled. Now we must rid ourselves of the lingering social corsetings bequeathed us by that long vanished society. We must move out from its shadows into the open air of a new time in which men and women can work together for mutual fulfillment through individual growth.

The Concept of Open Marriage

Open marriage means an honest and open relationship between two people, based on the equal freedom and identity of both partners. It involves a verbal, intellectual and emotional commitment to the right of each to grow as an individual within the marriage.

Open marriage is a non-manipulative relationship between man and woman. Neither is the object of total validation for the other's inadequacies or frustrations. Open marriage is a relationship of peers in which there is no need for dominance and submission, for commandeered restrictions, or stifling possessiveness. The woman is not the caretaker, the man is not the dictator. Because their relationship is based on mutual liking and trust, each one has enough psychic space, which is to say mental and emotional freedom, to become an individual. Being individuals, both the woman and the man are free to develop and expand into the outside world. Each has the opportunity for growth and new experiences outside the marriage. Through their growth as separate persons and their supportive love for each other, they vitalize and increase their couple-power. The union grows stronger and richer through a new dynamic principle. Because each one is growing through freedom toward selfhood, adding new experiences from the outside and at the same time receiving the incremental benefit of his mate's outside experiences, the union develops constantly in an upward spiral. Open marriage thus draws on the idea of synergy—that one plus one equals more than two, that the sum of the parts working together is greater than the sum of the parts working separately.

In a closed marriage, the couple does not exist in a one-plus-one relationship. Their ideal is to become fused into a single entity—a couple. Separate experiences, beyond those forced upon them by the fact that the husband goes to an office or a factory while the wife remains home to clean and shop, are not allowed, except for occasional, generally resented outings with "the Boys" (for the husband) and "the Girls" (for the woman). What often happens, in fact, is that the husband continues to grow at a greater pace than the wife, since he has greater exposure to the outside world. An imbalance is created, and the one who is restricted in his growth tends to resent the other's development.

The open marriage, in contrast, encourages growth for both husband and wife. Therefore their union thrives on change and new experiences. With change, new constellations of behavior, new ways of relating, new knowledge of the self, and an increased dynamism of interaction between the two become possible. Even falling in love with the other can become a cyclically recurring event. As each becomes more attractive to the other by means of their individual growth and their developing knowledge of one another, their union grows in strength, constantly revitalized, constantly expanding.

By contrast, closed marriage is conceived of as a trap. Our cultural attitudes toward the closed marriage are revealed in the colorful metaphors used to allude to the customary marriage: "she hooked him," "they got hitched," "you won't get me in that straitjacket," and "the ball and chain."

There is no doubt that innumerable contemporary couples are looking for some way out of the trap of their closed marriages. In the past few years, many therapeutic fads have come upon the scene, each offering some temporary relief from marital tension. Couples are taught how to channel hostility and aggression in therapeutic fighting with rules; they learn how, in the mounting number of couples' encounter groups, to ventilate their accumulated guilts and imprisoned feelings in an effort to break down the barriers and reach a communication with each other through turbulent and often violent physical and verbal exercises. Or they learn how to give themselves an annual emotional checkup, the way you tune up your car or take a business inventory. Some do find comfort and release in these exercises. But, like bathroom-cabinet medications that alleviate the indigestion but do not cure the ulcer, these remedies offer only emergency relief for marriage.

What we propose in open marriage is a complete revision from within the marriage—a revision that depends upon the two people involved, not upon what has been traditional in the past. Open marriage is not an abstract ideal—it is a suggestion for rewriting your contract into a viable life style according to your individual needs.

The meaning in marriage today must be independently forged by a man and a woman who have the freedom to find their own reasons for being, and for being together. Marriage must be based on a new openness—an openness to one's self, an openness to another's self and an openness to the world. Only by writing their own open contract can couples achieve the flexibility they need to grow. Open marriage is expanded monogamy, retaining the fulfilling and rewarding aspects of an intimate in-depth relationship with another, yet eliminating the restrictions we were formerly led to believe were an integral part of monogamy.

We have come a long way during the past century toward freeing ourselves from the restrictive, Victorian idea of marriage as a gilded cage. In the past decade alone, we have discovered, at last, that each mate should both enjoy himself sexually and endeavor to please the other; and we now know a great deal about how to achieve such a mutual giving. But we have also learned that "having sex" is not all there is to a good sexual relationship. More importantly, we have learned that good sex is certainly not all there is to a good marriage—it had only seemed that way so long as distortion and myth prevented men and women from understanding their sexuality. But, as Albert Ellis has pointed out,

Sexual arousal . . . is most importantly . . . the result of brain processes: of thinking and emoting. The art of sex is therefore, as Ovid properly called it many centuries ago, the art of love—that is, the art of being considerate, kind, loving, interested, self-confident, communicative, imaginative, permissive, and experimental.

Quite clearly, it is the nurturing of these underlying qualities that must be our most important task. We believe that the concept of open marriage, properly applied, can lead to the building of a relationship between a man and a woman that promotes the growth of these qualities. In the course of the century, the gilded cage of Victorian marriage has become just a cage, the gilt worn off, and rust setting in. It is time to throw it out altogether, and to make our marriages in the open light of day.

2 Who Has the Open Marriage?

Don't Judge from the Obvious

The following "film clips" are a test of your ability to recognize an open marriage in action. We survey the lives of three different couples, looking in on each of them at about 6 P.M. on an average evening.

COUPLE I

Setting: A luxurious seventeenth-floor apartment. Large picture windows overlook the lights of the city below. The living room is expensively furnished in contemporary style.

Elsa, an attractive blonde in her early thirties, regards herself as a liberated woman. As buyer for a large department store she could well afford to live alone in equally elegant surroundings, but for the past six years she has chosen to share her life with Stewart, a lawyer, in an unofficial relationship. They consider themselves married, and their friends think of them that way, too. Elsa has arrived home this evening shortly before six. She straightens the living room, closing the heavy drapes and plumping the pillows on the white leather couch. She has already prepared the salad and laid out the steak to be broiled. Changing into a long skirt for dinner, she is ready to greet Stewart as he comes in the door a few minutes later. Pitching aside his briefcase, Stewart says, "Golly, do I need a drink." Elsa kisses him, in a way that is at once flirtatious and motherly, and makes his drink for him.

COUPLE II

> Setting: A one-bedroom apartment in an eight-story building put up in the twenties. In untidy but comfortable confusion, samovars and East Indian bric-a-brac mingle with stacks of books, Mexican straw furniture and overstuffed chairs.

Laura has been married for eight years to Paul, a successful executive of a firm specializing in office design; they met while in art school together. Laura is busy in the kitchen, trying to get dinner on the table as close to six o'clock as possible, so that she and Paul can sit down shortly after he gets home. Paul gives her a hug as he comes in. "I'm starving," he says, taking off his coat. Laura has already dashed back into the kitchen. "Come make a drink, while I finish," she calls. Paul comes into the kitchen and they talk animatedly about their respective days while Laura fries the pork chops. Then they sit down to a hasty dinner. She has an eight o'clock class to make, and Paul is going to an art gallery where a friend of theirs is having an opening.

COUPLE III

> Setting: A small suburban house whose façade is replicated ten times down the block. The inside, though, is personalized by an interesting mixture of antique, art nouveau and ultramodern furnishings.

Bill, an assistant professor of literature at a nearby university, has just received a call from his wife Cathy in the city. She will be late. Before they married five years ago, Cathy had been working for some time in a publishing company, and she has continued to work there in spite of the problem of commuting, which often makes her late. Bill, who shares her enthusiasm for her work, and loves having a literate companion in his own field, obligingly starts to prepare dinner. He has, after all, been home for hours—his last class was over at three. They shopped together on Saturday, and the refrigerator is full. By the time Cathy gets back, the table is set and the dinner is almost ready to serve.

Have you guessed which of these three couples has the open marriage? Can you tell which one has revised the old marriage contract to suit their present needs? Don't judge from the obvious, for there is more than meets the eye in each of these three examples. Before you draw any conclusions, let's roll the reel a bit further on each of our couples, to cover the remainder of their evening.

COUPLE I

After a candlelight dinner, Elsa efficiently sweeps the dishes into the dishwasher, while Stewart throws himself on the couch to watch color television. When Elsa is finished in the kitchen she joins him, cuddling against him while they talk disjointedly above the sound of the television. He then goes off to his study to work on a brief. Elsa continues watching television, stretched out on the couch. The phone rings and she talks enthusiastically for several minutes. Stewart walks out of the study and hangs over the phone—she reaches out and caresses his arm as though to reassure him. When she hangs up, Elsa explains that it was a man from work about some new designs, but Stewart sulks, only half believing her. "I can't see why that job always has to follow you home. You're all so damn clubby." "But, darling," Elsa answers, "things have to be settled as they arise—why you're actually jealous!" Stewart snorts and returns to his study, slamming the door. But then minutes later he is back out again, suddenly in the mood for sex. Elsa obliges him.

COUPLE II

While Laura goes off to her class (she's working for a master's degree in art history), Paul does the dishes and then takes off for the gallery opening. He arrives at the tail-end of the showing, spends half an hour there and then goes on to a party he and Laura have been invited to, arriving long before Laura, who doesn't get there until ten-thirty. He introduces her to some new people he has met there, and they stay on for another hour. Home by midnight, they sit over the dessert they missed earlier and compare notes on their hours apart. It's late and Paul has to get an early start in the morning, but even so they make love before going to sleep.

COUPLE III

Cathy and Bill have a leisurely dinner while Cathy unbends from the day's tensions. She appreciates what he has cooked, and they both join in to do the dishes. But she is exhausted and sprawls out on the Victorian divan. Bill reminds her they have been invited to a party. He would like to go but Cathy says she is too worn out. "Well, what about a movie, then?" But she is too tired even for that. She would just fall asleep in the theater. In fact she falls asleep there in the living room, while Bill does some reading for the following week's classes.

It's Not Who Does the Dishes

Which couple has the open marriage?

If you guessed Couple I, you are wrong. In spite of Elsa's career and the fact that she lives with Stewart without the formal seal of marriage, their relationship reflects in every way a closed marriage contract. She is a "handmaiden to god," waiting on Stewart hand and foot. He manages to combine the authority of the patriarch with the petulance of a little boy. He was jealous when Elsa received her telephone call, and it was this jealousy that triggered their sex together. For all her ability to support herself financially, she is emotionally dependent on him, and uses her household services to keep him dependent on her. Their intimacy is based on this mutual dependency—he depends on her to reinforce his masculinity and provide his creature comforts, while she depends on him to make her feel needed.

If Elsa were actually married to Stewart, and they had two children, say, then she would be just a typical housewife, carrying out a typical contract—which might then be based on true economic dependency. As things stand she is dependent upon him in other ways; without his possessive, demanding love for her, she would feel lost. She could easily afford to hire help if she wanted to (a cleaning woman does come in once a week), but she is afraid that if she did not cater completely to Stewart's every physical need, he would lose interest in her. Stewart, on his part, demands her total attention, just as he once, an only child, got it from his mother. He even monitors Elsa's relationships at work, and when they attend a party he follows her around, as attentive as a radar scanner to every nuance of her behavior. She, of course, is aware of his overbearing interest and curbs her spontaneity. Both have opted for the traditional, tight marital contract of total dependency, he behaving with authoritarian restrictiveness, she with the "expected" feminine passivity. Elsa and Stewart have, in fact, the most completely closed relationship of any of these three couples.

You would also be incorrect if you were to guess that Couple III had the open marriage. Despite their ability to switch the traditional marital roles around, taking on tasks according to common sense and the need of the moment, regardless of whether they are male or female by custom, they are still tied up into a knot of togetherness and exclusivity. He has at least granted her identity, feeling that he has a lot more to gain from a woman who is growing and who has a sense of her independent worth. As he puts it, "I don't believe in a complementary theory of marriage, with each doing different jobs that are labeled masculine and feminine—ultimately it means we live in two different worlds, become different species and end up not being able to communicate with one another. Two people, each of whom does everything, means more sharing."

But while he has developed to this point, in respect to Cathy, she on her side is depriving him of certain requisites of identity and independence. Since she works with people all day long, relaxation to her means being alone with Bill —and resting. For Bill, who spends much of the day by himself, or giving formal lectures, relaxation means socializing, getting involved in give and take with other people. But the traditional marriage contract insists that couples must do everything together—if one is too tired to go out, then the other must sacrifice himself, and also be unoccupied, or tired. The old contract allows for no differences in mood, need or simple desire. It dictates that the couple operate in tandem, that even if we don't feel the same way at the same time, we *should* feel, or at least should act as though we do. Bill and Cathy continue to follow this rule. If Cathy doesn't go, then Bill mustn't go either. For all their openness and flexibility in other ways, they still have not achieved a true open marriage.

Cathy's means of achieving growth and satisfaction, her career, is her responsibility, not Bill's. If that means that she is always tired, then she must be willing to let Bill go his own way, instead of chaining him to a form of relaxation that ties in with the demands of her career but not with his. They both have identity outside their marriage, but Cathy is depriving Bill of his identity inside the marriage. They are slaves to the concept of the couple-front. If one doesn't go, then the other doesn't go either.

Couple II have the true open marriage. Couple I, Stewart and Elsa, have sacrificed identity and equality to their dependent relationship. Couple III, Bill and Cathy, have achieved some of the necessary equality and identity, but they have not moved on to the true *mutual trust* that grants real freedom. As you may have noticed, equality, identity and trust in the open marriage cannot be measured simply by who does the dishes or prepares the dinner. On alternate nights, for instance, when Laura has her class at six o'clock and doesn't get home until eight-thirty, Paul prepares the dinner for himself if he is hungry or has it ready for both of them to eat together when Laura gets home. Whoever is at home first on a particular night does the job. But they are not only flexible about their roles at home. They are also flexible in their social life.

It is more important for Laura to go to her class than to the gallery opening. But that does not mean Paul has to stay home. If he wants to go, she wants him to do it. He will have the pleasure of the event, and she will be able to share in it when he tells her about it later. If anyone at the gallery who knows them should be so foolish as to assume there was trouble between them because Paul was alone, Laura's feeling is that such a person's opinions are of no value anyway. Paul arrives early at the party, equally unconcerned about presenting a couple-front. If Laura had been tired and not shown up at all, he would not have been upset. She *chose* to go to class, miss the opening and be late for the party. Unlike Cathy, however, she does not force the consequences of her choice on her husband as well. When they finally do get together later in the evening, they are able to exchange accounts of their separate experiences, and have far more to talk about than would a closed-marriage couple who have to do everything together. And since there is complete trust between them when they are apart, they are able to open themselves to one another far more fully than Elsa and Stewart, who must guard their experiences for fear of antagonizing or hurting the other.

These three couples illustrate one of the most important facts about open marriage: it is not a new set of rules, telling you what you can and cannot do, but consists rather of a new way of *looking at* what you do. Open marriage is looking at your life together as a cooperative venture, in which the needs of each can be fulfilled without an overriding dependency that cripples the other's self-expression. Love can then be understood as a sharing of one another's independent growth rather than as a possessive curtailment of growth. Equality in open marriage is a state of mind, supported by respect and consideration for each other's wishes and needs. Roles can thus be flexible and interchangeable. In open marriage the wife may often cook dinner. In open marriage the husband and the wife may often attend parties as a couple. But when they do so, they are doing it out of choice, not because their mate *requires* them to do it. The difference between closed marriage and open marriage is the difference between coercion and choice.

3 Rewriting the Contract

*Psychological Commitments
of the Closed Marriage*

Marriage is a contract. But it is more than just a legal contract between the marital couple and society at large—it is also a psychological contract between husband and wife. This psychological contract has been determined for us, to a very considerable extent, long before we begin our first day of married life. It is in many ways an unconscious contract, agreed to by default in the sense that it is unwitting. But that does not make it any less binding upon our interaction with our chosen mate, upon our public behavior as a couple, or upon our attitudes toward the meaning of marriage.

In our marriages we act according to the way we were brought up, with some modifications based upon personal experience. We are guided by ideals from the past. If our parents had an unhappy marriage, we may try in some ways to insure that our own will be different from theirs, but even such differences will be worked out within the context of the closed marriage that has served Western society for the past several centuries. You may determine not to go out drinking every Saturday night the way your father did, because that was a cause of friction in your parents' marriage, but when you do no more than change such surface manifestations, you are treating only the symptoms and not the disease itself.

The traditional, closed marriage is a form of bondage, for both husband and wife. (The fact that your father went out drinking may in fact have been his way of rebelling symbolically against that bondage.) So rigid and unrealistic is the closed marriage contract that the late Dr. Henry Guze, a professor of psychology, was moved to write,

It is possible that in accepting the contract, persons are agreeing to behavior which is beyond their personal nature and perhaps beyond human nature. This unreality creates a breeding ground for neurotic interaction and permits the development of increased interpersonal exploitation.

Instead of acquiescing to the old contract, simply because our parents did, or because our neighbor is doing so, we should be writing our own marriage contracts. Each of us is different, each of us has different needs, and our marriage contracts should be tailored to fit each particular couple. If we rewrite our own marriage contracts in openness and honesty these new arrangements can minimize neurotic interaction and conflicts, and marriage can become a relationship for mutual fulfillment of realistic needs and growth to maturity.

But before we can begin to write our own unique contract, one flexible enough so that it can be changed as we go along, as we grow both within and outside our marriage, we must understand some of the hidden demands and dictates of the closed marriage. What, in fact, are the psychological commitments we make within a closed marriage?

THE CLOSED MARRIAGE CONTRACT

Clause 1: Possession or ownership of the mate. (Both the husband and the wife are in bondage to the other: "You belong to me." Belonging *to* someone, please note, is very different from the feeling that you belong *with* someone.)

Clause 2: Denial of self. (One sacrifices one's own self and individual identity to the contract.)

Clause 3: Maintenance of the couple-front. (Like Siamese twins, we must always appear as a couple. The marriage in itself becomes your identity card, as though you wouldn't exist without it.)

Clause 4: Rigid role behavior. (Tasks, behavior and attitudes strictly separated along predetermined lines, according to outdated concepts of "male" and "female.")

Clause 5: Absolute fidelity. (Physically and even psychologically binding, through coercion rather than choice.)

Clause 6: Total exclusivity. (Enforced togetherness will preserve the union.)

You may not agree that this is the kind of psychological contract you agreed to at all. *You* married for love, warmth, companionship. Of course you did. But, subtly, insidiously, often without your even knowing it, the clauses of the closed marriage contract begin to foreclose upon your freedom and your individuality, making you a slave of your marriage. Additional subclauses of the main six listed above come into play, governing your conduct within your marriage.

Let us take a look at how easily the closed marriage encloses you, cutting you off not only from the outside world but from your own natural desires. We will follow a young couple, newly married, through a week of their daily routine, pointing out the situations in which they succumb to the rules of the closed marriage contract, sometimes in spite of their better judgment. At the same time we will make clear, in parenthetical interpretations, the particular psychological clauses governing their behavior at any given moment.

The Ties That Bind: Eight Days in the Making of the Closed Contract

John and Sue, very much in love, have been married two weeks. Most of that time was spent on a honeymoon vacation in the Caribbean. Before their marriage, John kept house for himself in the same apartment in which they are now living as husband and wife. He works for an architectural firm, and Sue is going to continue with her secretarial job. Over the threshold they carry not only their vacation suitcases, but also the cumbersome (even though invisible) baggage of their respective pasts, weighted down by their personal experiences, their cultural conditioning and their idealistic expectations. Unconsciously, with only the desire to please one another and to express their love, this young couple begins to bind themselves to a closed marriage contract. They are happy, smiling and in love, for their pleasure in each other is new and fresh, but they are unknowingly painting themselves into corners and guaranteeing themselves future frustration and unhappiness. Let us see how it happens.

DAY 1: It is Sunday morning. Sue wanders sleepily into the kitchen and begins to make breakfast. John follows after bringing in the paper from the hallway. While Sue fries bacon and scrambles eggs, John sits at the kitchen table reading the paper. Every time Sue passes between the table and the stove, he reaches out affectionately to give her a quick caress. It is, in one sense, a charming scene. But under the surface, binding assumptions are being made. (CLAUSE: The woman is the cook.) As a bachelor John quite often cooked for himself, not just breakfast but dinner as well. But now that he is married he will never cook again, unless they eventually make enough money to have a summer house, in which case he can probably be expected to grill the steaks on the backyard barbecue. It is not even that John would mind cooking. He never prepared anything very elaborate for himself, but he found the actual process of working in the kitchen relaxing. Yet here he is, simply assuming that Sue will always do the cooking. And though he is keeping her affectionate company now, the day will come when he will start reading the paper in the living room, where there is more room to spread it around. When that time comes, Sue may very well begin to feel some resentment about her role as constant cook.

Later in the day the telephone rings.

"Darling," Sue whispers, "it's my mother. They want to come over and say hello. You know how much they want to hear about the trip. Is it all right?"

"Sure, honey," he answers obligingly. (CLAUSE: When you marry, you marry not only a husband or wife but an entire network of relationships and responsibilities.) John suddenly remembers that they had promised to get together with Linda and Bill, who first introduced them and are their closest friends. Here, of course, is another network. Most of these networks, which each partner in the marriage has separate connections to, are fun and rewarding. But they also can present problems. One of those problems is evident here; we shall discover others further on. Clearly on their first day back it is only to be expected that John will go along with the idea of inviting Sue's parents over. But having agreed this time, he will find it more difficult to say no next time, if Sue's parents should start pressing themselves upon John and Sue too often. This isn't to indicate that in an open marriage John would say, "Yes, they can come over this afternoon, but don't get the idea I want to see them every Sunday." Quite the contrary is true. In an open marriage there would be no need for John to make such a statement because Sue would not make the assumption that he's always going to say yes. In fact, it is in the closed marriage situation that John really should make such a protestation, to make matters clear. Yet, obviously, a young man very much in love with his new wife isn't going to say any such thing, and she, on her part, is going to assume that when she wants to see her parents, they will both see them. Sue makes a further assumption, too. "Don't worry," she says, "I'll give Linda a call. We can see them during the week but Mom and Dad can only get free on weekends." (CLAUSE: It is the wife's role to make decisions concerning the couple's social activities. And this presumes the wife's right to decide how the husband's time is going to be spent.) In the open marriage, such assumptions do not exist. Each partner retains control over the way he or she spends his or her free time. Sometimes they will spend it together, but sometimes they will spend it separately. And because neither presumes to dictate to the other how such time is to be spent, frustrations and resentments are drastically reduced.

DAY 2: Sue cooks breakfast, leaving the dishes in the sink, and they both rush off to work. At his office, John is confronted with a new project, as well as some leftover problems from an old one. The old problems involve personality differences and the blueprints for the new project are inaccurate; it's all very depressing. That evening, John arrives home before Sue and makes himself a drink. Sue comes staggering in with two huge bags of groceries. (CLAUSE: Shopping is the wife's job.) He helps her unpack them and then mixes a drink for her while she does the breakfast dishes and prepares dinner. (CLAUSE: Mixing drinks is the husband's job, but the dishes, as well as meal preparation, are the wife's responsibility.) John is preoccupied with his problems at work, but he tries to pretend that everything is just fine. (CLAUSE: The husband must always be strong; if he has problems, he must never communicate them to his wife, because to do so might make him vulnerable.) They eat dinner, making small talk, mostly about Sue's job and when to see Linda and Bill. John, however, continues to be upset about his problems at work. Still, he refrains from saying anything. (CLAUSE: You must always live up to the ideal conception of your role as husband—or wife.) Anyway, he tells himself, Sue probably wouldn't understand what in hell he was talking about—she doesn't know anything about blueprints. (CLAUSE: Women's minds are *different* from men's—the male's is abstract, the female's intuitive.)

Even if it were true that Sue would not understand the nature of John's problem (although the assumption that she won't understand is a throwback to the Victorian view of women) that is not to say that she couldn't, one way or another, make John feel better. Just to talk about it might relieve some of his tension. By not talking about it, John instead is guaranteeing himself future tension; the underlying, hidden clauses in the psychological contract are binding him to a position of non-communication with his wife. He is shutting his wife off from one of the most important parts of his life, and at the same time making it impossible for himself to truly relax even in his own home. If he cannot tell his wife what is wrong, then he must pretend that everything is all right—always. And although he may be able to so pretend, the strain of doing it is bound to increase over the years. She will recognize the strain, eventually, even if she doesn't know what causes it, and will feel shut out. Misunderstanding between a husband and wife becomes inevitable in this kind of situation. And it is all based upon an attempt to live up to the clauses of an unspoken, crippling psychological contract.

DAY 3: Sue calls John at his office to suggest dinner out with Linda and Bill that night. Although John had hoped for some time alone at home that evening to wrestle with some of his professional problems, he says, "Sure, darling," and they eat dinner out. (CLAUSE: Husband and wife must always see friends as a couple.) John is dead tired, having tramped over a new piece of property with a client all afternoon, and by the time he and Sue get home from dinner, he falls into bed without giving a moment's attention to the blueprints he has dragged along from the office.

DAY 4: When John arrives home from work, Sue isn't there yet. She can't be shopping since the refrigerator is still stuffed with food from her Monday marketing. John likes to eat around 7:00, but by 6:15 Sue still isn't home. He's tired and hungry and he begins to get irritated. (CLAUSE: Cooking is the wife's job.) In spite of the fact that John made perfectly creditable meals as a bachelor, it never even occurs to him to start preparing the dinner himself. Now that he is married he thinks of the kitchen as Sue's territory and responsibility; he is completely bound by an antiquated concept of proper roles for husband and wife. Not only does he fail to bend with the situation, doing the sensible, practical thing and getting dinner started, he is sufficiently disturbed by Sue not being around to do what he sees as her job that he is unable even to sit down and concentrate on *his* job now that he finally has a few free minutes to give full attention to his blueprints. (CLAUSE: Husband and wife must surrender their selfhood, or identity, to the couple unit.) John is already so caught up in the myth of couplehood that he is losing his power to act independently.

A few minutes later, Sue breezes in happily. She's late because she ran into an old friend from college just as she left the office. "Harry Bigelow, I've told you about him. Anyway, we had a drink and I told *him* all about my marvelous husband." John smiles and gives Sue a hug, but at the back of his mind he is still a bit piqued. (CLAUSE: Each partner in the marriage belongs only to the other and not anybody else.) This kind of possessiveness, since it is based on an unrealistic ideal (CLAUSE: I will be everything to you and you will be everything to me), leads to a basic lack of trust and to a sense of insecurity. Every couple knows, deep down, that they cannot be everything to each other, but since this admission is not made on a conscious level, it finds its way to the surface in terms of mistrust. John, for instance, cannot resist asking, "Did you have to have a *drink* with him?" Sue answers, "Oh, well, the bar was right next door, and he probably won't be in town again for ages."

This is fertile ground for further misunderstanding, though. John, preoccupied with his job problem, is more silent than usual during dinner. His quietness leads Sue to mistakenly assume that he is brooding about her drink with Harry. "You're not mad at me, are you?" she asks. And John, who had been about to ask if she'd mind if he did some work by himself for a while after supper, now feels he has to spend the evening watching television with her. If he said he wanted to be alone, she'd be hurt, and be convinced that he *was* mad at her. (CLAUSE: Togetherness is one of the most important things in marriage. You must always be willing to sacrifice your own needs on the altar of togetherness.)

Here you can see how entirely different clauses of the psychological contract interact to bind the partners ever more tightly within their closed marriage. Had John been sufficiently open with Sue in the first place about his job troubles (instead of being concerned about his role as "provider") the likelihood of her misunderstanding his silence at dinner would have been greatly reduced. Instead of asking "Are you mad at me?" she would have had the awareness (and the confidence that goes with it) to ask, "Are you still worried about those blueprints?" Then John would have been able to say, "Yes, I think I'd better work on them for a while after dinner." He would not even have to say "Do you mind?", for in the open marriage it is not necessary to ask permission—you know in advance that your right to the fulfillment of your own needs is freely given.

DAY 5: Morning dawns. John is bleary-eyed from lack of sleep. He lay awake until 3 A.M., too tense to fall asleep but at the same time too tired to give any coherent thought to his problems. He doesn't mention his insomnia, though, nor does he tell Sue that he really isn't hungry. He manages to get down the hot breakfast she cooks him, but it gives him heartburn all morning long. In fact, if he had only known it, the last thing Sue felt like doing was cooking breakfast. Each, in the name of love and at the expense of self, has done something he didn't want to do, and that it was unnecessary to do, simply because they both were being controlled by the unwritten clauses of the closed marriage contract. Each is responding according to what he *thinks* the other expects of him, instead of trying to find out what is actually expected.

During the day, Lenny, an old friend of John's, calls him to suggest a drink after work some evening, or maybe dinner on Saturday when Sue could join them. Much as he would like a little change of pace, and though he's very fond of Lenny, John refuses the drink, for that evening, anyway, and says he'll see what Sue has planned for Saturday. (CLAUSE: The husband's time belongs to the wife, except when he is actually at work.) He has misgivings about Saturday because Sue has always been put off by Lenny's forthrightness and brash sense of humor. And, as he suspected, Sue turns the idea down. "I really don't enjoy Lenny much," she says, and reminds him that the Millers, a couple down the hall, have invited them to drop in at their open house Saturday night. (CLAUSE: All friends of the married couple must be *mutual* friends.)

DAY 6: Friday, at last. Sue reminds John that she will be late getting home because she is having her hair done. And when John calls Lenny to say they won't be able to make Saturday night, Lenny suggests instead that John join him and his new girl for a drink after work. Since Sue will be late anyway, John agrees, but he feels guilty about it from the start. If Sue really doesn't want to see Lenny, then it's likely to seem kind of pushy of John to have a drink with him the next day—as though he were telling Sue off in a subtle way, which he doesn't want to do at all. If Sue really can't stand Lenny, then he'll just have to give up the friendship.

John has such a good time with Lenny and his girl, though, that it gets to be even later than he realized. He calls Sue to tell her why he's behind schedule. She's just been home a few minutes herself but was beginning to worry about him, she says. He stops at the florist to pick up a dozen roses, beginning the pattern of appeasement that develops inevitably in the closed marriage. It is not, of course, *only* to appease her that he buys the roses. He is newly married and very much in love. Nevertheless, there is an element of guilt involved—for not being at home when she got there and for seeing Lenny at all. There is also another kind of guilt at work here—for at the back of his mind John is aware that next time it will be even more difficult to see Lenny, that in fact he will have to give up the friendship. Since he is genuinely fond of Lenny, that makes him feel guilty too.

In an open marriage, neither of these two distinct but interlocking guilts would be necessary. In an open marriage the clauses pertaining to ownership of the mate and to the maintenance of the couple-front do not operate, and neither partner need feel guilt at having a friend the other doesn't like or at being "late" getting home. Such friendships and occurrences are accepted in the open marriage as being a normal part of life, as indeed they are. No two people can be realistically expected to like exactly the same friends. Yet in the closed marriage it is exactly this kind of unrealistic expectation that each partner has been taught to believe can be fulfilled.

DAY 7: In the morning, while Sue cleans house, John takes the laundry to the laundromat. Laundry is something he would usually consider one of the wife's jobs, but he is not actually going to sit there and watch it spin around in the machine—he will leave it with the attendant and pick it up later in the day, paying extra for the service of having it done for him. Besides, the laundry bag is heavy and awkward, and Sue would have a hard time carrying it. (CLAUSE: The husband must never do anything out of line with his image of himself as a "man.") John's rationalization about the heaviness of the laundry is ridiculous, of course —but that is just the kind of thinking that an excessive concern for role leads into.

That evening, as they get ready for the Millers' party, Sue asks John what she should wear. "You look good in anything," he says. But when she appears in a slinky, spangled gown, looking very 1920s, he says, "My God, Sue, where are you going, to a costume ball?" (CLAUSE: Husband and wife are reflections of one another; neither is allowed, therefore, to wear clothes that don't suit the other's taste.) Although Sue actually looks terrific, and right in keeping with the tone of the party, John's words are enough—off comes the dress. Both John and Sue are demonstrating their lack of personal identity, or selfhood, here. Sue had the right instinct as to what she should wear, but showed her lack of confidence in herself by asking John's approval in the first place and changing when he disapproved. This is not to indicate that in an open marriage the partners would never ask one another what they should wear. If Sue were really not sure, and honestly wanted John's advice, then it would be perfectly sensible to ask him. But to ask when she knows already what she wants to wear is to play a foolish, self-destructive game. And John, in making her change, is simply illustrating his lack of confidence in himself: if what his wife is wearing can so easily embarrass him, then his sense of himself as an individual is sadly deficient.

At the Millers' party, John and Sue spend most of the evening moving around as though they were chained to one another. (CLAUSE: Husband and wife exist primarily as a couple, and must always maintain the couple-front. Otherwise someone might think they were not married, or worse still, that they weren't getting along.) Nevertheless, they eventually get separated when Judy Miller asks Sue to give her a hand in the kitchen for a moment. When Sue gets back to the living room she sees John sitting on the sofa talking intently to a woman Sue doesn't know, who apparently has only just dropped by. Sue rushes over to join them. (CLAUSE: Neither husband nor wife is ever allowed to show interest in a member of the opposite sex unless the mate is right there too.) When John introduces her, Sue is perfectly polite. But her physical action in charging over to join them has clearly indicated to the other woman that she is regarded as an intruder. Sue might just as well have said, "He's mine. Get away from him." And, indeed, the woman takes the hint and excuses herself after a moment or two. In fact it turns out that she is also an architect, and had worked before with the client who's been creating John's problems. She was giving John some helpful hints on how to handle the man, but Sue's instant jealousy has brought the conversation to an end. Sue's actions said to the other woman, "He's mine," and to John they say, just as clearly, "I don't trust you." Of course she doesn't trust John—how could she? She has been taught to believe fidelity consists of a rigid, mechanical rule: Never take an interest in any member of the opposite sex. Deep down, Sue knows, as all of us do, that this is a standard impossible for John to live up to. In respect to such a rigid view of fidelity, what mate *could* trust another? Sue would do better to question the rigidity of the rule.

DAY 8: It is Sunday again. And just as last Sunday, Sue's

parents call and suggest coming over. "You don't mind, darling, do you?" Sue asks. John had been hoping they might go to a movie, but if he were to refuse to see her parents, she'd be hurt. "Fine," he says. And the pattern becomes more deeply implanted.

The hidden contract has been accepted by both.

4 Open vs. Closed Marriage: the Guidelines

The Preformed Mold

John and Sue, without so much as a word of discussion, have in their first week of marriage set the pattern for a contract that will govern their behavior for as long as they are married. Sue does the cooking and housework, John carries the laundry to and from the laudromat, neither has any privacy and each monitors the other's friends. They appear always as a couple, to the exclusion of their own interests. And with time they can be expected to "grow together" even more. What "growing together" means under the closed marriage contract is that they will stamp out individual desires and potentials, encouraging only those that are mutually pleasing and acceptable. In the name of their love for each other they steadfastly eliminate exactly those individualistic qualities in themselves that should be the basis of the further personal growth without which any marriage is bound to stagnate.

The mold into which they have squeezed themselves was preformed, its contours determined by social traditions long outdated. John expects his home to be run in much the way that his mother ran hers. He is willing, of course, to make some concessions to changed circumstances. His mother did the family laundry at home, but she had her own washing machine in which to do it, and a back yard to dry it in. Sue has been taught by social custom and media advertising that the good wife does her best to run her husband's home the way he wants it run. The fact that she works full time, something that neither her mother nor John's ever did, is simply not considered. Eventually, of course, Sue will consider it, and come to resent it, when she discovers how exhausting it is to accomplish in a few odd hours here and there what her mother devoted full time to. But by the time Sue makes that discovery, the pattern will be so firmly established that it will take a major blow-up to change it.

Young Architect Marries Household Drudge

When both partners in a marriage work, the problem of keeping house becomes a crucial one. And since more and more women are (and should be) pursuing independent careers, the problem becomes increasingly common. Sue and John each had their own apartment before they were married. John knows how to cook and clean; in fact, although Sue is the better cook, you could equally well say John was better at cleaning, to judge by the comparative neatness of their bachelor establishments. Yet as soon as they marry, John expects Sue to take on the entire load of household chores. That's part of a wife's job, or so he has been taught. And since Sue has been taught the same thing with even greater thoroughness, she will try to live up to that ideal. If John should offer to help with the dishes once in a while, well, that is a gesture of purest magnanimity on his part. He has been so thoroughly indoctrinated that he can actually feel noble when he carries the laundry bag two blocks to the laundromat.

Given this attitude on John's part, Sue has only two choices—to acquiesce or to resist. If she acquiesces, it probably will mean that she'll eventually give up her job and become just a housewife, falling back into the most rigid of closed marriages. If she resists, then the household duties will become a battlefield. Household tasks are not just simple everyday nuisances that everyone has to contend with unless both partners agree to look at them that way. If such an agreement is made, if doing the dishes or dusting under the bed is seen as part of a whole complex of daily impediments that must be taken care of in order to live comfortably, then they can be made light of. They can be shared, exchanged, or taken over by the one who minds them least. Housework becomes important only when it becomes symbolic of an expected role performance.

The woman who holds a job but also has to do all the housework is being told (and is accepting) that her status in the marriage is less than her husband's. Unfortunately, the frustration of many women over this question has led to absurd overreactions. Some women are now setting up a hue and cry for a new kind of contract that is just as rigid as the old one: these would-be wheeler dealers of the toilet brush and the scouring pad are demanding that men should pay their wives in hard cash for the household services they perform. But the substitution of one rigidity for another is not going to solve the problem. The true equality of a husband and wife cannot be measured by *who* does the dishes, or whether or not a specific reward is given for doing them. It can only be measured by *what our attitudes are* toward the doing of the dishes. As long as a man rates his status by the old rules, in which his time and effort are seen as more valuable than his wife's, the frying pan will remain a weapon of war and the dishes can be expected to turn into missiles. But if the roles of man and woman are flexible and interchangeable, and true equality exists, then the everyday tasks will find their own, secondary level of importance.

Darling, You're Everything to Me

John and Sue are so hooked on togetherness, so filled with the expectation that each can supply all the needs of the other, that the idea of arranging for some mutual privacy would probably seem absurd to them. But already John has had a few moments of frustration when he couldn't get off by himself for an hour to work on his blueprints. Such moments will increase as constant togetherness takes its inevitable toll. Everyone needs space in marriage. Not just physical space, in the form of a den or sitting room where one or the other partner can get away by himself for a while (although physical space can be helpful), but psychic space. Psychic space might be described as a mental room of one's own. Without that space, growth is impossible. And without growth even the most loving couple will eventually become bored with one another.

But the need for psychic space is something that John and Sue are going to have to learn for themselves, probably painfully. Having been duped into believing that they can be everything to each other, John and Sue will fall all over one another trying to live up to the false ideals of another day. As the months go by the pattern of their closed marriage will become more and more deeply entrenched. By the time they begin to discover that the ideals are unobtainable, the demands upon them exorbitant, and that their growth is being stunted, the way back out of the maze of clauses and subclauses in their contract will be extremely difficult to find.

At the beginning each thinks that love will conquer all, and both are too busy striving to please to analyze what they are doing or why they are doing it. The imposed social and psychological contract is never *verbalized*, never evaluated. There is nothing wrong with most of their acts as such. To ask what you should wear, spend more time than you would like to with your in-laws, always do the dishes yourself, or give up a friend: all these things can be done without harm to you or your mate, even with benefit to both, provided that the reasons for doing them are out in the open and full responsibility for them is accepted. But they are wrong, and harmful, when they occur as part of a preset pattern, carried out to fulfill a litany of expectations, when they are based on self-deception and unwitting self-denial. If you must sell yourself into slavery and deny your individual growth and freedom, at least be aware that you are doing it.

But when none of John and Sue's interactions is verbalized, when they do not analyze their own actions, when neither tells the other how he really feels, what he really wants or needs, then the unacknowledged clauses of the closed marriage contract will quickly take effect. And they will inevitably lead to trouble, because they are based upon false expectations.

Resentments will be small at first: a few complaints, a little nagging here and there. But as frustration mounts, the resentment will grow, and eventually it will explode. Sooner or later, Sue will scream "I'm sick and tired of doing all the housework myself and working too," and John will yell "For Christ's sake, can't you see I need some time to myself?" After too many weekends with the in-laws, John may still be smiling on the outside, but he will be seething inside. He will begin to criticize her parents, then accuse Sue of being just like her mother, and finally burst out with, "Who in the hell did I marry, anyway, you or your family?"

Most of us don't like to think of the sharing of our lives with a loving mate in the unromantic terms of a contract. But, like it or not, that is exactly what we are getting involved in when we marry. If we refuse to face up to this fact, refuse to examine what is wrong with the psychological commitments of the traditional, closed marriage contract, then we are accepting that contract and whatever it brings. It will, of course, finally, bring communication—but in the form of fighting. When we refuse or do not know how to communicate directly and rationally, then the suppressed tensions find release indirectly through irrational explosions of anger.

By the time John and Sue begin to communicate through fighting, it will be too late for their garbled cries of resentment to have any constructive effect. The best they can hope for is that through their fighting they will be able to effect a compromise. They will put into practice all those tired concepts so dear to the marriage counselors and therapists of the togetherness cult: they will "give in," "sacrifice," and bargain and haggle over their rights as if marriage were a commodities market. John and Sue will finally "adjust" to one another.

But the adjustment they make will be to the demands of the closed contract, and it will come about only through painful experience. In today's world, when change is so rapid and so constant, flexibility is an absolute necessity. Our marriage contracts must be sufficiently open so that adjustment can be made quickly and easily—not through drawn-out trauma and compromise. We must be able to change our contracts to suit new circumstances: a new job, no job, having a child.

Let's look at what happens when John and Sue have a child. Under the old, closed marriage contract, the advent of the first child usually brings on a crisis—it constitutes the biggest adjustment that a young couple will have to make. If your mate expects exclusive attention from you, to say nothing of total fulfillment, and you expect the same back from him, how is the child going to break into this closed circle of love? A review of the research surveys conducted during the 1960s on the subject of marital happiness came up with this surprising conclusion: "Children tend to detract from, rather than contribute to marital happiness." Surely we shouldn't blame the children for this problem, but rather look for its causes in the ways we go about achieving marital happiness. Obviously, John and Sue will have to change and expand their concept of love as possession in order to absorb the child into their unit. Exclusivity of love and psychological ownership of the mate are hardly the proper prerequisites for parenthood—yet closed marriage is based on them. How can John and Sue bring up their child to be a responsible, mature adult with a sense of his own identity if they have not experienced selfhood themselves within their marriage? How can they give their love to their child in an expansive and growing way if all they know in their marriage is a love created out of dependency and self-effacement?

Clearly, for the good not only of themselves but of their children, John and Sue should strive to escape the bondage of the closed marriage contract with its constricting secondary clauses. But how do we get out of such bondage, short of canceling the contract altogether?

Writing the Open Contract

Instead of surrendering to the hidden clauses of the old, closed contract, you can write your own, individual open contract. You can agree to look honestly and openly at what you are doing and why you are doing it—whether you are going to get married tomorrow or have been married ten years. The power of the hidden clauses of the old contract to constrict your marriage lies in the very fact that they are hidden. We have seen how those clauses operate through our examination of the relationship between John and Sue. We have seen the dangers of unconsciously accepting those hidden clauses. Look at your own marriage. Get the hidden clauses out into the open. Then you can begin to rewrite your contract *as you go along,* starting new, from scratch, today.

You can rewrite your contract as a commitment to individual freedom and mutual growth instead of as a commitment to mutual slavery. By being open with one another about your needs and expectations, you can modify your marriage contract to suit your own unique requirements as a couple. You can tailor your contract to your own specifications. What is more, because you keep that contract always open before you, it can be constantly revised to allow for future changes, for continuing growth.

The open contract does not substitute new regulations for old ones, but rather suggests ways in which you can learn to communicate freely with one another, in order to arrive at a consensus for living, mutually and fully understood. Let us compare, once again, what the old contract demands with what the open contract offers:

The Old Contract Demands	*The Open Contract Offers*
Ownership of the mate	Undependent living
Denial of self	Personal growth
Playing the couples game	Individual freedom
Rigid role behavior	Flexible roles
Absolute fidelity	Mutual trust
Total exclusivity	Expansion through openness

The old contract, with its hidden demands, leads to stagnation. The open contract, with its incentive to mutual growth, leads to the development of synergy. Synergy is the combined, cooperative action of two people working in concert. When one grows, he not only benefits from that growth himself, but gives the other partner a stimulus that will assist in his or her growth. In the closed marriage, possessiveness forces both partners to forego experiences that could enlarge their world. John must give up Lenny's friendship; Sue clings to John's side at parties instead of seeking out new people who might be of interest to her. Stagnation is inevitable in such a marriage. But if each were free to follow his own instincts, to keep up with the people who may interest only one of them, then the growth that each experiences in the course of such contact with others can be channeled back into the marriage. Both must also be free to follow up the potentials of their own personal development in other ways, whether they involve career choices, intellectual interests or other modes of self-fulfillment.

Everyone can understand that as long as the increments to the marriage are financial (as in a raise in salary) or convey new status, both partners benefit. But what must also be understood is that intellectual or emotional growth on the part of each one also benefits the other and their marriage. The marriage contract is not just a financial arrangement, a legal document creating a particular social unit. It is also a psychological contract, and as such, the personal and emotional as well as the material development of each partner will vitally affect the marriage. The opportunities for personal, intellectual and emotional development are even more important to partners in a marriage than material gains. The synergy released by mutual growth, in a personal sense, can bring far more dynamism to a marriage, far richer and deeper benefits, than can simple material advances. This is not to deny the importance of the material world, but simply to say that without personal growth no amount of material success can bring a true sense of mutual fulfillment.

We have found eight cardinal guidelines to aid you in individualizing your marriage contract as you work toward the achievement of an open marriage. Each of the guidelines is important, and if you are to make the fullest use of one, you will have to put the others into effect also. But they can be taken one at a time, developing your strength in each area at your leisure. As you move from one guideline to another, you will find that the implementation of one guideline will assist you in putting another into effect, and vice versa. The guidelines themselves interact in a synergistic way.

The guidelines are as follows:

1. LIVING FOR NOW AND REALISTIC EXPECTATIONS
2. PRIVACY
3. OPEN AND HONEST COMMUNICATION
4. FLEXIBILITY IN ROLES
5. OPEN COMPANIONSHIP
6. EQUALITY
7. IDENTITY
8. TRUST

Where do love, sex, and fidelity fit in? Are these not guidelines too—the basic components of any marriage? Important, yes; guidelines, no. Many of the problems with the closed marriage stem from a false concept of the part that love, sex, and fidelity play in the relationship between a man and a woman. The guidelines of open marriage listed above form the basis upon which love, sex, and fidelity achieve their meaning, not vice versa. If personal identity is based on love, equality measured by sex, and trust defined as fidelity, then identity will be crushed by a lessening of the initial romantic fervor, equality diminished by a temporary failure in sex, and trust destroyed through even the appearance of infidelity. But if personal identity, equality and trust exist in full measure, then the normal fluctuations that occur in any relationship between two human beings can be taken in stride.

A Word about the Guidelines

The eight guidelines form the heart of this book. They are designed specifically to help you develop competence and skill in relating to your mate. We recommend reading them in the chapter sequence in which they are presented, to gain the clearest understanding of their interrelation, but that does not mean they must be approached in this sequence when you begin to make actual use of them in your daily life. They progress from the simplest to the most complex aspects of human relating, but you may find one of the more complex to be most useful to you at the beginning and most pertinent to your particular marital situation. The guidelines are suggestions, not magic formulas or sets of rules. Our object is not to outline a specific format for you to follow, but to show you how you can develop a constructive life style specifically suited to you and your mate.

5 Living for Now and Realistic Expectations

Now for Now

"Now for now" is a colorful expression used by the islanders of Trinidad to sum up their belief that the immediate moment is all any man can count on in life, and that the man who doesn't make the most of that moment is, in effect, throwing away his life. Open marriage draws upon this philosophy: to live an open life with your mate and to rewrite your contract as you go along, you must relate to one another in the here and now. Yesterday is gone; tomorrow has not yet arrived. But you have today, and you should make the most of it, seeking a vital awareness of what you are doing, how you are feeling and acting, and what is happening to you in the *now*.

An overriding obsession with the future is a hallmark of the closed marriage. When John and Sue get married they immediately take out a subscription on the future, tying themselves down to expectations. New furniture, a new car, a down payment on a house, a trip to Europe, a first child, a summer cottage, a second child—there are so many future things to save up for, events to plan for that the *now* is forgotten and becomes nothing more than a time you pass through on your way to the future. The expectations, the goals, take over. John and Sue lose their personal selves and the sense of the moment in striving to attain those goals, to bring about the fulfillment of those expectations. But marriage should be for the people involved, not for the material goals of the future.

There is nothing wrong, of course, with knowing what you want out of life in a material sense, in dreaming of a sailboat or skiing vacations in the Alps or a house by the sea. But if these material goals are allowed to become the central focus of your life instead of personal growth, the chances are that by the time you have that house by the sea you won't be sharing it with the same mate you originally dreamed about it with. A couple's commitment should be to one another rather than to goals that may or may not be achievable. In an open marriage, partners know that *they* are the most important ingredients in the marriage, know that personal, immediate awareness of the self and of the mate's self are more important than any future possibility. Time consumed in looking forward to tomorrow's achievements, or in either lamenting or glorying in the past, is time lost in the vital present. And the loss of that present time cuts down on your awareness of what is happening between you and your mate.

Past and future are certainly relevant, but it is necessary to ask how relevant they are and to give them no more than the appropriate amount of attention. You can, for instance, learn from your past mistakes, but no matter what your problems may be, or how much they may stem from your past, those problems exist in the present and must be dealt with in the present. They can only be worked out in terms of your day-to-day actions. How you solve your problems *now*, how you experience joys and pleasures *now*, your immediate feelings and emotions and the degree to which you share them with your mate will determine the nature of your relationship. Your interaction with your partner in the now is what makes for a meaningful relationship. If there is no relating in the now, how can there be in the future?

The importance of this "now for now" orientation was expressed by a young couple whom we interviewed. The wife, Jean, said, "Ken used to be very unhappy; he planned ahead outlandishly. He was always in the future, anticipating, planning for the eventuality that never happened. Trying to make everything happen before it was ready to happen, securing the future was what he called it. Scaring me to death was what I called it. I began to worry along with him, not as much as he did, but too much. Well, it almost ruined our relationship. He would call me at work five or six times a day—he was afraid for tomorrow on today's time—he just couldn't let things *be*. That is, until we had some hassles and I made it clear that I *was* here now but wouldn't be in the future if he kept it up."

"Well, I finally learned," Ken said, "to let things be. And I found that was a lot better than worrying about them, about what they might or might not become. It took a few rough times to shake me up, but now I live in today. Absolutely each day is to be faced in and of itself. A bridge is something to be crossed only when you come to it, and meantime Jean and I are building right where we are in the here and now. And it's funny, but not only has our relationship become more than I dreamed it could, my career has just zoomed out of sight, too."

The Security Blanket

Couples would find it easier to relate in the present, and to live a more dynamic, open life if marriage were not held up to them as a symbol of security. Most of the unrealistic expectations surrounding marriage are cast in the form of promises of security. Couples depend upon marriage to *give* them a purpose and meaning in life, to give them love and affection, social acceptance, status and a happy family. Actually, of course, these are all things which the partners must *create* for themselves within their marriage. Marriage in and of itself provides none of these securities. Many couples refuse, however, to face the facts, and try instead to make of marriage a kind of security blanket, like children who drag around with them some frazzled remnant of their baby blankets. Having been told all their lives that marriage will bring security, they insist upon clinging to that false notion even when everything is falling apart around them. Such couples will seek for the cause of their troubles anywhere but in their own distorted views of what marriage should be.

Many couples use material acquisitions (the house, the bank account, the car, the appliances) to flesh out this illusion of security. But material security can of course evaporate overnight, or disintegrate in excruciatingly slow dribs and drabs, as neighborhoods change, values drop, inflation rises, and jobs change or disappear. Children offer no security—in fact quite the reverse, they are a great responsibility. The promise of perpetual love and care from our mate that is set forth in the marriage vows and enhanced by our unreasonable "ideals" becomes a cruel deception when we find that people change, feelings fluctuate, romance cools, marriages fail and mates leave. Affection and love must be nurtured if they are to grow; they wither in the harsh light of excessive expectation and demand.

Thus the promise of security in and through marriage is a myth. Security and the constancy of love can be found only in ourselves, not in the institution of marriage. No one can offer to another a security he does not first possess himself. And just as the child discards his ragged security blanket as he grows up, so too must we put aside our unrealistic expectations, our fairy-tale ideals, if we are to achieve the belief in ourselves that can alone provide any real security, that alone is worth offering to a mate or to a child.

He May Not Be the Father to Your Child

"Until death do us part" we promise when we take the marriage vows. But we know full well, or ought to, that other things may part us much sooner. Divorce now occurs with such frequency that marriage has become a revolving door through which marital partners pass on the way to the next promise of fidelity forever, exchanging one partner for another in a way that makes a mockery of our culture's scorn for polygamy. The man you marry today, sad to say, may not be the father of your child tomorrow.

Nor will your wife necessarily be the mother of your children. She may be, but don't count on it. This may seem a harsh and unpleasant way of looking at things. But we are not suggesting that you assume the person you marry *won't* be the mother or father of your child; we ask only that you resist making the assumption that she or he *will* be, that you recognize that she or he *may* not be. This is not negativism, only realism.

The assumption that your mate will definitely be the parent of your child is not positivism but a kind of self-delusion and fantasy that may tend to get in the way of the kind of genuine relationship between you and your mate upon which any strong, healthy and lasting marriage must be based. Parenthood today is optional anyway, and the person you marry should be enjoyed for what he is, loved as a person and not just as a potential parent. Partners who can stop living in a future devoted to raising a family and concentrate on building a good relationship *first* are far more likely to have a happy family in the long run.

Even if you do have children, and do manage to stay married for life (assuming you marry at twenty and live to age seventy-five), you should remember that child-rearing will take up only approximately one-third of your married life—a whopping two-thirds of it (or over 12,700 days) will be spent in intimate relationship together as a couple rather than as parents. So even if he *does* become the father of your child, or she the mother, your relationship to one another should remain of primary importance to you. The better this relationship is, the more meaningful it will be to your function as parents. It is vital therefore to concentrate on each other as individual persons instead of as parents-to-be, to enjoy one another in the here and now instead of looking to the future. The future will be here all too soon as it is.

The Package and the Packaging

Premature anticipations of parenthood and false hopes of security are only two among a whole panoply of unrealistic expectations that prevent us from living in the now and from actively *seeking* freedom, growth and love in our relationships with our mates. Without a close look at the expectations foisted on us by the old, closed contract, it is impossible to try to rewrite a new, open contract more suited to our actual needs. The closed marriage is designed to eliminate thinking. You are sold a complete bill of goods —not only a set of expectations but even rigid rules as to how to fulfill those expectations. Since the expectations in themselves are unrealistic, and since there is only one approved way to fulfill them, an inevitable pattern of disillusionment is set up, ready-made. The expectations lead to demands, the demands to manipulation, manipulation to frustration, and frustration to bitter disappointment. This vicious progression can only be stopped by cutting it off before it begins: by eliminating the unrealistic expectations that are the root cause of the trouble.

We are conditioned to instant perfection in our society, from instant orgasm to instant therapy. We buy a product and if it is not perfect we return it immediately. Often the product turns out to be different from what we expected; we have been misled by the packaging. The closed marriage also comes wrapped in misleading packaging, not in the form of styrofoam or plastic, but in the bright colors of idealization. The packaging for closed marriage would lead us to believe not only that it will fulfill our dreams, but that it is the only way our dreams can be fulfilled. Naturally, when we find that it doesn't deliver, that it is something other than what it was advertised to be, we feel cheated. Then we do one of three things: we live with our purchase in resignation and disappointment, we throw it out and buy another which we hope will be an improvement (and which may be one simply because we've learned not to expect so much), or we throw it out and, vowing never to get suckered into buying outright again, settle for short-term rentals instead.

What follows is a list of unrealistic expectations of marriage. It will be contrasted with what we believe you can legitimately expect of an open marriage. Some of the unrealistic expectations may not seem so to one reader or another. But we hope that in the course of the book, the reasons for including each of them in this list will become abundantly clear. We even venture to predict that as you go along many of you will discover that it is exactly those expectations you do not recognize as unrealistic at first glance that are the cause of problems within your own marriage.

UNREALISTIC EXPECTATIONS, UNREASONABLE IDEALS, AND MYTHOLOGICAL BELIEFS OF CLOSED MARRIAGE

- that it will last forever
- that it means total commitment
- that it will bring happiness, comfort and security
- that your mate *belongs* to you

- that you will have constant attention, concern, admiration and consideration from your mate
- that you will never be lonely again
- that your mate would rather be with you than with anyone else at all times
- that your mate will never be attracted to another person and will always "be true" to you
- that jealousy means you care
- that fidelity is a true measure of the love you have for one another
- that sex will improve with time if it isn't already the world-shaking experience it is supposed to be
- that good sex will in fact (if you can just get the positions right and learn the proper techniques) solve all your problems in marriage
- that all problems in marriage revolve around sex and love
- that you are not complete persons without becoming parents
- that the ultimate goal of marriage is having a child
- that having a child is the ultimate expression of your love for each other
- that having a child will bring new vitality to a sagging marriage or rescue a failing one
- that you will adjust to one another gradually without fights, arguments or misunderstandings
- that you don't love each other if there is conflict between you
- that any change in your mate will come gradually with the maturity of age
- that any other kind of change is disruptive and means loss of love
- that each of you plays a different part in marriage, a role for which you were biologically designed
- that you therefore have the right to expect one thing of a husband and another of a wife

- that sacrifice is a true measure of love
- and last, but most important, that the person you
   marry can fulfill all your needs, economic, physical, sexual, intellectual and emotional

Every single one of these ideals, beliefs or expectations
is false in one way or another, and practically impossible to
attain, much less to sustain. Yet the clauses of the closed
marriage contract are specifically designed to make these
expectations come true. Any of them that you do manage
to make come true, unfortunately, are almost certain to be
at the cost of personal freedom and individual development, with consequent damage to children and to the
overall success of the marriage itself.

The real problem is that the closed marriage is conceived
of as a *static state of being*, a pattern that once established
will mean the fulfillment of all expectations. But when expectations are rigid and the means to them restrictive,
spontaneity is lost and creativity stifled. Open marriage, in
contrast, is a *process*, in which a dynamic interaction takes
place between husband and wife, in which both realities
and expectations are constantly changing. We believe, in
fact, that the only realistic expectations partners can have
for marriage revolve around *change* and *growth*.

REALISTIC EXPECTATIONS
OF
OPEN MARRIAGE

- that you will share most but not everything
- that each partner will change—and that change can
   occur through conflict as well as through a gradual
   evolvement
- that each will accept responsibility for himself and
   grant it to his mate
- that you cannot expect your mate to fulfill all your

needs, or to do for you what you should be doing
for yourself
- that each partner will be different in needs, capacities, values and expectations because he is a different *person*, not just because one is a husband
and the other a wife
- that the mutual goal is the relationship, not status
or the house by the sea or children
- that children are not needed as proof of your love
for each other
- that should you *choose* to have children, that you
undertake the role of parents knowingly and willingly as the greatest responsibility in life
- that liking and loving will grow because of the mutual respect that your open relationship engen-
ders

In contrast to the unrealistic ideals of undying love, security and fulfillment through another person that are the
hallmarks of closed marriage, the ideals of open marriage
are:

intimacy	responsibility
intensity	learning
creativity	stimulation
spontaneity	flexibility
growth	enrichment
respect	freedom

and

the liking and love that grow
out of all of these

These ideals are not achieved by placing demands on
your mate, as is the case with the ideals of closed marriage.
Instead, they are the natural fruit of an open relationship,
a relationship that may differ greatly from couple to couple,
a relationship that you build yourselves, by yourselves and

for yourselves—both your individual selves and your collective selves.

We think that the open relationship, out of which the above ideals will grow, can be achieved through the application to your individual case of the guidelines we have assembled here:

- through realistic appraisal of your situation and living in the now
- through the giving of privacy and freedom to one another
- through open and honest communication
- through the shedding of inflexible roles
- through open companionship
- through identity, equality and trust

There may be other guidelines that you will discover for yourself. But none of them can be of use *unless you take the first vital step*: make an exploration of your expectations of marriage and then, each couple acting according to their judgment, decide which of them are real, honest and open, and which are unrealistic, confining and limiting. Discover which of them are preventing you from living in the now, from enjoying the present moment with your mate and then, with the help of the guidelines, begin to shape an open relationship for yourselves.

6 Privacy

For Chrissake Leave Me Alone

When Sam screams at Lucy to leave him alone, he probably means it literally. The problem is that Lucy, at the end of a long day spent amidst squabbling children, carrot peelings and dirty laundry, looks forward to the few evening hours she and her husband can spend together. He is, for one thing, her major contact with a larger, non-domestic world. But she is forgetting that the larger world makes its demands upon the husband, too. People have been on his back all day long, and now he comes home to discover that his wife has turned into an octopus. In pure exasperation, he blows up.

"What's eating him?" Lucy wonders. "Does he really want to be alone or does he just want to get away from me?" Immediately, she has turned a genuine need on her husband's part into a personal affront. He puts an arm around her to offer reassurance. "It isn't that I love you any less, it's just that I've got to have a little time to myself. Can't you see?" She tries to see, but she still feels rejected. After all, one of the reasons you get married is so that you can spend as much time as possible with your mate. And here he is at home but acting as though he wished he weren't.

The housewife frequently has the opportunity to find a few intermittent moments for herself during the day. The demands of the husband's job are much less likely to allow him any moments of real privacy, when he can relax and think about whatever he feels like. Working wives are in a better position to understand such pressures. After a full day's work, a short period of privacy can be far more of a restorative than anybody's company, no matter how much we may love him. The housewife often doesn't discover that there can be such a thing as too much togetherness until her husband spends three or four days at home ill with the flu. Then the same woman who regards her husband's at-home time as belonging to her by marital prerogative is likely to howl, "My God, he's driving me crazy. I can't wait until he goes back to work."

If husband and wife both understand the need for privacy, then there need be no hurt feelings or fear of rejection on either side when one or the other closets himself away for a while. One young couple whom we interviewed had worked out personal guidelines about the privacy question during their first year of marriage. Both Mike and Fran work, but Mike's job frequently involves overtime, so that Fran generally arrives home before him. When he comes in the door they share a kiss and a greeting, but neither pounces on the other with the news of the day. Instead, as he relates in his own words, "Sometimes I need a few moments of privacy, just to myself, when I get home. Those moments give me time to remove my tensions, so that afterwards I can share myself better with Fran.

"Let's say I come home disgruntled from the job," Mike goes on. "If I am immediately forced to do something, to talk or work, then I carry these tensions right into the conversation or activity and they build up even more. If I can have just a few minutes, just to get my head away from my tensions, then I don't have to bring them to her. She can help me remove them by letting me unwind at my own pace, by waiting and not making excessive demands on me." Mike and Fran also spoke of the moments of solitude they allowed one another on weekends. They felt they were essential to a good emotional relationship. "Without them I am depleted," Mike said. "I give her less than myself."

Most young couples with a family will admit that they need time off from their children. One busy young New York couple periodically pack a bag and check into a hotel for the weekend, right in the city. They are only a taxi ride away from their children should anything arise that the babysitter can't handle, yet they are able to have two days of privacy. The same couple, however, would be reluctant to recognize that they might sometimes need some time off from one another, as well. This is not necessarily to suggest that married couples should spend an occasional weekend apart, although such agreements, extending even to separate vacations, have turned out to be the solution to the privacy question for some couples. But the husband or wife who completely denies his or her mate's need for privacy is contributing to the buildup of a tension that can spill over into other areas of the relationship. The need for privacy is one that we all share—the only exceptions are people in whom dependency has reached neurotic proportions.

An American Peculiarity

No other society in the world has promoted or propagandized the idea of togetherness for married couples to the extent that we Americans have. In an ethnographic survey of 554 of the world's societies, Dr. George Murdock found that in about one-fourth of them the mother and her children occupied a household in which the father was present only occasionally. In some primitive societies, husbands and wives do not eat together and cannot display tenderness and affection in public. In others, menstrual and postdelivery taboos require husband and wife to sleep apart for long periods of time.

Obviously, these behavioral patterns are at the opposite extreme from our own, and we are not urging that they be emulated. But since marriages under such conditions are as stable, if not indeed more stable than, those in our own society, it should be abundantly clear that togetherness is not the vital element in making a marriage work. An argument can be made, as pointed out in chapter 1, that the togetherness mystique developed largely as a counter-force to the new mobility and freedom of women, providing the wife with a new reason to stay in the home and under her husband's thumb. The taboos in primitive societies that prevent married couples from eating together or sharing sexual pleasure at certain times act as a limitation upon the pleasure that can be derived from an intimate relationship between two people. But the togetherness mystique has its taboos, too. When it is taken as a personal affront if one mate closes a door on the other to do anything other than go to the bathroom, then we are talking about taboos. When a taboo runs counter to such a strong psychological need as our "instinct" for occasional privacy, tension is bound to result.

Psychic Space

It took Martin, a musician, twenty years of crowded togetherness before he discovered the true importance and real meaning of being alone. His statements are a striking testimonial to the crushing pressure of too much togetherness. "Now I love my wife and my kids, but there were many times when I wanted to be alone," he explained. "But, see, I thought, my God, that's immoral. Even though I needed it, I still felt guilty. We've got three kids, a jumping family, my work is always with people, playing at night in crowds, and my students call up at 4 A.M. I never knew what privacy meant until about three years ago. Well, I had a concert to play in Virginia and had to drive down alone. The trip took nine hours on the road. It was a revelation.

"I stopped in the mountains, got out, and climbed to the top. For the first time in twenty years of marriage I was alone. All alone, just me, and the mountains. I found myself up there. I liked myself. This was three years ago, and ever since, I take time to be alone. I have a soundproof studio at home, and now I go in, not to play, but just to be alone. I will sit there in my studio and I feel a charge of energy, a self-communication I find nowhere else. Maybe that's what you call liberation."

Man fluctuates between a desire for gregariousness and a desire for solitude. It is in the moments of aloneness that we can recharge, take stock of ourselves and revitalize our energies for further encounters with others. To give all of ourselves, all the time, to those we choose to live with is a denial of our separate identities and of our individual needs for self-renewal. To demand that your mate interact with you constantly is not only an invasion of his right to privacy but a barrier to his growth.

There are, as the psychologist Dr. Clark Moustakas has pointed out, two major pathways to growth. One pathway is through our interaction with other human beings; the other is the route of self-discovery through solitude. "Some kinds of self-discovery," Dr. Moustakas writes, "emerge only through self-reflection, self-confrontation, and meditation, and in no other way . . . The personal relationship is just what must be abandoned in some of life's critical moments."

Privacy can provide a way for coping with problems. One young husband commented, "Privacy means that you have to have the guts, when your mood is really down, to break loose from the other and find your own way to pull out of the mood—take a walk, just brood if you want." His wife added, "I respect his desire for privacy, for I know there are places I cannot go with him—just as there are areas of myself that are for myself alone. When he has worked out his mood, then we get together and share it, but only when he is ready for it." This couple has recognized that everyone has an individual way of leveling with himself, and that both partners in a marriage must respect the integrity of the spouse's method.

Too much togetherness in marriage leads to the denial of both partners' need for psychic space—which can be either intellectual "thinking space" or emotional "feeling space." Time apart from the mate gives each partner the opportunity to explore his own preferences, private perceptions, insights, beliefs and values. If you have no time alone, you will never know yourself. And, ultimately, the most valuable thing you have to give to your marriage is your self. If you don't have the opportunity to discover, continuously, what that "self" is, then you cannot openly give of it to your mate.

The Golf Hat and the Bandanna

An eminent psychologist and teacher worked out a signal system with his wife to indicate the need for privacy. If the professor was thinking through a particularly difficult problem, when any interruption to his train of thought would be disturbing, he would put on his favorite golf hat. To his wife, this hat conveyed the message, "Leave me alone for now, I'm thinking," just as clearly as if he had worn a sign around his neck. His wife tied on a particular bandanna when she was in a similar mood. Sometimes they would wear the golf hat or the bandanna for only a few hours, sometimes for much longer periods. Each respected the other's need for privacy and left the one wearing the headgear strictly alone.

Since the professor often worked at home, and because his work involved him with complex psychological theorems, he had a greater than average need for privacy. But each of us has moments when a certain amount of time apart is necessary, when no amount of tender concern or well-meant advice can help us and may indeed simply make matters worse. Any couple who can set up a non-verbal signal to indicate the need for privacy will find it a great help in eliminating hard feelings and furthering their understanding of one another. If the relationship between two people is such that either one can openly say, "Don't bother me for a while," without the other being upset, then they will have no need for a non-verbal system. But if either mate is likely to take such a statement as a form of rejection, or demand an explanation, then a signal system can be very useful. Verbal explanations or requests can be misinterpreted, but a golf cap makes itself instantly clear.

Being Alone Together

Wearing their respective pieces of symbolic headgear, the professor and his wife could have privacy even though they were occupying the same room or eating at the same table together. Privacy does not necessarily involve going off entirely by oneself. Indeed, a couple's ability to be together in the same room and yet alone indicates a fundamental respect for one another. In such a situation, "togetherness" takes on a new meaning. As one wife put it, "I can still be with Reggie, yet very alone when I am absorbed in making jewelry and he is doing something else. We work side by side, yet I can feel alone and think alone. Some of our best sharing comes from allowing each his own total involvement with his own project."

Donald and Marilyn, on the other hand, are typical of

the couple who have failed to communicate their needs for privacy. Don has a thriving and demanding law practice. His wife manages their ten-room house and tends the growing family more than adequately, but understandably likes to stretch out on the couch and relax after dinner. She wants Don to share this time with her, but his needs are different. "You know how busy the office is and the chaos here at home with four kids," he says. "Well, just for the purpose of privacy I fixed up the attic. But fat chance I ever get to use it. Marilyn mopes and sulks when I go up there and I just can't make her understand that sometimes I need to get away. So just to be with her, I haul out the bills, the calculations and plans for investments I'm involved in. But that isn't enough for her. Not that she wants to share these aspects of my job with me. Oh, no. Instead she complains that I never talk to her. Well, how can I win? So what do I do? I stay over at the office more now, or go in on Sundays. And if I really want to escape I go and play golf."

The wife who is without resources to entertain herself, and who doesn't understand her husband's need of privacy, is more than likely to do just what Marilyn is doing to Don —drive him out of the house. Since Marilyn refuses to let him off by himself within the house, and does not have the ability to take pleasure in his presence beside her in the same room without badgering him to talk to her, he is left with no choice but to seek escape routes for himself. Eventually, of course, he is likely to seek the ultimate escape—divorce.

Learning to be alone together will be particularly important to couples living in small, cramped quarters, where it is difficult to arrange to be physically alone. But even couples with the space for a sitting room or den, to which one or the other partner can retreat, will find that being alone together offers special pleasures—the possibility of being private in a way that simultaneously enhances the couple's sense of sharing. The real point of "togetherness," surely, is to create such a sense of sharing; yet many couples, by assuming that sharing means demanding your mate's constant attention, destroy the very thing they are attempting to achieve.

The Self-sufficient Spouse

Gordon was a psychotherapist who had been divorced for two years following twenty years of marriage. At the time we first interviewed him, he was involved in a semi-committed, non-marriage arrangement with Carol, also divorced. They were companions in most of their activities, including entertaining together and sharing vacations. Yet Gordon refused to live with her. "Carol is a great gal," he said, "and we share many things together, almost all our spare time. But to live together . . . that's another thing. All my life I've been beholden to other people and my profession reinforces this. I spend my entire day in intense involvement with the problems of my patients. I *like* the idea of being by myself at times—the freedom of not having to put myself out. If I want to go to bed and read a book, I can. In fact, I *need* the time to be by myself. If I were to live with Carol, and I know her pretty well by this time, she might see this as withdrawal, which it isn't. The question is her ability to accept this as *me*, not as a withdrawal. Perhaps two people in a long-established relationship can reach this agreement—the acceptance of each other's individuality—but in a newly established relationship it takes a very secure person to accept this. I doubt if Carol is that secure. My wife certainly wasn't. Now that I have this freedom, I'm not trading it in for the same old thing again."

Gordon's situation, and his feelings about it, emphasize the extent to which the guidelines for open marriage presented here interlock with one another. Privacy is an important ingredient in open marriage. It is, to begin with, an actual need that the traditional closed marriage ignores, indeed tries to repress. In addition, privacy is vital to the continuing personal growth that is one of the chief ends of open marriage. But, as Gordon makes clear, it takes a secure person to grant privacy to his mate. That kind of security can come only from having a strong identity, and the self-sufficiency that goes with it. Identity, of course, is another of the guidelines. And identity cannot be achieved unless one has sufficient time alone, the necessary privacy, in which to seek the self-discovery of which Dr. Moustakas writes.

To return to Gordon, and his reluctance to marry Carol because he feared that she lacked the self-sufficiency, the identity, to allow him the privacy he needed, there is a further chapter to the story. Since the time we interviewed him, Gordon has in fact remarried. But he did not marry Carol. Rather, he married a woman working in his own field, a busy professional with a strong sense of self, who not only understood Gordon's need for occasional privacy, but shared that need herself.

All Things in Proportion

The need for privacy should not of course be confused with outright avoidance. The aloneness that is an integral part of all of us, which gives us our sense of self, is very different from the neurotic loneliness of deprivation and alienation. One woman we interviewed complained bitterly that her husband went off to bed immediately after dinner every night. "He says he's exhausted, but it means that he never sees the children. In fact, I hardly see him myself, because by the time I'm ready to go to bed, after spending the whole evening by myself, he gets up and watches old movies half the night." Obviously, the husband in this case is not seeking normal privacy, in order to restore himself, but is simply withdrawing from his family and his responsibilities to them.

Outright avoidance, as in the case of Don's escape to his

office or the golf links in order to get away from the demands of his wife Marilyn, is often a symptom of trouble in the old, closed marriage. The person who is freely granted his times of privacy by his mate does not feel the need to escape. The sense of perspective and the feeling of independence developed by both partners when their mutual need for privacy is accepted serves to reinforce the strength of each personality and makes their partnership all that much more vital in the long run. For some, the granting of these moments of privacy to the mate may be a difficult, even painful step, and the time thus spent alone seems to weigh heavily. But such difficulties in accepting one's own moments alone can usually be taken as an indication of how much they are needed. Privacy is an essential component of a healthy marriage, and if you find that you can't bear to be alone with yourself, the probability is that you have not yet achieved, through confrontation with yourself, the kind of strong identity which will lead to personal fulfillment with your mate. If you can't make it alone, you will have trouble making it together, too.

7 Open and Honest Communication: Verbal and Non-Verbal

HelloHowAreYouI'mFine

Your father may be in the hospital, your ten-year-old son may have lost two front teeth in a fight at school yesterday, and you yourself may have a sinus headache—but if a casual friend should ask you at the office or in the supermarket how you are, you will probably reply, "I'm fine." Much of what passes for communication is merely ritual, and our responses are often determined by a kind of habitual defense mechanism. In most situations, there's nothing wrong with this kind of superficial exchange. When people ask how you are they're merely trying to express their general friendliness; they certainly don't expect you to bend their ears for half an hour with a full account of your state of health. The trouble is, though, that over the years these shallow, ritualistic responses, little white lies, and defensive prevarications become so ingrained that we find it difficult to communicate directly, honestly and openly even when we want to do so with people who are important to us.

We are taught from birth that the image is more important than the reality. As children we watch with amazement as our parents break off a furious argument to talk perfectly calmly on the telephone when friends call up in the middle of the battle. We hear Mommy tell Daddy that she had a very nice day when in fact she broke down and cried right in front of us only an hour ago. The examples increase as we grow older, and we learn to do the same thing ourselves. When we try to be honest we often get into hot water: nobody is at all pleased with us when we announce that the reason we don't like to visit Aunt Martha is that her house smells. We learn to keep our mouths shut and to hide our true feelings. That, it appears, is the only way to get along in the world. And there is no question that it helps grease the wheels of ordinary day-to-day living. We continue to assure ourselves, however, that when it comes to anything really *important*, we will be able to go back to being forthright. Unfortunately, it isn't that easy.

The examination of John and Sue's first week of marriage in chapters 3 and 4 illustrates how we bring our tendency to put a good face on things, and hide our true feelings, right into our marriages. We do so, like John and Sue, out of love, because we don't want to hurt our mate or to disappoint him by appearing less than perfect. While growing up we have absorbed from our parents and the world around us the lesson that to preserve those ideal images gentle deception is often necessary, and that outright cunning may even be required. To preserve the fraudulent ideals demanded by the closed marriage contract, we stoop to deception, further undermining our ability to communicate openly and truly with our marriage partner.

Honest, free-flowing communication is crucial to the building of an open marriage. But how do you break through the wall of self-defense that has been erected over the years? How do you clear away the tangle of habitual minor deceptions? How can you get back in touch with your mate?

Let us begin by getting a better understanding of what communication between human beings consists of.

Non-verbal Communication

Research has indicated that about 70 percent of our communication with others is carried out on a non-verbal level. The most profound form of non-verbal communication is, of course, sex. But the ways in which your mate walks, stands, holds her head, drums his fingers, smiles or frowns are important, too, and can often tell you far more than words. Every action provides a sensory cue that can be read by others. Some of us are so acutely aware of these cues and responses that we are frequently able to add up the sensory data and then intuit beyond them to another level of understanding, leading us to say we feel "vibrations" from other persons. We can pick up such vibrations from people we've never met but simply exchanged a glance with across a room. Yet in our relationships with those closest to us, we tend to ignore these signals. In many cases we simply become so used to our mate's non-verbal signs that they cease to affect us on a conscious level. Sometimes, too, we deliberately screen them out, either from impatience or because we don't want to recognize the message that is being sent.

Even though body language is often ignored or misread, non-verbal communication is still less complicated than verbal. For this very reason, it should be easier to correct some of our mistakes in this area first. You can make a conscious effort to be receptive to your mate's non-verbal signs and to act according to what they tell you. When Helen comes home from the dentist with a swollen jaw and her eyes dulled with pain, it is sheer sadism to remind her that a pail of dirty diapers has been sitting at the foot of the basement stairs since yesterday.

Timing is a crucial element in life—not only in choosing the right moment to grasp an opportunity, but also in learning when to avoid the wrong moment. If you insist on bombarding your husband with all of your aggravating grievances of the day the moment he comes in the door crumpled from a heat wave and a discouraging day at work, then you are deliberately ignoring non-verbal cues and asking for a fight.

Of course, part of you may be just spoiling for a fight, even though the other half of you would like to avoid it. If you keep your eyes open, and look for the telltale physical signs and body cues that reveal your mate's state of mind, then you will have a much better chance of controlling your responses when your own feelings are divided. Helen's husband, for instance, may indeed feel a degree of unconscious sadism, wondering why the devil he had to marry the woman with the worst teeth in the state, so that he's always up to his neck in dentist's bills. Because he unconsciously wants to upbraid her for something that he consciously realizes she can't possibly help, he seizes on the diapers as a substitute rebuke. But if he opens himself to her non-verbal signals, thus allowing himself to recognize her genuine pain, he will feel sorry for her, and the unconscious urge to hurt her will be squelched.

Discrepant Messages

Learning to read the non-verbal cues of your mate can also help you untangle the confusions caused by discrepant messages. Discrepant messages occur when our verbal and non-verbal forms of communication *contradict* one another. Bill may say to his wife, "I'm listening, I'm listening," but his body is hunched over attentively in front of the television set. Arthur may tell his wife, "I love you," over and over, but she has good cause to wonder if he means it when he never listens to her attentively, gives her only a peck on the cheek, and is perfunctory in bed.

Whatever we may *say*, it's the *non-verbal message* that usually tells the truth. A verbal lie is all too easy to tell. Controlling your body sufficiently to make it back up your lie is much more difficult. And frequently, even when we ourselves believe our own verbal messages, our bodies may tell a different story.

The discrepancy between a body message and a verbal message may well indicate a problem area in the relationship between husband and wife. Couples who are trying to develop a new openness and move away from the restrictive conditions of a closed marriage may find the pinpointing of discrepant messages in one another a useful method by which to improve communication in general between them. Discovering the contradictions in messages can uncover and bring to light unrecognized needs, feelings and desires.

In the open marriage there should be no need for saying things you don't mean. Bill should not have to say "I'm listening, I'm listening," when he isn't. If he is intently watching television, it is obviously not the time for Mary to start a discussion or rattle on about unimportant matters. However, if her verbal mesage and a discussion of it is terribly urgent *she* should be able to say so, and Bill should be able to turn off the TV set and listen. If not, *he* should be able to say openly, "Could we wait till later, Mary?" and Mary can respect his desire to delay the conversation, for she will expect the same kind of consideration from him at another time.

The ability to recognize discrepant messages in one another can provide the couple with important clues as to those areas of the closed marriage that are most restrictive to both. This is not to suggest, of course, that Bill's wife should immediately cry out, "Aha, caught you in the act, you're sending a discrepant mesage, you don't really want to listen to me at all!" Instead, a frank discussion of the contradictory message that each notices in the other can lead to a much fuller understanding of just how the contract is affecting them. Pinpointing the real message Bill was sending from the TV set could well lead into a discussion of the "your time is my time" clause of closed marriage, and lead to a new respect for each other's privacy.

Creating a Non-verbal Language

Learning to read your mate's non-verbal signals can help you to understand him or her better, and guide you in choosing the best time for and the best kind of verbal communication. But partners who become aware of the tremendous importance of non-verbal communication can use it as a language in itself. Since our understanding of this type of visible communication is still in its infancy, most of us have been alerted only to *reading* the body messages of others. But body language can, with sensitivity, training and skill, be used as a direct means of communication. From becoming increasingly aware of each other, partners can learn to read, interpret and respond to each other's silent signals. Couples can set up a prearranged system of non-verbal signals for all kinds of situations, such as the golf hat and bandanna we mentioned under Privacy or the signals couples give each other at parties to indicate boredom, silence on certain topics, or "it's time to leave." They can even develop a silent language of their own, a kind of shorthand that cuts across other barriers and which will in the long run become an important aid to better verbal communication.

Sensuality as Communication

Visual communication with body messages is only one kind of non-verbal language. Another method of communicating without words is to use our bodies directly. The need to reach out and *touch* one another, if only for a moment, has created a new national pastime. Sensitivity training and encounter groups flourish from coast to coast. Why their sudden popularity? It is because we desperately need to reawaken our physical senses.

The infant first learns about the world through his sense of touch. His feelings of confidence, trust and warm intimacy are first established by being held, supported, touched, caressed and attended to physically. But in our society this deep need for physical intimacy—the need to reach out and touch, to *feel*—is trained out of us as we grow up. Physical demonstrations of emotion are frowned upon, and we are taught to curb our sensual and erotic sensitivities from earliest childhood. Is it any wonder couples have trouble expressing the simplest affection—or even compassion and sorrow—in a physical way? Is it any wonder that so many couples have difficulty in achieving sexual compatibility? You can't train someone *not* to respond for twenty-five years and then turn around and ask him to perform responsively in bed.

Couples need to relearn the full use of physical expression as a means of intimate communication and to reawaken their sensuality. The dictionary defines sensual as "voluptuous" or "devoted to pleasure of the senses and appetite," and adds, as a final caution, "sometimes lewd." Thus disapproval of sensuality is built right into our language. But sensuality, far from being lewd, is absolutely necessary to good physical communication. The sensuous exchange bettween partners is the manifest physical expression of caring.

There are many kinds of exercises to assist men and women in rediscovering their physicality and developing their sensuality; we are not going to recommend any particular approach or method for the simple reason that what may be helpful to one couple can easily seem silly to another, and vice versa. But, short of embarking on an actual program, you can still work together as a couple to increase your capacity for sensual sharing: first, by becoming more aware of your own and your mate's physical needs and responses, and second, by reaching out to each other physically, and actively exploring together new means of sensual awareness—through touch, smell, sight and sound. We are not necessarily speaking here of explicit sexual experimentation, although that certainly is a very important way of getting back in touch with your physical selves. Becoming more sensually aware and communicating it in sex can bring greater sexual enjoyment and sharing for couples.

Another dimension of sensitivity and sensual awareness can best be explained in the words of a young wife whom we interviewed:

"Most of us," she said, "are brainwashed into thinking that orgasm is one of the best outlets for tension—well, it doesn't always work that way. There are times when I'm in a low mood, not keyed-up tense, but low-keyed tense and sex just won't work for these tensions. At these times I have a great need to hug, to be close. Jim hugs me and understands. It's almost as if his energy is flowing into mine, and if I can just squeeze him I feel better. Sex isn't what I need at that point; it's for an entirely different kind of mood."

Jim himself added, "I can sense the times Elaine needs to be hugged, and we both share them. I'm not much up on these Oriental philosophies, but somehow we do transmit spiritual and physical energy through our bodies. At other times, when I am drained, at a low ebb, or worried, she knows. She reaches out to touch me or hold me and I gain strength from her." This kind of communication may sound simple, and in a sense it is. But it requires a far more open awareness of your mate's moods and non-verbal messages than many couples are accustomed to sharing. It requires, of course, not only an ability to read your mate's signals, but a willingness to have your own read. It means not only mood tolerance but mood sharing. The intimate, physical sharing that can be gained by such openness is a pleasure denied to those who will not let down their guard, or betray their "image," even long enough for their mates to discover what in fact they do need and want. But within the context of open marriage, the willingness to be "read" develops naturally, in conjunction with your fulfillment of the other guidelines.

All That Talk

The mastery of non-verbal communication, learning to decode your partner's body language and becoming a sensuous, sensitive partner able to physically express your feelings can help you greatly in attaining an open marriage. But the remaining 30 percent of your communication that is verbalized is even more important than the 70 percent that is unspoken. The real bridge that makes it possible for partners to know and love one another in intimacy and to sustain a relationship in depth and through time is the verbal one. All marriage relationships must ultimately be distilled in the crucible of words.

Good sex, for instance, vital though it is as a form of non-verbal communication, has never yet by itself settled a real difference between marital partners or preserved a marriage that wasn't working out on other levels. It is spoken language—all that talk, all those words you send back and forth—that must serve as the primary means for marital partners to come to know one another in depth. The degree to which a couple can open up and explore their relationship verbally is the degree to which they will achieve individual growth and true commitment to one another. The following chapter, therefore, will concern itself with the psychological bases of good verbal communication, and will detail five principles whose application can help you to achieve more open and honest communication with your mate.

8 Communication: Self-Disclosure and Feedback

Guessing Game

Many couples believe that they know a lot more about one another than they in fact do know. This finding has arisen out of a number of recent studies and research projects, whose results point up the need for greater communication between husbands and wives. Several years ago at the Merrill-Palmer Institute, for instance, Dr. David Kahn, a clinical psychologist, presented couples with a sentence-completion test made up of statements such as "Personal habits of mine which annoy my mate most are . . ."; "My mate's decisions are influenced too much by . . ."; "Things would go better if he (she) would tell me . . ."; and "Trouble between us would not have arisen if . . ." The husbands and wives each filled out two forms, one in which they completed these statements for themselves, and another in which they answered as they *thought* their mates would answer. When comparisons were made, certain couples in certain areas came quite close in their answers. But, in general, there were wide discrepancies in their answers which demonstrated a lack of understanding and knowledge of each other.

Guessing won't work. Unless you *tell* your mate how you feel, he or she will be forced to guess, and the strong likelihood is that the guess will be wrong. Communication cannot be carried out on the basis of supposition; mindreading is best left in the hands of nightclub performers. Unfortunately, in this age of pop Freudianism, in which everybody knows a few phrases of psychoanalytic mumbojumbo, people are more likely than ever to believe that they have their mates all figured out. But if you treat your mate according to what you *think* his underlying motives are, all you will accomplish is a further muddying of the already swirling communicative waters. *Mutual* analysis, with both partners opening up to receive the other's messages, and with both attempting to communicate his own feelings as honestly as possible, can be rewarding, provide insights, mutual support and greater understanding between partners. But guessing will get you nowhere.

Communicating with Yourself

If you want your mate to stop guessing about your feelings and motives, you have to be prepared to reveal yourself. And in order to reveal yourself you have to know yourself. You can't talk openly and honestly with your mate until you have tried being honest with yourself first. Take time off to be alone. Use that time not simply to engage in passive meditation, but to carry on an active inner dialogue with yourself, between the person you think you are and the inner you that operates at gut level. Communicating with yourself involves revelation, self-analysis and re-evaluation. Change is impossible otherwise. No architect of change, in any field, will attempt to make new plans without assessing the present situation. So, too, each of us can

and must make an assessment of our own assets and lia-
bilities.

Level with yourself. Remove your inner as well as your
outer mask. We all put on some sort of mask when we face
others. But we have inner masks, too, behind which we hide
from ourselves. Take a fresh look at yourself. What do you
really feel, about yourself and others? Try to view yourself
and your actions objectively, without praise or blame,
simply trying to understand why you behave as you do,
analyzing yourself as though you were an observer and not
the doer. What would the judgment of an impartial observer be concerning a given action of yours?

If you are honest with yourself, you may come up with
an unflattering objective analysis of your behavior. And at
that point you will probably start arguing with yourself,
rationalizing your actions, seeking external causes that impelled you to act as you did. The boss yelled at you, you
weren't in a position to yell back, and went home in a
temper. At home you then yelled at your wife, who subse-
quently yelled at the children. And so on. But there's nothing wrong with attempting to rationalize your behavior so
long as it's part of a debate with that other "objective" part
of yourself. Which half of you "wins" the debate is beside
the point. It is the debate itself that is important, because
it gives you an opportunity to get to know yourself better.
If you happen to be a person who is easily depressed, with
a tendency to run yourself down and take too much blame
on yourself, then you should try to reverse the procedure,
using the "objective" part of yourself to praise your actions
and point out the redeeming aspects of your behavior.

Some people are naturally given to analyzing themselves,
having discovered long ago that doing so gave them added
confidence—other people's criticism is far less likely to hurt
you if you have already gone over the pros and cons in
your own head. If the criticism is just, then you will be
able to more easily admit your mistake and move on without wallowing in self-pity or guilt. On the other hand, if

the criticism is unjust, then you will be able to better defend yourself, since both sides of the argument are clear in your own mind.

In devising other exercises for getting acquainted with yourself, you can provide your own best guidelines. Professional analysts' books on the subject may be a help, but they are generally made up of case histories of people whose situations may be very different from your own. More useful, because it is more personal, is the analysis of your own dreams. An interesting and effective method of analysis is presented by Dr. Fritz Perls in *Gestalt Psychology Verbatim*. The book is based on taped sessions in which Dr. Perls demonstrates how to use dreams as a vehicle for self-exploration. You need only a segment of a dream. From that segment you take each element and *become* it, personifying it and giving a voice to it. You assume the role of the train, the butterfly, the menacing stranger, whatever— each object or person in the dream. In this way you can learn to recognize your inner conflicts and translate your own private symbolism in terms that are more readily understandable.

The usefulness of such devices will depend upon the kind of person you are. But you should try to discover some way in which to communicate better with yourself. To understand why you acted as you did in one case is an important step toward the prevention of future overreaction or miscommunication in your relationship with your mate. Your insights become part of you, unconscious as well as conscious, and the more knowledgeable you are concerning yourself, the easier it will be for you to communicate that self to your mate.

Self-Disclosure

All the discoveries that we make through communicating with ourselves—our thoughts, beliefs and concepts of self—are only ideas until we crystallize them and give them meaning and substance in words. Thus we come to know ourselves even better through disclosing ourselves to others. "Full disclosure of the self to at least one other significant human being," writes Dr. Sidney Jourard in *The Transparent Self*, "appears to be one means by which a person discovers not only the breadth and depth of his needs and feelings, but also the nature of his own self-affirmed values." Revealing ourselves openly and honestly to others is the most important means of knowing the self.

Furthermore it is one of the most important means by which our mates come to know us. "Through my self-disclosure," writes Jourard, "I let others know my soul. They can know it, really know it, only as I make it known." True intimacy between mates, and mutual growth, is based on the ability to open up and share your inner selves without fear of judgment—not only your likes, but your dislikes, your doubts as well as your hopes. We become authentic beings to each other by "taking the first step at dropping pretense, defenses, and duplicity."

But inevitably we hesitate. We fear that revelation may expose our vulnerabilities to others, even our mate. There is no question that discretion in self-disclosure must be exercised in ordinary communication with the larger world, but how much censorship and restraint should we use with the person we love and live with?

It is easy to argue that you hold back your true feelings out of concern for your mate, but generally the concern we feel is also for ourselves. We are afraid that we will seem less "good" or "strong" than our mate expects us to be, or that he will not approve of our feelings. What is really in operation here is a lack of personal identity—and the sense of insecurity that goes with it. That insecurity leads us to maintain the façade, to try to appear as the ideal husband or wife. But people are not ideal, they are only human. And to hide what we really feel only makes it more difficult to grow and to achieve the knowledge of each other that is only possible through self-disclosure.

One of the neglected areas of communication between partners, and the most important for a loving relationship, is disclosing positive feelings. When partners have been deeply moved by something, or touched by a tender observation that strikes a note of response in them, they should try to express it, to disclose it to the other and capture the moment before it is gone. With positive self-disclosures, that is, telling the good things you feel, husband and wife can open up the way for honesty in more critical areas of feelings and knowledge of each other.

Is Honesty the Best Policy?

Some people will insist, of course, that mates must not "tell all" to one another, that honesty hurts, that our innermost revelations are sometimes too devastating to be faced, and that most of us cannot bear to hear the truth. The truth, it is said, is often brutal.

Blunt or "brutal" honesty, however, is seldom a disclosure of intimacy. It is usually an indulgence in destructive and unnecessary criticism. The "brutal" or blunt truth, in fact, is often an exaggeration. If Tom has been waiting for his wife to finish dressing for almost an hour and says, when she finally appears, "I don't know why that took so long, you look as frumpy as ever," he is not "telling all" but simply being cruel. On the other hand, a very similar remark can, under different circumstances, be rewarded by a laugh and a kiss: if, after being out partying until 3 A.M., Dick and Susan find themselves looking blearily into the bathroom mirror the next morning, there will be truth but no cruelty in Dick's remark, "I'm afraid it's hard to say which of us looks lousier, honey. I guess it's a toss-up." It is all in the context.

There is no place for what might be called "vicious truths" in marriage or in any good relationship. But honesty about your true feelings, if they are shared with someone equally as honest, is the best way (and really the only way) to establish a relationship of openness and trust, provided respect and concern for the other's ego is maintained. In such a relationship, the truth as you initially see it may alter its shape in the light of your mate's responses to your honest self-disclosure. Neither will know the truth as it exists between them until each has communicated to the other his individual *perception* of the truth and compared the two points of view. Each of us assumes that the way we perceive things is the way they are, and we expect that others see them the same way.

The real nature of "truth" and the way you perceive it is illustrated by the following story. A reporter asked three umpires how they distinguished a ball from a strike. The first umpire answered, "There are balls and there are strikes and I calls them as I sees them." The second umpire answered, "There are balls and there are strikes, and I calls them as they is." But the third umpire replied, "There are balls and there are strikes, *but they ain't nothing until I calls them.*"

This story points up the fact that each spouse has a different frame of reference, and that the balls and strikes of life are determined by what they think they are. Notice that the third umpire is the one who is aware, who knows that reality exists in terms of the way he *perceives* it. Thus what you *think* it is determines *what* it is for you. If a husband thinks all women spend too much money, even though in reality his wife is very thrifty, then he will think that her $2.98 purchase is extravagant. She may think that her $2.98 purchase is a bargain.

You and your mate are both umpires in respect to the events of your life together. If you, to yourself, call a ball when your mate, to himself, calls a strike, and you never openly communicate your calls (i.e. your perception of the event) to each other, then you are allowing a misunderstanding to exist between you and you will never get to know one another or be able to approach honesty together. John and Sue, if you remember, each saw John's conversation with the lady architect from their own differing perspectives. Disclosing your perceptions—your opinions, beliefs and feelings—even if it means confrontation, is fundamental to intimacy and honesty in an open relationship.

The importance of honesty between husband and wife was strikingly demonstrated during our interview with Martin, the musician whose remarks about his need to be alone some of the time were quoted in the chapter on Privacy. Martin's wife Gloria was present at the interview, and contributed to it. At one point, after we had been talking for some time, Martin complained of the pace of his life over the twenty-three years of their marriage. And suddenly, he and Gloria discovered that they had both been wanting the same thing but had not even known it. The interchange went as follows:

MARTIN: God, but my life was a rat race—I traveled this country at night, in the daytime, on weekends—always out making a buck, never home at night. It's changed now—I'm at home more—and I really like it better. I've gotten very choosy about the jobs I take.

INTERVIEWER: (*To Gloria*): And how did you feel all those years when he was traveling and away at night a lot?

GLORIA: How did I feel? Well . . . I suppose lonely.

INTERVIEWER: Were you concerned and uneasy?

GLORIA: Yes. That's right. Sure I was. Damn lonely and worried.

MARTIN: But, Gloria, why didn't you tell me? Why didn't you say so?

GLORIA: You never asked. I thought that was just the way it was. You were gone, working. I stayed home. What should I have done, shouted to you, stay home, Martin, please stay home, I miss you?

MARTIN: But you never *told* me how you felt. How did I

know? I thought I had to accept every job that was offered me—if I didn't, I felt like I was letting the family down. If I had known *that*, it could have changed everything. I didn't want to travel that much, playing every night, but I thought I had to, had to be out there bringing the dollar in. Hell, I could have found another way, but you never told me.

The waste of time, energy and potential happiness through the years of Martin and Gloria's marriage, when what they both *really* wanted was so much more similar than what each *supposed* the other wanted, is appalling. Yet this same kind of waste, to a greater or lesser extent, clearly affects millions of American marriages. And that waste occurs for the very simple reason that husbands and wives are not honest with one another about their real needs and desires, and because they do not communicate them.

A marriage relationship gives you no license to make childish confessions of past misdeeds, or to turn your mate into a dumping ground for your personal guilts. That is not honesty at work but neurotic insecurity. The open marriage, however, does require honesty about how you feel *now*, in relation to the life that you and your mate are making together. Without such honesty, you will find it far more difficult to avoid the restrictive clauses of the traditional closed marriage contract, and almost impossible to rewrite the contract according to your own specific needs. You cannot work toward the meeting of needs whose existence you are afraid to admit. Without honesty you leave yourself vulnerable to the kind of sad waste of happiness that afflicted Martin and Gloria.

Self-knowledge, self-disclosure, and honesty—these comprise sound psychological foundations for good communication between mates. To build upon this foundation, we suggest the use of the following five principles of effective communication:

1. Understand the context
2. Timing
3. Clarity
4. Open listening
5. Feedback

We will discuss each of these principles in turn.

Understand the Context

Every communicative exchange takes place within a web of circumstances which determine the meaning of what is said. We have already seen how similar comments about a wife's appearance can take on different meanings in different contexts—in one case a harsh putdown, in the other a shared joke. Another example involves the use of the word "scatterbrain." When Harry says, "Hi, scatterbrain," and pulls Pam down onto the couch with him, the word is a term of endearment. But if he uses it when she arrives home from the supermarket without the charcoal briquettes he asked her to buy for the barbecue, she may well take offense.

Rose is a great kidder. It's a quality her husband Ben is well able to appreciate most of the time, but unfortunately she doesn't know when to stop. Even when he is genuinely concerned about something, a problem at work or the number of unpaid bills in the desk drawer, she goes right on making her little jokes. She may only be trying to cheer him up, but under the circumstances it seems to him that she is belittling him for taking his problems so seriously. What is meant to be helpful thus comes out seeming like criticism.

Such examples may seem trivial. But a large part of any relationship with a marital partner does in fact consist of what can only be called trivia. And if you can't get along with your mate on the level of trivia, you are certainly headed for larger problems. Many misunderstandings and disagreements can be avoided if you simply pay attention to the context, and are sensitive to the conditions under which you are attempting to communicate. Sometimes the context is obvious, as when Pam forgot the charcoal. At other times, the *real* context may become apparent only if you read your mate's non-verbal signals.

You may at first feel self-conscious, even foolish, in attempting to become aware of the context. But if you make a genuine effort to increase that awareness, it will in time become second nature to you, something to which you do not even need to give conscious attention. Most of us have bad habits in this regard; we ride roughshod over the context when talking to people in general and particularly to our mates. In correcting, or giving up, any bad habit, whether it is excessive smoking or talking a blue streak at breakfast (when all your mate wants to do is read the paper in silence), there will be a period of self-consciousness. But in the long run the benefits will prove worth it.

Timing

Timing is allied to context. As you become more aware of context, and attune yourself to your mate's non-verbal signals, you can set about timing your verbal communications on difficult matters accordingly. Instead of letting yourself in for unnecessary and unpleasant confrontations, you can hold off for the proper moment to speak. The time to tell your wife she's shooting the budget to pieces with the amount she spends on clothes is not when she comes rushing home full of pleasure with a new purchase. Since she's going to have to deny herself future pleasures, there's no point in spoiling her present pleasure as well. That merely adds insult to injury.

The art of timing is really a simple one. Children make use of it constantly, although in a negative way. The savvy kid reads his parents' moods and saves his confessions of wrongdoing or his requests for extra money until he thinks the circumstances favor him. He zooms in when you're harassed or confused, knowing perfectly well that you'll say "yes" just to get rid of him; and if he's lost another pair of gloves, he'll be sure to tell you when there's company present, since you're much less likely to bawl him out in public.

This negative, manipulative approach is one that many people unfortunately never grow out of. As adults, they discover that the restrictive clauses of the closed marriage contract make it necessary for them to try to manipulate their mates just as they did their parents. Open marriage, however, makes such maneuvering unnecessary. When it is possible to communicate openly and honestly with your mate, there is no need to trick him into giving you your way. "Your way," in fact, is something that will be freely granted you, provided that it does not involve restricting your mate's way. But timing remains important as a positive technique. You read your mate's non-verbal cues not in order to choose the best moment in which to manipulate him, but rather in order to pick out the best moment in which to fully and openly discuss the question that concerns you. In the closed marriage the art of timing is too often used to disguise one's real desires; in open marriage it is used positively to further the chances of honest communication.

Clarity

Verbal communication is very complex, at best. We add greatly to its complexity, and to the possibilities for misunderstanding, by being unclear in what we say. Sometimes we say one thing when we actually mean another. "Did you pick up the laundry today?" Mary asks Bob. Since Bob has arrived home without the laundry, Mary's question didn't even have to be asked. But what she was really saying was, "Why are you so late? You damn well didn't pick up the laundry!" Or Bob may say to Mary, after spending the evening at the home of friends, "Alice certainly comes up with unusual meals, doesn't she?" What he really means, of course, is, "Why don't you cook a few more interesting dishes?"

Some spouses may understand what is really meant in such situations, but if they do they are likely to react with hostility. For almost always when we say one thing and mean another the message we actually want to get across is a criticism of some sort. Try to think before you speak, making sure exactly what it is you really want to say. If it sounds rude or unpleasant when directly, clearly expressed, then it's probably better left unsaid. On the other hand, if it seems upon reflection something that must be said, even though unpleasant, try to hold back for the moment, and bring it up for discussion at an appropriate time.

There are occasions, of course, when you are so angry or upset that you must say something immediately. But instead of making some snide comment, full of hidden meaning, or shouting a muddled accusation, say exactly what the fact of the matter is: "I'm very angry." When you are emotionally upset, you are less likely than ever to be able to express yourself clearly. The chances of unnecessarily hurting your mate, or further confusing the issue are very great. If at such a moment you must say something, to relieve the pressure, start out by stating how *you* feel, instead of by accusing your *mate* of wrongdoing. In many cases, your mate will know immediately what it is that he has done to upset you, and will apologize. If you begin by attacking him, however, probably hurting him in the process, his natural reaction will be to either defend himself (even though he may know he is wrong) or to strike back.

What we are describing here is a technique modeled on the principles of communication that Dr. Haim Ginott has delineated in his best-selling book, *Between Parent and Child*. Although his concepts have been popularized as "childrenese," they are nevertheless applicable in a reciprocal type of communication between husband and wife (which could be termed "matese"). The principles he outlines are sound advice for good communication between any two people, no matter what age. Dr. Ginott's directions (which can be interpreted in the simplified motto: say what you see, tell what you feel, but do not criticize) are based on respect, consideration and what he calls extending "emotional hospitality" to others. Although his methods involve many other aspects of good communication in interpersonal relations, we can stress only a few of them here, in terms of clarity and consideration in communication between mates.

If you think your husband is giving the plants too much water, if you think your wife is stirring the martinis too much, don't say, "Here, dear, this is the way to do it." That sounds perfectly clear, even polite, but in fact it implies that your way of doing it is right and your mate's is wrong. Whenever there is a hidden message, you are not being as clear as you can be. And whenever there is a hidden message, the possibility of an altercation lurks. You may not in fact be right. Everyone is wrong some of the time. So work at avoiding criticism. Say, "I usually only give that plant half a glass. Do you think it needs more?" That gives your husband a chance to say, "Well, it was drooping a lot this morning," if he has a reason for what he is doing, and an opportunity to retreat with grace if he doesn't have a reason.

The technique of "saying what you see and telling what you feel without criticizing the other" makes it possible to state your own point of view, when it is at variance with your mate's. The main idea is to avoid accusation and destructive criticism of the other. If you make a direct attack on your mate, impugning his judgment or taste, you are invading his *ego territory* and you must expect a counterattack. Using these principles allows you to delineate the boundaries of your own ego territory, by clearly stating what you think and feel, while at the same time acknowledging the boundaries of your mate's ego territory by refraining from direct attack. It may require patience, skill and practice, but if you can get out of the habit of criticism and attack, we believe you will find that you can sharply reduce the number of domestic confrontations. At the same time, of course, you will be taking another step toward granting your mate the full right to his own identity.

A different application of "telling what you feel" develops in respect to the communication of your deeper feelings and emotions. In our adherence to good manners and the niceties of convention, we have lost the intimate language of feeling. We tend to leave it to the poet—or the songwriter—to express our joy, frustration, despair or exaltation. A few of us, because of our ethnic background or a particularly outgoing personality, are more expressive than others, but by and large the language of emotion, having been sacrificed on the altar of conformity, now lies buried beneath it in a casket of purest embarrassment.

The feelings are still there below the surface, but they seldom make themselves fully known except when we explode in anger—moments which find us at our most incoherent. Men in particular are taught to believe that they should not express their feelings, that to do so is somehow unmanly. In fact, the very opposite is true—what could be more cowardly than to be afraid to admit what one most deeply feels? It is important to fight the embarrassment that prevents us from saying what we feel. Unless we say it out, clearly, our mates cannot know that we feel it. And if we will not tell them how we feel, how can we expect them to respect those feelings?

Open Listening

Open, clear expression of what we feel is vital to a healthy relationship between marital partners. But it will go for nothing unless it is complemented by open listening.

Most husbands and wives seldom really listen to one another at all. They conduct what the philosopher Abraham Kaplan has called a duologue. In a duologue two people dutifully take turns expounding their separate lonely litanies. Everyone knows how such "conversations" go: Susan and Mark discuss the activities of the day, Susan talking about the fact that their son Bobby is going to have to have braces, Mark wondering aloud about the rumors that his company may be involved in a merger. Each is listening to himself rather than to the other. Susan is concerned about the cost of the braces, as well as their nuisance value, and Mark is concerned about what a merger might mean to his position in the company. Since Mark will have to pay for Bobby's braces, and since Susan will also be affected if Mark's job situation changes, they will eventually have to stop their separate soliloquies, and start all over again asking one another to repeat what has already been said. We have all been through it a thousand times.

In open marriage if you really do not want to listen, at a given moment, it is possible for you to make that desire known to your mate, and you can expect to have your desire respected. But if your mate is going to continue to respect your desire for such moments of privacy, then you must be prepared really to listen when you indicate a willingness to do so. You must be prepared to enter into a *dialogue*, as opposed to a duologue. Kaplan describes the true dialogue, in which both partners listen and respond to one another, as communion rather than communication. In a true dialogue, each partner is, certainly, communicating with the other, but because he is also listening, and responding to what he hears, the final result is a form of communion. Good communication, when coupled with open listening, results in communion.

Open listening requires that you become, in effect, transparent, thus letting the other in. You cannot respond properly unless you open yourself completely to what is being said to you. Unless you listen, actively, you cannot hear. Unless you hear you cannot enter into a dialogue. And no true meeting of a husband and wife can occur unless they both enter willingly into such a dialogue.

Feedback

Your response to someone's attempt to communicate with you can be as simple as a nod of the head. Sometimes that is enough. But too often, when a fuller response is really necessary, we settle for that nod, for a mere "uh huh," or a "yes, dear." You cannot create a dialogue with your mate unless you provide a lot more than a few grunts in the way of feedback.

Feedback is a term that is part and parcel of the new computer technology. In technical terms it can be described as the automatic furnishing of information on a machine's output to a control device, so that errors can be corrected. Thus a feedback system is self-correcting. In more human terms, when a man sets a glass down on a table, his nervous system provides him with the visual and sensory feedback necessary to guide his hand. This is the hand-eye-brain feedback system at work. If the man is drunk, the feedback is likely to be incorrect, so that the man drops the glass on the floor. This concept of feedback can easily be applied to communication between human beings. You can give your mate feedback by paraphrasing his statement to make sure you understand it, by asking questions, or by making your own responsive statement that tells how you feel about the matter.

You need open and honest feedback from your mate in order to know that he has understood you, in order to discover how he feels, and in order to adjust your own feelings or perceptions in light of his. Many husbands and wives short-circuit the feedback cycle, through deception or overt criticism, or by withholding their response altogether. Sullen silence might be described as negative feedback; like a failed monitoring system on a moon rocket, it tells you that *something* is wrong, but it doesn't go very far toward telling you what. Unless you indicate what is wrong, through positive feedback, your mate will not know how to proceed further.

For couples who need to learn feedback on an elementary level, there is a simple exercise called "completing the communication," as described by Lederer and Jackson in *Mirages of Marriage*, that they can make use of. While it may seem unnatural and even rather silly at first, it will get you in the habit of providing feedback and increase your sense of the importance of responding to your mate. There are three elementary steps to the exercise: Person I makes a statement. Person II acknowledges the statement. Person I confirms the acknowledgment.

For example:

MARY: Did you pick up the laundry?
DICK: No, I didn't. No parking space.
MARY: Maybe I can do it tomorrow, then.

Or:

DICK: I ran into Bob Bartlet today.
MARY: How is he these days?
DICK: He seemed fine.

The two initial statements made by Mary and Dick above are of the sort that frequently evoke no more than a word. Other simple statements (such as "What a beautiful sunset") evoke no more than a nod, a grunt or a mumble. But each one, when you begin these exercises, should be acknowledged and have the acknowledgment confirmed. Making a specific meaningful response to such minor statements is a step toward improving your ability to provide feedback in other more important situations. It will also help stimulate you to open listening. Open listening is, of course, absolutely essential to providing proper feedback.

With feedback established, you can approach real self-disclosure that will implement growth. We change and grow by *re-forming* our concepts of ourselves and the other through our own disclosures and through our mate's feedback to us.

All five of the principles of good communication that we have discussed in this chapter—Understanding the Context, Timing, Clarity, Open Listening and Feedback—are vital to open and honest communication. As you have seen, each of them reinforces the others. Your timing cannot be improved unless you understand the context. All the clarity in the world means nothing unless your mate is committed to open listening. And proper feedback both depends upon and aids the exercise of the other four principles. With these interrelated principles as a background, we will discuss in our third and last chapter on communication some additional techniques that can be of help to you in achieving truly open verbal and non-verbal exchange.

9 Communication: Productive Fighting and Fantasy Sharing

Productive Fighting

There are few healthy couples who do not occasionally, when the chips are down, communicate by fighting. Unfortunately, this is the only method some couples use to achieve an intimate exchange. Couples who do not fight may be among those rare few who have reached the promised land of complete understanding and synchronization. But it is more likely that they just don't care enough anymore, that they have given up the struggle, accepting all the clauses of the closed contract and succumbing to homogenization. Constant and total marital harmony is a myth. Open marriage, we believe, can bring you as close to that kind of harmony as it is humanly possible to get, provided you seriously endeavor to put the guidelines to work for you. Still, there will be times when the need to fight, or at least to argue, will overwhelm you. So let's explore the marital battlefront.

Fighting in marriage can be a respectable and even healthy method of communication, *if* the bouts are conducted fairly. Fights can reduce tensions and clear the air by ventilating pent-up feelings. A fight can be a way of leveling with your mate, better understanding your differences, and can mark a new phase in the development of your relationship. But it can also be devastating, a session for the venting of mutual aggression or individual hostilities resulting only in destruction. The difference between these positive and negative results lies in knowing how to fight fairly and in a constructive manner.

In *The Intimate Enemy*, Dr. George R. Bach, with the assistance of Peter Wyden, thoroughly explores the topic of fighting and describes a system of rules for constructive fighting developed in his training clinic for married couples. Some of his pointers with some comments and examples of our own are outlined below:

1. *Choose your time and place by mutual consent.* Context and timing, as explained in the previous chapter, are just as important—if not more so—when you want to argue as when you are embarking on a less emotional discussion. It may be difficult, and sometimes impossible, but "gripe hours" *can* be negotiated.

2. *Keep your anger focused on current issues, on the present moment rather than the past.* Too many couples fight dirty. One common way is to dredge up the past, using yesterday's failures as today's ammunition. Men particularly accuse women of this tactic. But both men and women are guilty of nursing past grievances and resurrecting them in the heat of battle. The woman may resort to this tactic more frequently because she *does* in fact have more grievances. The closed marriage, with its unequal status, frequently places the wife as low partner on the marital totem pole, and in an unequal match she hauls out invectives and blanket criticisms. But the husband has just as many blanket criticisms based on past ideas of the feminine and

wifely role, of her volatile "feminine nature." In fact, aggression and hostility are the natural outcome of a typical closed marriage and its clauses. To fight constructively, partners should forget past fights and criticisms and focus on the here-and-now issues.

3. *Know what you are fighting about.* Trivial issues may be just blowing off steam over petty annoyances and, if recognized as such, can become fun fights. But sometimes trivial issues become decoys, allowing you to evade the real issue and perhaps leave unsettled deeper more central problems. As an irate husband, for instance, are you really fighting over your wife's method of disciplining the children, or are you upset because she isn't giving you enough attention and respect? As an irate wife, are you really arguing over the fact that your husband is sloppy and never picks up after himself, or are you suspicious of all his overtime hours? Whatever you're really upset about is what you should be fighting about. Otherwise it is a waste of time and energy which could better be spent on fighting fair over the real issue.

4. *Be as candid as you possibly can.* The authors call this leveling: "one should be transparent in communicating where one stands and candid in signaling where one wants to go." Everything that was said in the previous chapter about honesty applies here.

5. *Don't try to win, ever.* If one of you must win, then the other, obviously, must lose. And if one of you loses, then both have lost, in terms of increased resentment and greater strain on your relationship. As Dr. Bach puts it, "The only way to win intimate encounters is for both partners to win."

What both partners can win in marital fighting, by following these rules, are greater insights, new information, and new methods by which to resolve future conflicts. People forget that there is almost always more than one answer to any single problem; one conflict may have many resolutions. We believe that if both partners have identity and equality, there is no overriding need for the release of aggression. As you progress further and further toward the achievement of a true open marriage, it should become more and more possible for you to approach differences between you as questions of problem-solving, to be worked out by consensual agreement. The essence of open marriage lies in finding an answer that will benefit both partners and bring harm to neither one. Along the path to the full realization of this essence, fighting can be a legitimate, educational and, obviously, invigorating method of communication, provided you fight openly and honestly, concentrate on the now, and seek to develop better problem-solving skills out of the experience.

Sharing Dreams and Fantasies

In the previous chapter we discussed the possibility of using your dreams to achieve a better understanding of yourself. Dreams, and fantasies, can also be used to increase the communication between husband and wife. Many couples do share dreams—daydreams, or dreams of the future. Such sharing is fine, as far as it goes, and provided that the dreams are reasonably realistic and do not interfere with living in the now. But what about the dreams of sleep?

Couples can considerably deepen their intimacy by sharing their sleeping dreams. Dreams do, after all, reveal things about our unconscious selves which we might not otherwise know. Don't bother, however, with specialized books that try to label dream symbolism, telling you that ladders are sexual or garden tools aggressive. You will learn much more by trying to interpret your own dreams—and you'll have a good deal more fun at it, too. It's *your* dream, and no one else has ever had one quite like it. There may be general similarities with other people's dreams, but your own past history and present conflicts will provide a crucial difference.

Tell the content of a dream to your mate and explain

what it means to you—then let your husband or wife give his interpretation. By sharing your dream, verbalizing it and making it concrete, you will make its meaning clearer to yourself. At the same time, you will be able to gain the additional insights of your mate. His interpretation may well be different. Not only will you find out more about the ways in which he sees you, and gain a clearer idea of the extent to which he really understands you, but you will also learn more about his own attitudes and beliefs. Thus each of you will learn more about the other through this form of self-disclosure.

Sharing your fantasies with your mate is a much more drastic form of self-disclosure. Rarely does anyone share a fantasy with another except on the analyst's couch or in the therapist's chair. We may not need therapy, but each of us does have a need for someone to whom we can tell almost anything. Why shouldn't that person be your husband or your wife? Clearly such self-disclosure would not work in a closed marriage, whose restrictive clauses so drastically limit communication. But in a well-developed open marriage, the partners should have sufficient self-security not to be threatened by the imaginative world of one another's fantasies.

Fantasies sometimes deal with "forbidden" desires. The fact that your husband fantasizes his involvement in group sex, or that your wife likes to imagine, in technicolor detail, what it would be like to sleep with Paul Newman, can be very disturbing if you are not sure of both yourself and your relationship with your mate. Even your husband's desire for his own plane, or your wife's for a $10,000 coat can be threatening in the sense that you cannot provide them and to the extent that they reveal your mate's sense of being unfulfilled. We can be tolerant of a child's fantasy desire for an Italian sportscar, understanding that this wish is not based on reality. But the same fantasy in an adult can seem like a rebuke. If you are secure, however, you can grant in fantasy what you can't grant in reality, and both you and your mate can enjoy laughing at one another's extravagant desires while at the same time you learn something more about one another. If either of you feels uneasy about this form of self-disclosure, however, don't even try it. This kind of sharing is intensely private and must be considered highly optional.

The value of discussing your fantasies, aside from what you can learn about one another, is that their shock value is dissipated. We all have fantasies. But often we feel guilty or embarrassed about them. Just as with dreams, the foreboding aspect of fantasies disappears when you bring them out into the light of day and discuss them in the context of shared reality. By sharing dreams and fantasies before you are ready to do so, or while feeling uneasy about it, you can create problems for yourself. But if you can do it with a sense of balance and security, you will open up a whole new area of communication with your mate and enrich your understanding of one another. Use your own discretion— you know yourself and your own situation best.

Tape Recorders Can't Argue

Tape recorders cannot argue or deceive—they merely record. They are no substitute for face-to-face communication, but they can provide you with valuable information about how you communicate. If you are just learning how to communicate openly they can serve as excellent learning devices.

Try taping your own voice first. Tenseness, irritability, sleepiness, joy, love, and doubt are all reflected in the tone, quality and speed of your speech. Do *you* enjoy listening to yourself? If you don't, perhaps your speech also affects others adversely. We don't mean your accent or pronunciation—these are part of you and should be enjoyed and accepted as such. But monotonous voices can become boring, high-pitched voices can become irritating. Evaluate how you sound in general, not according to the idiosyncrasies of your speech.

More importantly, if there is something that you can't yet tell your mate about—because you are too shy or too angry, or because your mate gets too angry when the subject is brought up—try recording what you want to say on tape. Then let your mate play it back, listening to it in privacy. Talking into a tape alone does of course deprive us of watching the body cues, the physical attitudes, of the person we are trying to communicate with. But in the early stages of your attempts to improve your communication this can be an advantage. In a face-to-face conversation, the non-verbal cues you receive from your mate may be inhibiting your attempt to communicate, substantially altering what you mean to say. By using the tape recorder you can get the message across without the interference that your listener's body stance, movements and gestures inevitably produce. When you have reached the point of more relaxed and honest communication, you can start putting your understanding of your mate's body language to its proper use. But let the tape recorder act as an intermediary for you on touchy subjects that you haven't yet learned to talk about easily in direct conversation.

Record your discussions with your mate about any burning issue in your marriage. Play back an argument or a decision-making session. Then sit down, either together or separately (preferably the latter), and listen to it when you have cooled down. If you are alert to what's happening on the tape, new discoveries will emerge. A tape winds back time and lets us look at ourselves and our interaction with others objectively. You can now, for the first time, hear the argument as though you were a third person, removed from your emotional involvement in the immediacy of the situation.

While your husband was trying to tell you how he felt

about letting your daughter stay overnight at a friend's house after a date, were you really listening? In all probability you were not fully aware of what he was saying. You were preparing your next line of defense or rebuttal—engaging in a duologue instead of a dialogue. When we are actively engaged in a discussion or argument we translate and filter the other's words through our emotions of the moment. We too often respond not to *what* is being said, but to how we *feel* about it, sometimes even anticipating the other's statements. The tape playback enables us to listen without an immediate emotional response to cloud the picture.

One couple we interviewed had recently started making use of a tape recorder. The husband admitted that until he listened to a few tapes he had never realized how often he interrupted his wife's statements or how completely he ignored what she was saying until he finally shut up for a few moments. His wife, on the other hand, realized for the first time how much she whined, how defensive she was, and how circular her arguments were. Both felt that their communication with one another had improved a lot since they had begun to use the tape recorder.

Tapes can provide you with uncensored, mechanically objective feedback on how both of you come across to the other. You can listen to yourself. You can listen to your mate. You can come to appreciate better both what open listening is and how great the need for it is, and you can then try to practice it more completely the next time you have a debate.

None of the principles, guidelines or techniques of communication we have been discussing in the past three chapters can be completely grasped overnight. It will take time to put them into practice. But as you work toward implementing them, let the tape be your referee, your intimate advisor. It can tell you how you are feeling and reacting, whether you are attacking, retreating, defending, evading or blocking. And it will also make clear your improvement along the way, confirming the progress you both are making toward open listening and honest self-disclosure.

10 Role Flexibility: Masculine and Feminine— Which Is What?

Where Will It End?

Men have become kitchen scullions—some of them, some of the time. They are now washing dishes, pushing vacuum cleaners, diapering the baby and learning to knit. Women—more of them all the time—are aggressively trudging to work, making home repairs and studying karate. They are becoming jockeys, furniture movers and corporate executives. Single and divorced women think nothing of asking a man for a date or paying for his lunch. Among young people the trend to long hair and unisex clothing sometimes makes it hard to tell the difference between a boy and a girl.

Where, some people ask in alarm, is it all going to end?

In disaster, reply a few nervous sociologists, who see role reversal and the blending of secondary sexual characteristics as first steps along the bleak path toward a race of biological neuters. The merging of traditional sex roles is likely to lead to a decrease of interest in sex itself, according to their line of reasoning. Such predictions are nonsense, of course. It is interesting to note that those who make them are invariably men; and it is easy to suspect that their rather churlish views are related to the fear that if things get any further out of hand someone is likely to ask *them* to do the dishes.

To answer the alarmists, it should be clearly stated that the biological urge to mate has little or nothing to do with the roles that a given society ascribes to male and female. The hackneyed role stereotypes in our society (the male as aggressive and dominant, the female as passive and submissive) actually inhibit men and women from expressing the full range of sexual and sensual pleasure natural to human beings. The traditional roles have become obsolete, to the point where they hinder our ability to achieve psychological and sexual fulfillment. They exist not as a positive force in society but simply as stumbling blocks to our efforts to adapt to a changed and changing world. In fact, then, the truth is that we haven't yet progressed far enough toward a merging of the traditional male and female roles.

To ascribe mutually exclusive characteristics and occupations to male and female is to split husbands and wives into separate, and inevitably opposing camps. If men are to be only tough, strong, providers, competitors and abstract thinkers, and women are to be only soft, pliant, homemakers, cheerleaders and intuitive thinkers, then it is impossible for husbands and wives ever to really know one another—for you cannot get to know someone you can't understand. We must share these supposedly male and female qualities instead of dividing them, so that each of us at the appropriate time can be strong or pliant, competitor or cheerleader, abstract or intuitive, regardless of whether we are male or female. There will be a "war between the sexes" so long as we are divided into separate camps. Only through developing the common humanity that transcends our maleness or femaleness can we finally learn to understand one another and live in harmony.

The Marriage Crisis

Marriage is what anthropologists call a crisis rite, marking the passage of a couple from one kind of status to another. Like the passage from boyhood to manhood, or girlhood to womanhood, the marriage ceremony signifies that you have accepted new roles. You are no longer just a man and a woman, but a husband and a wife. Some couples find it easy to accept these new roles—at least at first, before the restrictions of the closed contract fully reveal themselves. Others have trouble from the beginning. Sometimes one partner in the marriage will accept his role much more quickly than the other. For some, marriage is a crisis of such proportions that it destroys the relationship between the man and the woman.

The exact nature of the crisis is often misunderstood. For one thing, we tend to confuse the issue by giving undue prominence to the sexual aspects of it. For even if the man and woman are both sexually sophisticated (and perhaps have been sleeping together for months or even years) another sort of crisis exists. Let's take a look at the marriage of Stan and Judy, for instance. They had lived together for six years before marrying, working out a comfortable design for mutual companionship that resembled marriage in every way except for the fact that they hadn't signed a contract. After six years of living together, they decided they wanted to make it legal. And a year later they got a divorce. We've all heard stories like that, or know couples to whom it has happened. But why does it happen?

Clearly the signing of that legal document constitutes a crisis all on its own. No comprehensive research has been done on this particular kind of marriage relationship, but it's possible to make some educated guesses about what happens. Once such a couple legally marries, the restrictive clauses of the old contract, including all the subclauses that govern the choice of roles, come into play. Gone is the non-binding commitment to stay together just because you want to, gone are the flexible, mutually compatible arrangements reflecting that voluntary commitment. In their place is a contract, a specific, binding agreement that carries with it an entire tradition of predetermined rights, obligations, and expectations.

One saddened casualty of the marriage crisis, whose long-term relationship had been spoiled by making it legal, put it this way, "Before we married, everything was free and easy and really great. So, okay, we marry, and right away she begins to take me for granted. Now I'm a husband, and should empty the garbage. Instead of working it out, like we did before, suddenly I'm *supposed* to do this, *supposed* to do that. You'd think she'd know me better, wouldn't you, after all we've been through together?"

The wife in this case had similar complaints. What had happened was that they had stopped being the *people* they were before and started playing the *roles* of husband and wife. Accepting those roles destroyed their flexibility, and imposed upon them a new set of rigid rules that they'd been able to avoid as a non-married couple. Such couples clearly demonstrate the overpowering impact of marital roles. So powerful are they that one couple who had lived together for thirty years as common-law mates, and raised two children in the process, were unable to make it through even a full year of legally married life. They separated and divorced.

When friends get divorced, or you yourself experience marital problems, there is always a tendency to blame any difficulties on personality problems. "Mabel always was a neurotic girl," we say. "If only Don weren't such a tyrant, I think everything would be all right," your best friend may say about her husband. Personality problems do of course cause many marriages to break apart. But the experience of couples with long-standing good relationships *before* marriage and nothing but difficulties *after* marriage, strongly suggests that there is another culprit to be named here. We believe, in fact, that the traditional roles of husband and wife are often destructive to marital relationships. However well those roles may have suited another, earlier society, they do not reflect the realities of today's world. We further believe that the power of these roles is such that they often aggravate any personality problems that individuals may have. Indeed, they may bring out into the open for the first time a neurotic tendency that has lain dormant for years. How many times have you heard the phrase, "He's not the same man I married." The reason he's not the same is that he is conforming to a predetermined role. He is no longer his *own* man, but belongs instead to his role.

These two chapters on role flexibility are dedicated to finding ways to help you remain your own man or woman after you are married, to help you escape the bondage of outdated role expectations. Let's begin by examining some of the reasons why the rigid roles of the closed marriage have such a hold upon people. There are three chief explanations: (1) We are trained into the roles; (2) Different status is attached to male and female roles; (3) Husband and wife, and man and woman are confused with definitions of masculine and feminine. We will examine each of these three subjects in turn.

The Training Period

From the moment we are born, and wrapped in blue (for boys), or pink (for girls), we are trained for our future roles. Little boys are taught to be aggressive and are given Erector sets; little girls are taught to be passive and are given dolls. There is no need to belabor the point—we all know how rigid the distinctions are between what is proper for a boy and what is proper for a girl. We all know how many pressures there are to conform to expectations. The girl who wants to play baseball is teased unmercifully, and the boy who doesn't want to play baseball (God forbid) is held in absolute contempt. We recognize these distinctions but often we fail to understand their full impact on our future lives. Children are not merely being taught what our society regards as masculine and feminine traits. They are being taught male and female roles; they are being instructed in male and female relationships. When a small boy and girl play house, the boy soon learns that his part is not to cradle the doll but to walk pompously through the imaginary door and say, "Where is my dinner?" If the game is playing doctor, the boy gets the stethoscope and the girl gets the bandages. And while the boy is off building model airplanes, the girl is helping her mother make cookies.

All these activities help shape the attitudes that the boy and girl will eventually carry with them into their marriages. Obviously, there is a much greater emphasis on the girl's training in the wifely arts than there is on the boy's training in the husbandly arts. In fact, the girl is taught to be a *wife*, while the boy is taught to be a *man*. The inequality of status is thus implicit from the very beginning: even in our language a couple is referred to as man and wife rather than husband and wife. But then, there is not nearly as much need to teach the boy to become a husband as there is to teach the girl to become a wife and alternately a mother. The husband will only be spending about a third as much time in the home as the wife will. His role as husband and father is a part-time role; hers as wife and mother is supposed to be full time.

Today, however, a great many wives are unwilling to accept that full-time role. They want a change in the balance between husband and wife, and by seeking it they force their husbands to try to adjust their roles also. More and more women, bored by the aimless confinement of their homes, are seeking employment. The woman who works is carrying a double burden, since more often than not she continues to do the major part of the housework in addition to her regular job. Husbands are often willing to help at home, but they find aprons demeaning and housework as repetitive as their wives always have. Why should he trade independence and challenge in the outside world for a dishmop or a toilet brush? Who can blame him for objecting? But, on the other hand, who can blame the woman for seeking those same outside challenges?

The world has changed sufficiently so that the training given female children is losing its effect—like an inoculation that doesn't take. Yet the male's indoctrination remains almost as effective as it has ever been. A disparity naturally arises in adult relationships between men and women. Their training is no longer complementary. The woman asks for a larger and larger share of the world that men have been taught belongs to them, but there has not yet been a sufficient shift in the men's training so that they are willing to accept their responsibilities in what they regard as the "woman's world." After all, the men have always known that the "woman's world" was less interesting than the one outside. In the past fifty years, as educational opportunities for women have steadily increased, they too have come to recognize this discrepancy between the two worlds. And they are no longer willing to put up with the inferior status accorded to women because of the world in which they have long been forced to live.

The Status Comes with the Job

The question of status has a crucial effect on the problem. Whether or not we like admitting it, the husband has higher status than the wife. The ascribing of such status has nothing at all to do with the individual people involved, but simply pertains to the *jobs* that go with their roles. Sally may be a lot smarter than Don, and a nicer person to boot, but her status is still less because she is a housewife and he earns the money. Of course, on a personal basis, the wife's status may be the same as her husband's. Certainly women are equal to men, any male will protest. But nevertheless the jobs that the wife does in her typical role as home-maker do not merit the same status as those her husband performs. If they did, he wouldn't be so reluctant to trade with her, or set up such a howl about sharing the house-work.

And men are right, of course. No matter how creative you are, or how many electrical gadgets you have to help you, there is a limit to the interest and pleasure that can be derived from housework. Housework must be put in its proper place, and thought of merely as a job that must be taken care of to achieve domestic comfort rather than as "woman's work." It is just work, whether a woman does it or a man does it. In the next chapter we will look at some ways in which housework can be separated from its ancient association with the woman's role—until such a separation is achieved, it will continue to be a source of friction.

Some will claim, no doubt, that the woman's low status as a homemaker is compensated for by the high status associated with motherhood. In fact, the importance of motherhood has been inflated out of all proportion, to the point where it begins to look suspiciously like a sop thrown to women to make them forget the other ways in which they are downgraded. Furthermore, the assumption that mother-hood is integral to the wife's role, and an absolutely essen-tial part of womanhood, serves very well to keep women in the home where it used to be said that they belonged. Con-cerning the importance bestowed on the role of motherhood, Dr. Alice Rossi, a sociologist, has pointed out that "... *for the first time in the history of any known society, mother-hood has become a full-time occupation for adult women.*" The idea that this is "only natural" is dispelled by historical examples and a study of primitive societies, in which motherhood is just one of several parallel activities among the life-sustaining tasks undertaken by women. Child care (that longest and most laborious aspect of motherhood) is a responsibility *shared* with kinfolk, husbands and older children. In many societies, the man is intimately involved in caring for and training the child, even in its very earliest years.

Aside from the actual bearing of the child (and even that, biologists indicate, may be carried on outside the mother's body within the next decade or so), the raising of children must be a matter of shared responsibility in our society, too. Motherhood and fatherhood should be equal parts of parenthood, not consist of unequal tasks assigned to the wife's or the husband's *role*. Motherhood must be disentangled from the wife's role. While it *is* an extremely important, rewarding and enriching experience in a woman's life, it certainly should not be falsely glorified as her only meaningful role in life. To so glorify it robs the last thirty or forty years of her life of their proper significance and worth; it robs her of the possibility of becoming a person in her own right in other areas; and it deprives her husband of enjoying full parenthood and sharing in companionship with his wife during the child-raising years.

Fortunately, change is already occurring in this area. Many more young couples are choosing not to have children. Women are no longer made to feel "incomplete" if they do not bear children. Motherhood and parenthood have both become optional, as well they ought to be in an already overpopulated world. Those couples who do have children increasingly appear to recognize that when parenthood is equally shared by husband and wife it is not only better for the parents but for the children as well.

Masculine/Feminine: Which Is What?

The greatest cause of misunderstanding, confusion and resentment over appropriate roles for husband and wife arises from the way in which they are linked up with American cultural concepts of maculine and feminine. What Americans regard as masculine they assume to be natural to all males. As we shall see, they are assuming too much. Furthermore, they assume that what is male is the exclusive property of the husband. Thus, if a wife comes on particularly strong in a marital argument or makes a decision on her own (and lets her husband know about it), he will often put her down with a remark like, "What are you trying to do, wear the pants in the family?" She has displayed traits of decisiveness, competence, and assertiveness that are supposed to be masculine, according to our society. And the husband reacts by reminding his wife of his exclusive male rights to those masculine traits. Conversely, if a husband always does the cooking, or lets his wife run the finances for the family, he is likely to be thought of as weak, or even unmanly.

To be feminine (or a wife) is to be passive, pliant, emotional, temperamental, loving, meek, receptive, and nurturant. To be masculine is to be tough, competitive, brave, calm, staunch, strong, and dominant. Or so the mythology goes. We all know men who are meek and women who are tough, of course, but we tend to regard them with suspicion, as though they weren't quite normal. Is there, in fact, any biological or psychological "proof" as to which qualities are normally male and which are normally female? The answers to that question tend to confuse matters further. There are certain basic physical differences in body, frame and musculature, and physiological differences that we all know about. There is the fact that men are usually stronger, in terms of what they can lift and haul, but that women have the edge in terms of life-span. But scientists are a long way from establishing that such physiological differences, or even the more complicated hormonal variations between men and women, have any effect on such matters of character as meekness or bravery. Psychological research is even less conclusive, for the simple reason that most of the differences which *are* found, are primarily those that society has trained its men and women to adopt.

If we turn to the field of anthropology, however, we find that the evidence is much more concrete and much more persuasive in demonstrating that behavior which we call "masculine" or "feminine" is largely culturally determined. That is, these differences are much more a result of training, according to the traditions of the society you happen to live in, than they are a product of basic biology or psychology. The most impressive anthropological evidence on the subject was amassed by Dr. Margaret Mead many years ago in her study of sex and temperament in three New Guinea tribes. The implications of that study, published in 1935, still go unheeded by many, to judge by current debates over the question. Thus, it seems pertinent to present some of that evidence again here.

Among the mountain-dwelling Arapesh, Dr. Mead found, the man as well as the woman was mild, compliant, responsive and cooperative. In sharp contrast, the nearby Mundugumor tribe trained its women to be as violent and as harsh as the men: "both men and women developed as ruthless, aggressive . . . individuals, with the maternal cherishing aspects of personality at a minimum." Clearly, then, other societies can set up prescriptions for male and female behavior that—even though as rigid as our own—are very different in form.

While, according to our standards, men act like women among the Arapesh, and women act like men among the Mundugumor, the third society that Dr. Mead studied had completely reversed what we consider masculine and feminine roles. Among the Tchambuli, the woman is the "dominant, impersonal, managing partner, the man the less responsible and the emotionally dependent person." If you think that sounds familiar, it's because it is *exactly the reverse* of what American women's magazines spent the postwar years telling their readers.

Tchambuli women provided the food by fishing, and also produced the highly prized mosquito sleeping bags widely traded in the Sepik River area of New Guinea. The husband went to market and traded the mosquito bags for shell money. Upon his return home, he had to bargain with his wife to obtain a share of the profit. Tchambuli wives are tough, brusque, practical, humorous and earthy. The Tchambuli husband, on the other hand, walked "with mincing step and self-conscious mien." He was catty, bickering, and mercurial in his relationships with other men, but charming toward women. He performed the ceremonial tribal functions in masked ritual dances and spent endless hours on his personal toilette, sporting delicately arranged curls and a handsome genital covering of flying-fox skin highly ornamented with shells.

What, then, are "masculine" and "feminine" in this context? Certainly, they are very different from our own understanding of them. Whatever the biological determinants may be, they have been overshadowed by cultural training. Margaret Mead's conclusion is to the point: "If those temperamental attitudes which we have traditionally regarded as feminine—such as passivity, responsiveness, and a willingness to cherish children—can so easily be set up as the masculine pattern in one tribe [The Arapesh: our note], and in another be outlawed for the majority of women as well as for the majority of men [the Mundugumor], we no longer have any basis for regarding such aspects of behavior as sex-linked."

Thus the rigidity of our own marital roles cannot be justified by arguments as to what is "naturally" feminine or "naturally" masculine. If men can adequately care for children, or do the cooking and weaving in other cultures, if women can carry burdens, build houses and collect the major part of the food supply, there should be nothing to prevent greater flexibility in the roles of husband and wife in our own culture. Indeed, as our society becomes increasingly mechanized and computerized, the allocation of most tasks according to gender looks more and more foolish: the electronic button really does not care whether the finger that pushes it is male or female.

The categorization of "masculinity" and "femininity" is needlessly arbitrary and restrictive in a psychological as well as a purely practical sense. Just as men and women are capable of doing one another's tasks, so they could benefit enormously if they shared and openly displayed the admirable qualities that each sex is supposed to have separately. Fortunately, the process is already underway. Our young are refusing to be herded into rigid categories, and are accepting a broader emotional definition of masculinity and femininity. A recent research report indicates that families in which both husband and wife worked outside the home fostered this development. In such families the children, whether male or female, saw themselves as possessing the desirable qualities of both sexes—much more so than children whose mothers were full-time homemakers. Seeing greater equality between their parents, when both worked, the children were able to develop a capacity for both assertiveness and tenderness, instead of just the former if a boy, or just the latter if a girl.

If this trend continues, it will be the men, interestingly enough, who will gain the most, since our concepts of masculinity are far more restrictive than those pertaining to femininity. Women can "cross the line," so to speak, from feminine to masculine traits with far greater ease than men can do the reverse. The girl who is a tomboy will certainly be teased, but she will suffer nothing like the trauma of the boy who is regarded as a sissy. Since masculinity must constantly be protected with an arsenal of ego-defenses, man's range of permissible feelings and sensitivities is much more circumscribed than woman's. By breaking out of the stereotyped roles, husbands could be more than disciplinarians, staunch providers and obliging handymen—they could be lovers and poets as well.

If husbands and wives could learn to see both male and

female as embracing the total range of human emotional expression and intellectual capacity, then the outdated cultural hangups that bind us to restrictive roles could be cast aside. The following chapter concerns itself with methods that can be used in achieving this more open outlook. By gaining and practicing greater flexibility in roles, *both* husband and wife can be compassionate as well as resourceful, nurturant as well as courageous, strong as well as sensitive. Thus those qualities that all of us treasure as most humanly valuable would belong to both.

11 Role Flexibility: Role Reversal and Role Exchange

Role-Free Behavior

In the search for freedom, self-expression and intimacy in personal relationships, some psychologists hold up as the ultimate goal a concept that they call role-free behavior. Unfortunately, this is a confusing term. None of us can be *totally* free of roles—to leave them completely behind would be to turn one's back on life. But even though the term may be misleading, many of the ideas associated with it are both important and useful. The primary objective must be to avoid being *controlled* by the role. Clearly, this can only be done by breaking down the rigid separations between the roles of husband and wife. If we say, no, I won't do that, because husbands (or wives) don't do that, we are being controlled by the role. What we do or do not do in our relationship with our husband or wife should be determined by what we feel as an individual human being, not by some predetermined set of restrictive codes.

In breaking down the artificial rigidities of the roles of husband and wife, you can't expect to achieve true flexibility overnight. But there are a number of techniques that can be helpful in working toward such flexibility, and the rest of this chapter will be devoted to them. Some of these techniques are designed to help you gain new insights into your role as husband or wife, illuminating the ways in which you are bound by those roles, and the extent to which they control you. With this new understanding, you will be able to make use of other suggestions that follow to establish fresh ways of approaching your role, gaining greater flexibility through a gradual process of redefinition.

Imitating Your Mate

Imitation is one of the most painless ways of learning. To a significant degree we model our behavior, from childhood on, by observing and copying the habits, attitudes and actions of others, which gradually become a part of our unconscious repertoire of behavior. We learn bad habits as well as good ones this way, of course, including many of the unspoken rules of role performance. But, by using imitation consciously, you can make your mate better aware of his own unconscious habits. By imitating one another, husbands and wives can hold up a mirror to one another's actions. If it is done without malice and in good humor, this kind of "game" can give both partners in a marriage a fresh sense of themselves.

Betty and Phil are sitting at the kitchen table, feeling lighthearted, kidding each other. Betty begins to mimic the way Phil behaves when she serves him some kind of food he doesn't particularly like. "Gee, these parsnips are great," she says, getting exactly Phil's tone of forced enthusiasm into her voice. Then she toys with her food, pushing the parsnips over to one side and tucking them under the lettuce. Phil, laughing, says, "All right, now watch me,

I'm *you* getting dinner." He moves around the kitchen, making as much noise as possible, banging the pots and pans, slamming the refrigerator door and, finally, with the water running in the sink as loudly as Niagara Falls, calls out, "Where are you, Phil, I'm talking to you? Can't you hear me?"

As you might expect, the typical reaction to this kind of imitation is, "Do I really do that?" The humorous approach and game-like atmosphere thus make it possible to tell your mate things you might not otherwise bring up. Certainly, it is a much pleasanter and more effective way of telling Betty how much noise she makes than angrily telling her off. Your mate may or may not respond to these humorous critiques by changing his habits. Some habits, after all, are much harder to change than others. But most people are willing to try to improve themselves, when a fault is pointed out to them in a sufficiently relaxed way so that they don't feel as though they're being attacked. That is why it is so important that both partners engage in this game of imitation at the same time, when both are in the mood for it. It won't work if one starts imitating the other on the spur of the moment, as another way of "getting at" his mate. That is simply a more sophisticated way of starting a fight.

If there are children in the family, particularly adolescents, the imitation game can become even more instructive—and even more fun. For then one member of the family can sit back and watch as another takes his place and interacts with the others present. A mother, for instance, might watch while her son took her part in acting out a typical dinner scene with the father and the daughter. Why doesn't the daughter play the mother? Well, there's no reason why she shouldn't, but remember that there's no reason why the son shouldn't, either. Don't let the typical confusions about the definition of masculinity, as discussed in the previous chapter, inhibit you; for one thing, when the role imitation is carried out by someone of the opposite sex, he is often able to pinpoint role habits more accurately than someone of the same sex would be able to do.

Role Reversal

Full role reversal requires more ingenuity and spontaneity than simple role imitation. Instead of just imitating your mate, you try to become him, thinking and feeling as well as behaving like him. Jenny becomes Bob, and Bob becomes Jenny, simultaneously. Since you will be interacting with one another, and must be actor and audience at the same time, you can avoid confusion by agreeing on some particular theme to serve as the focus of your role experiment. For instance, you might choose an area of conflict to discuss: whether the wife should continue working or not; whether or not your son should be made to give up playing baseball until his grades improve; whether or not you should buy a second car. Whatever the focal point may be, each partner expresses with feeling and conviction what he thinks the *other's* viewpoint on the subject is, as if he were in fact that person.

Perhaps even more effective is to use an actual argument as the basis of your role reversal. Say, for example, that Barney comes home from a grueling day, including three hours' overtime, and finds his wife Sally watching television and eating chocolate even though the kitchen sink is full of dirty dishes. Naturally, Barney loses his temper. And Sally, who has had a bad day herself and just didn't feel up to dishwashing, yells back. Some few couples may be able to stop the argument in the middle, change roles, and get a better understanding of how the other feels right on the spot. But if you haven't got the self-discipline to do that, at least keep the argument in mind and use it as the basis for a role-reversal experiment at a later date.

There is hardly any technique as effective as role reversal

for loosening up opinionated attitudes, exposing selfish habits or learning to appreciate other points of view. You can't really understand how your mate may feel until you try to defend his or her position. The husband who plays his wife in role reversal is after all doing far more than mouthing prepared lines like an actor. He must dig out of himself the lines that he believes his wife would speak. And in doing so he will find it necessary to justify her words and actions. Studies in social psychology demonstrate that appreciable attitude change occurs when subjects must defend viewpoints opposite to their own. Thus role reversal not only helps you to understand your mate's point of view, it also opens up and even changes your own attitudes.

Occupational Exchange

Really venturesome couples might want to try switching their primary occupational roles, not just as an exercise, but in actuality. The husband could become a house-husband, which the Swedish call a *hemmaman*, while the wife becomes the breadwinner. Most spouses get a small taste of this kind of exchange when they fill in for a mate who is sick or absent. Most husbands have had the experience of taking over the housework, however unenthusiastically, for a few days. But unless a husband has a grave illness or loses his job, the non-working wife seldom has a chance to experience the responsibility of providing the basic support for her family, and indeed only a minority of wives would be prepared to do so. But if more couples were prepared to take over one another's roles, crises could be far more satisfactorily faced. With the instability of job markets that currently exists (and which seems likely to get worse rather than better as technological developments continue to increase at an ever-expanding rate), a new flexibility in regard to primary occupational roles begins to look like plain common sense.

One couple recently carried out just such an exchange from choice. The husband, Samuel C. Brown, Jr., described it this way in *Redbook* magazine: "For two years my mind and body taught at school, but my heart stayed home. I was nervous and reluctant to leave its familiar, uncomplicated warmth every morning, and oh, so glad to return every night." He gave up his teaching job to care for the home and to write in his spare time. His wife, who literally "wanted out" of the home, took on a position teaching dance at a local college. Both are happy. Even with two young children and his domestic duties to attend to, the husband has more time for his writing than he did while teaching school. The wife, on the other hand, is able to enjoy the fulfillment that comes from working at her own career.

The couple described here may not continue this exchange of basic roles forever, nor is there any reason why they necessarily should. But for now each is experiencing a release from boredom, is coming into contact with new situations, and is expanding his individual talents. They are doing what they want to do for themselves, still being good parents, and reaping many other benefits besides.

Any husband who has watched his previously house-weary wife begin to glow again from the sense of achievement offered by a job or career of her own can testify to the benefits of expanding outside your typical role. Such a husband discovers that he has a more attractive and vital wife, a more stimulating conversational partner. Since both husband and wife have put in time in the breadwinning as well as the domestic role, there need be no competition over the relative status of home work versus career work, and they can share experiences on a new level of achievement and challenge. Also, wives who work outside the home have less opportunity to become too intensely involved with their children—to everyone's benefit. The child develops his independence more quickly when his mother starts living her own life instead of living only through her child.

At the same time, the husband who stays at home has a rare opportunity to get to know his children intimately in a new kind of fatherhood. As the young husband who gave up teaching put it: "What is more touching than a child's spontaneous kiss when his daddy 'feels bad'? How many other fathers really know the exuberant confidence—and the honest fear—with which their children greet life?"

Not all husbands, of course, may feel they'd really enjoy a try at the domestic role, but others might find themselves ideally suited for it. As one Swedish *hemmaman* claimed, "I like to play with children. My wife finds it hard to be six years old. I find it easy." Neither this husband nor the former teacher found the house-husband role in conflict with his masculinity for, being sure of their maleness in the first place, they had no need of external roles, clearly labeled "masculine," to prove that maleness. Those roles we feel most comfortable in are the ones we should choose for ourselves, if at all possible, rather than allowing ourselves to be forced into a role in which we feel uncomfortable. Not all women are temperamentally suited to motherhood. Not all men are cut out for the relentless struggle in the jungle of business competition.

There is a further reason for wives and husbands to acquire a multi-role facility. In most cases both the provider role in the family and the managerial positions in our society are filled by men. These are stressful positions, and the toll they exact from the men who hold them is demonstrated by the increasing incidence of the psychophysiological diseases induced by stress: coronaries, ulcers, colitis, allergies and hypertension. Such stress could be equally shared by men and women. To so share it will provide the double benefit of giving women an opportunity to actualize their capabilities, and of increasing the health and longevity of men. Our traditional separation of male and female roles no longer makes sense in a complex technological world.

It is time to stop overburdening our men while we deprive and under-utilize our women. While each of us in our own way can modify roles to suit our needs, the success of sharing parenthood and interchanging husband and wife roles will depend on the creation of new patterns in work and family arrangements which offer broader bases than the nuclear family for sharing and mutual support.

Chore Exchange

The full exchange of occupational roles is becoming more and more common—yet to many couples it may seem a drastic and, initially, even inconceivable step. But there is no reason why any couple should find it too difficult to try an exchange of chores, perhaps only for a day or a week or on a regular rotating schedule. Henry, for instance, can do the dishes and mop the floor, while Jane repairs the screen door and balances the bank account. Any task normally undertaken by one mate can be exchanged with the other. None is likely to be glamorous, but all are necessary, and by shifting these chores back and forth, marital partners can relieve boredom, learn something new, become more versatile, and gain additional respect for the other's efforts.

It is important, though, to carry out such exchanges in a relaxed way. One couple we interviewed had carried this simple form of role-switching to extremes. They made an elaborate list of all the minutiae of their daily routine—from cleaning the refrigerator to replacing light bulbs. From this list they prepared a detailed schedule for sharing chores, making certain that both had a crack at each task. Tacked up on the bulletin board, this chart, whose complexity would have staggered the computations of a time-motion expert, came to rule their lives just as rigidly as their former roles had. Such charts can of course be helpful, but keep in mind that the central idea is to be *flexible*, to flow with the situation, avoiding rigid patterns. There's little point in making a chore of keeping track of the chores.

The benefits of chore exchange were made especially clear by one couple we know. George had taken over the shopping for three weeks. At first he bought only what was on the list, listlessly wandering up and down the aisles until he found each particular item. "Then I thought," he said, "after getting stuck in line and being bored, why in hell should I buy only what she wants? So I looked around for what *I* liked. First we had mushrooms in our omelet, something Marge never makes. Then it was spaghetti with clams." George learned to imbue the shopping trip with his own personality, instead of merely carrying out an errand for his wife. He has become very knowledgeable at selecting ripe avocados, tender cuts of meat, etc., and his wife, who thought he was a bull in the proverbial china shop looks at him with amazed respect. His awakened pleasure in the task meant that the job got done not only efficiently but with fresh culinary results in which both he and his wife could share.

Such accomplishments may seem minor—but remember how often friction arises between a couple over just such domestic details. The household chores must be done, and by sharing and exchanging them in a free-flowing way, they can be made light of. In addition, this kind of exchange helps to break down our prejudices about "masculine" and "feminine" categories. Each partner can increase his own sense of competence while gaining the further respect of his mate. By trying out some aspects of the other's role, each learns more about the responsibilities and demands placed on his mate, and he, himself, expands and extends his own capacity in coping with and accepting the challenge of something new.

Naturally, there are some jobs that are number ninety-nine on an individual's list of preferred tasks, that he either doesn't want to do or simply can't do. But enough flexibility can be achieved so that a greater understanding of one another's roles is developed, and so that neither remains an absolute slave to the role traditionally determined for him by the closed marriage contract.

New Perspectives in Housework

Switching chores is one way of discovering something new in the area we all label "work." There are other ways too, once household duties have been separated from their old role associations and both husband and wife share them.

We've all tried at one time or another to find ways to vary our daily tasks, and relieve their repetitiveness. Most can be varied in some way—either by changing your timing, using a different technique or simply by approaching them from a different point of view.

One of these is the aesthetic pleasure gained from accomplishing a task. The gleaming sink or tidied-up room provides some small measure of gratification and pleasure, even though tomorrow it will be back in the shape it was before. Even housework can be sensual if you are willing to let yourself go and look at it that way—sudsing the dishes, smoothing the sheets, sloshing big sponges and water over the car, smelling the tangy lemon oil polish and smoothing wax over the warm and satin-hued wood of a table top, can be just as sensual as enjoying the touch of velvet or satin, or enjoying an exotic or fresh perfume. Sensuality includes touch, smell, sound and visual awareness but it also can be enjoyed by experiencing your body in movement—by becoming completely physically immersed in the task. We are all physical as well as emotional beings, and enjoying your body and the sense you have for awareness can be used in all aspects of life—housework as well as sex and other pleasures. Sensual housework may not turn you on, but how do you know until you've opened up and tried it?

It is, at the very least, another way of getting back into the *now*, of experiencing yourself in the moment fully for what it is in the here and now.

Perhaps the greatest pleasure that can be derived from housework, if you are so inclined, is to use your ingenuity in reducing it to a minimum, in figuring out ways to do it more efficiently so as to leave valuable life energy and time for more meaningful and productive pursuits. For some tasks, like weekly housecleaning, you and your mate can team up, work out a routine, get things done in half the time and have fun doing it.

By limiting ourselves to a strict list of traditionally masculine or feminine tasks, we rob ourselves of such pleasures. Relentless repetition is bound to dull our response. The wife who has cooked three meals a day for five years naturally becomes blind to the beauty of a pile of vegetables—fresh green peppers, plum tomatoes, firm white mushrooms and glistening eggplants—set out on a cutting board. Similarly, the husband no longer delights, after endless Saturdays, in the smell of fresh cut grass and the feel of the sun on his back. The pleasures to be taken in ordinary tasks are many, if we will only open ourselves to them. But so long as we allow ourselves to be bound into a role that requires us to undertake the same chores forever without end, we will inevitably lose our perspectives, seeing only the drudgery and none of the pleasure.

Play and Creativity

By exchanging roles, even on a limited level, we give ourselves a chance to bring a sense of play back into our daily lives. The growing child lives in a world of perpetual wonder, because he is always discovering something new. Desmond Morris, author of *The Human Zoo*, puts it this way: "Each bout of playing is a voyage of discovery: discovery of itself [the child], its abilities and capacities, and of the world about it. The development of inventiveness may not be the specific goal of play, but it is nevertheless its predominant feature and its most valuable bonus."

In open marriage, it is possible for a couple to continually discover more about one another, and through such discovery to continually renew their marriage. By freeing themselves from the restrictions of their customary roles, they will have a better chance of reawakening the sense of play that lies buried beneath the responsibilities of adult life, to find again the childlike "sense of wonder and curiosity, the urge to seek and find and test," of which Morris speaks. Open marriage depends upon such qualities—the openness to seek out new ways of relating to one another, the urge to test one's commitments, accepting those aspects of the old marriage contract that work for the individual couple and rejecting those that don't, to find new ways in which to make each marriage a creative, growing union rather than a static, even stagnating form of bondage.

Creativity, Morris reminds us, is "no more than the extension into adult life of these vital childlike qualities. The child asks new questions; the adult answers old ones; the childlike adult finds answers to new questions. The child is inventive; the adult is productive; the childlike adult is inventively productive. The child explores his environment; the adult organizes it; the childlike adult organizes his explorations and, by bringing order to them, strengthens them. He creates."

Yes, No and Wow

The psychologist Eric Berne, author of *Games People Play*, once mentioned three words to live by—Yes, No, and Wow. The ability to say "yes" or "no" means that you know what you want and what you do not want. The guidelines for open marriage presented in this book, whether they concern open communication or living for now or role flexibility, are intended to provide you with special techniques or new approaches by which you can determine exactly what it is you want and do not want as a couple and as individuals. Having made that determination, and put into practice the relevant methods for change, you should find it possible to react to your lives more and more often with the constantly new and fresh dimensions expressed in that single word, "wow!"

We live in a world of expanding options. Technology has brought us a pace of change that can be dizzying, but on the positive side of the ledger it has also brought us increased diversity of choice. But you cannot discover the nature or extent of those choices if you simply accept the role model for husband or wife that has been prescripted for you by tradition. You may not feel ready to go so far as to exchange occupational roles with your mate—you may never want to do that, indeed. That is fine. As in all these guidelines, we are merely setting down possible ways to open your marriage up. No particular method is required. But if you wish to have an open marriage, it *is* necessary to make some attempt, whether large or small, to gain a new perspective on the roles you play. Without being exploratory, without developing some degree of flexibility, you cannot discover what is best for you either as a person or as a couple. And if you cannot answer "yes" or "no," if the answer is provided for you ahead of time, allowing you no choice in the matter, then the number of "wows" in your life is bound to be small.

When husbands and wives strictly adhere to separate, completely distinct roles, true understanding between them becomes virtually impossible. By sharing and exchanging roles, that understanding can be achieved, and with it, a new closeness and intimacy. Dr. Jack R. Gibb, a consulting psychologist, puts it this way: "Neither a role nor a role-taker can fall in love, communicate deeply with another person, or be creatively interdependent." But to become role-free, or at least role-flexible, means that perhaps for the first time you can drop your roles within the intimacy of your marriage, and show yourself to your mate as the *person* you are. As roles disappear, says Gibb, "the person appears . . . Persons, who experience themselves as persons, can be free, creative, and deeply *with* another person." And that is what open marriage is all about, being *with* your mate, and not just beside him.

12 Open Companionship

The Couples Game

Joyce had just come to New York to take on a college teaching job. Being new in the city and lacking information about the local academic scene, she decided to call Phil, a former colleague from graduate school at the University of Chicago. Phil's wife answered the phone when Joyce called, and Joyce explained who she was. "But do you know what happened when I finally got together with Phil for lunch?" Joyce said. "He told me, 'Look, Joyce, don't call me at home, I don't want trouble with my wife.'" Joyce was surprised and angry at being considered a threat to the wife of an academic colleague; she herself was recently divorced, and was not yet used to the reaction she aroused in married women. "It's absolutely archaic," she groaned. "Why, I can't even talk too long to someone else's husband at a party, now that I'm single—they begin to hunt him out and I get those piercing stares—my God, they're so cold they'd freeze over the hot springs in Yellowstone."

As a divorced single Joyce was experiencing something she had not noticed so acutely when she herself was married—the tight *couple-front* of the closed marriage. The couple-front is the outward manifestation of the clause in the closed marriage contract that calls for the two partners to be all things to one another, to fulfill all of one another's needs—emotional, psychological, intellectual and physical. This "fantastic notion," as anthropologist Dr. Ray Birdwhistell calls it, is blatantly unrealistic, and an impossible dream. Throughout life, from infancy through adolescence and into young adulthood, we are taught to reach out to others in order to learn, to grow, to enrich and vary our existence. We are open to the world around us. Suddenly, with marriage, all that comes to an end. The bondage of closed marriage requires husband and wife to turn off the outside world, and to turn on only to one another. They must restrict their contact with others, not only with those of the opposite sex but also with any friends of the same sex of whom their mate does not approve. Is this kind of circumscribed life necessary to marriage? Is it inevitable?

Let us listen to the words of a couple whom we interviewed, Frank and Janet. Frank is a chemical engineer by profession, a researcher and innovator respected in his field. Janet, still trim at thirty-nine, had once been a dancer, but is now actively involved in a teacher-training program for social workers. Both Frank's and Janet's interests span many areas. Some overlap, but not all are the same. Frank, a tall, lanky, gray-haired man, explained to us his open relationship with Janet. "For our marriage to stay together we both have to be alive—living, functioning human beings. Both of us have shared interests along with different individual interests. So how can we live our whole lives attached to one another? Her to me, me to her? Is she going to get all her humor from me, all her sympathy, all her intellectual interests from me. Christ, I can't fill that role. I'm smart, but let's face it, I'm not God. So when you get down to it, what does that mean, that I can't be everything to her. It means she has to live with other people, too. So if she meets another person, another man, say, who is a musician, if she finds intellectual interests with a friend who is a musician, it's all right for her to go to dinner with him. Is it all right for her to go to a ballet or a concert with him? Sure. Sometimes we go to the ballet together, too. But I can't possibly supply the same type of stimulus and companionship at a ballet or concert that she can get with a musician."

"Nor can I be everything to him," Janet said. "Frank has some interests, like discussing philosophy and working out mathematical puzzles, that I am just not enthusiastic about. He met a friend recently, a woman, who's just as fascinated in these things as he is—they have a running competition about who solves which puzzle first. Sometimes they get together here in the apartment, other times at other places. Why should I deny him the fun and pleasure of sharing these things with someone who likes them too? Once in a while I get excited and try to follow through with them on the puzzles, but sometimes I make other arrangements for the evening and go out."

All very well, you may think. But don't they ever get jealous of one another? Don't they ever wonder what the other one is really doing when he or she is out with another woman or another man? Frank and Janet discussed these questions frankly, but before we take a look at how they manage to avoid such fears and jealousies, let's investigate further the need for the kind of freedom they allow one another. Unless that need is fully understood, unless the "why" of open companionship is clear, the "how" cannot be properly conveyed.

Your Hook-up Points

Each of us is unique. There is no one else in the world who has exactly the same combination of memories, personality characteristics, and potentials—whether they be potentials already known or as yet undiscovered—as you do. Each of us, then, is a human being with a multitude of facets: likes, dislikes, experiences, talents, whatever. And each of us is unique in the patterning of these facets, and in the quantities and kinds of them that we have.

But let's make this idea more concrete. Imagine each person as an organism covered with thousands—literally—of these facets, sticking out like multiple antennae. Each of these facets, or antennae, is a hook-up point that makes it possible for us to reach out and connect with other human beings. These are our points of contact, of validation and confirmation and sharing, which make interpersonal relationship possible. If you don't share any hook-up points with another, then you can't make a connection; and it takes a sharing of many such points to establish a full-fledged relationship.

So there you are, a person, a particular identity, with your unique pattern of hook-up points. And there next to you is your mate with his own particular identity and his own unique pattern of hook-up points. You become joined together because you find that numerous, perhaps even a majority of your hook-up points match. You grew up together, you speak the same language, have the same values, both like potted plants, Mozart piano concertos and candied sweet potatoes. Some of your hook-up points may be in areas of profound feeling, sex, for instance; others may be entirely frivolous. But however many hook-up points you share, there will be others that you do not, simply because you are unique individuals.

What then happens to those hook-up points you and your mate cannot match? Whether they are actual needs that your mate cannot meet, or unrealized potentials that your mate cannot stimulate to further growth, they are part of you. And if they are not used, if they remain untouched, unvalidated or unfulfilled, they will become brittle from disuse. Eventually, to continue the image of these hook-up points as external antennae, they will become so deadened that they will simply drop off, making you a diminished person with fewer points of contact. These lost hook-up points leave you less of a unique person, less than you once were or could in the future be. If one of these hook-up points has roots deeply imbedded in your personality, stemming from a major need, it may be impossible to simply shed it like a porcupine's quill. Instead it will fester where it is. If it is of sufficient importance to you, an unmet need can become like an open wound in your being. Abraham Maslow, the psychologist, put it this way: "Capacities clamor to be used, and cease their clamor only when they *are* well used. That is, capacities are also needs. Not only is it fun to use our capacities, but it is also necessary for growth. The unused skill or capacity or organ can become a disease center or else atrophy or disappear, thus diminishing the person."

Yet in our closed marriages, we allow only those hook-up points that match those of the mate to be fulfilled. Only those facets of Sue's personality that match John's are utilized and John is limited in the depth, breadth and scope of his potentials to those experiences Sue can share with him. John, through his job, may be able to make use of a few, but not many, of the hook-up points that Sue does not share with him: Sue herself, confined to the home, will have even less opportunity to exercise the hook-up points she has but John does not. The importance of the guidelines concerning privacy and role flexibility become obvious here. But while the proper application of both these guidelines (role flexibility in particular) can help you to make greater use of your hook-up points, something more is necessary.

The Need for Others

All of us have profound needs for a wider range of interpersonal relationships and for a greater variety of companionship than the closed marriage permits. Marriage, by combining the resources of two individuals, *ought* to increase our opportunities for discovering the pleasurable companionship of new people, but in fact it does just the opposite. The closed marriage contract demands that all friends must be acceptable to both partners. This, of course, is a perfectly logical extension of the clause that all social functions must be attended jointly — the only trouble being that the insistence upon joint attendance is restrictive and unrealistic in the first place.

Each partner in the marriage is thus forced to give up any former friends his new mate doesn't like, or else sneak off to see them outside the house, meeting at the bowling alley or the hairdresser. And *that's* something you can get away with only if the friend is of the same sex. Premarriage friends of the opposite sex you'd just better forget about. In fact, if you really want to keep a premarriage friend, he should not only be of your sex but he really ought to get married about the same time you do, so you can keep up the couple-front together as a happy foursome. For the first two or three years of a marriage, a young couple may occasionally invite for dinner two unmarried friends, an old girlfriend of the wife, and a long-time chum of the husband, but as time passes, most closed marriage couples find themselves keeping company with other couples only. Unmarried people at a party tend to make the couples nervous; the women, especially, look with hard-eyed mistrust at any single girl who tries to talk to their husbands. It's easier to forget about your former friends, unless they soon get married too and your mate likes not only the friend but his or her new mate.

In the closed marriage, endless shuffling takes place even

concerning which couples are to be permitted, for the circle of friends is limited to those couples that both partners find mutually compatible. Naturally, few couples find both members of another couple equally palatable, so they eliminate ruthlessly. Since couples come only as package deals (John-and-Mary, Sue-and-Brad) if Brad is disliked then Sue must also be ticked off the list. When the final homogenized list of agreed-upon couples is assembled, it turns out that most partners don't even agree on the value of those "friends" that are left. In a recent study conducted by sociologist Nicholas Babchuk, 116 married couples were requested, separately, to make lists of their closest friends. In an astonishing result, when their lists were compared, only *six* couples had produced identical listings. And this brings us to a crucial question. If they can't agree on who their close friends are, then do they in fact have any close friends?

The traditional married couple is hardly likely to share any deeply personal relationship with another couple: in preserving the couple-front, marital partners surrender their individual identities. When the individual identity is lost or muffled, communication becomes extremely difficult on anything more than a superficial level. (One of the reasons for the popularity of encounter groups probably lies in the impoverished level of experience that married couples usually have in their impersonal relationships with other couples.) Couples do of course get together socially, but few share their deepest feelings or even expose the full breadth of their personalities to one another. The problems and triumphs they share with one another are only the most public and superficial of their concerns: overcrowding at the local school, deteriorating garbage service, the wonders of the new radar cooking range, the acquisition of a new sportscar. But how can more be expected of them? Trained to exclusivity, governed by the jealousy that inevitably accompanies "ownership" of one another, how can they possibly dare to open up and share intimately with one another?

Since no two people can possibly match all of one another's hook-up points, and since both premarital friendships and contact with other couples are subject to the veto of either partner, it is inevitable that the husband and wife in a closed marriage will both become diminished persons, in Maslow's phrase. Dr. Jane Pearce of the Sullivan Institute has in recent studies conceptualized our continued need for others. From our first moments as infants we have a constant need that continues throughout our lives for validation, for sharing our experiences with others. And all those feelings, observations, explorations and capabilities that *do not* receive validation or confirmation by others become collected into what Dr. Pearce calls a "central paranoia." Central paranoia is like a huge reservoir containing the sum total of our self-losses through the years, self-losses incurred by not sharing our experiences in rewarding interpersonal relationships with others.

As Dr. Pearce articulates it, the larger this reservoir of unshared experiences, the less is our capacity to share intimacy and tenderness with another. Looking at marriage in the light of Dr. Pearce's ideas, we believe that to the degree that a marriage limits a couple's growth and validation through others, it limits the marital relationship itself in its range and depth of intimacy. Of course, two people can be many, perhaps even most, things to one another over a certain period of time. The exclusivity of newly married couples, for instance, is to be expected, for they are still learning to know one another. A process of discovery in the case of a new relationship takes some time to run its course. But with exclusivity imposed upon the relationship over an extended period of time, after each has come to know the other thoroughly, growth will inevitably be curtailed.

"It is the natural and constructive sequence that when

the fulfilling aspects of a relationship have run their course and no longer contribute to mutual growth, the relationship, as a going concern, comes to an end," states Dr. Pearce, writing with Dr. Saul Newton. In terms of a marriage relationship, the goal is to keep it going and, clearly, the best way to achieve that goal is to promote the continued growth of both partners.

If each partner is allowed to grow individually, in directions that he may find interesting and fulfilling but which his mate does not, if he is allowed to seek in others outside his marriage a response to those of his hook-up points that are not matched by his mate, then each partner will continue to grow and change, so that there will always be new things for his mate to discover in him. If discovery between two people is continuous, if each is always growing, then the fulfilling aspects of the relationship will never run their course. Thus couples who insist upon exclusivity, who continue to believe that any husband and wife can be all to one another, are in fact only insuring that their relationship will eventually cease to be fulfilling in a mutual way. To commit yourself to this ending, by accepting the traditional closed contract before you have even begun, seems a tragic error, especially since it is such an unnecessary one.

What about the Risks?

Even though you may by now be convinced of the need for open companionship, for allowing your mate to have relationships, whether with men or women, that do not necessarily include you—even having admitted that need—you may still have strong reservations about allowing your mate that kind of freedom. So let us go back to our open couple, Frank and Janet, and listen to what they have to say about the risks involved.

"This freedom," said Janet, "means a lot to both of us.

The real problem I've discovered in marriage is that we deny parts of ourselves. Most people try to set themselves in a mold because if they got out of it, they're afraid they might fall apart or find someone else better that they may love more."

Frank cut in at this point. "Sure," he said, "inherent in this freedom, of course, is the risk that some day Janet, or me, is liable to meet someone much handsomer, much smarter, much richer, much more stimulating intellectually and that's the end, maybe, of the marriage. But life is like that anyway. There's no guarantee in life about *anything*. If I lived in fear, afraid of Janet seeing anybody else, or talking to another man without someone else around—well, that's a weakness. It comes from being afraid of competition, right? But I'm not afraid of competition. I can't be more or different than I am. And I can't keep Janet tied on a halter, either. I know what I have to give and the love we share together."

"You know, people frequently make a case of this," Janet added, "this fear that you will find someone better, more beautiful, all that stuff, but then that's the mold I spoke of, people are *afraid* of their own relationship. If they don't trust *themselves*, how can they trust others? The fear of finding someone better is because they doubt what they have in their own relationship. We've built up a secure and honest relationship; it's hard to come by, but when you have it, then the freedom you have is really an extremely strong bond between you. Our honesty and freedom is really a bond that holds us together."

This last point of Janet's seems to us an extremely important one. The bond of honesty and freedom is a positive bond. The bond of possessiveness and jealousy is a negative one. And a positive bond is invariably a more durable one. In closed marriage, the coercive restriction of the exclusivity clause provides a breeding ground for dependencies and insecurities, and leads inevitably to jealousy and suspicion.

By setting up possessive boundary lines on the mate's behavior, and thus implying ownership of the mate, the closed marriage creates the conditions necessary to jealousy. If I own you and you are "mine," I am bound to be jealous of your separate interests and of any attention you give to others, or that others give to you. You are making use of yourself in a way that excludes me, and are taking something away from me. In truth, of course, no one person can ever *own* another—he can only be responsible for himself and for his own feelings. But the closed marriage creates an artificial semblance of ownership, and jealousy follows inevitably.

"Jealousy," Janet said, "is the hardest part for other people to understand. I've been accused of not being in love because I am not jealous of Frank. These people reason that the mate who owns his partner and keeps him under lock and key is the one who loves most of all. Well, that's just nonsense. How can I be possessive and jealous when I know what Frank and I share by *not* being that way? What he shares with someone else is something different. It's not going to make what we share together mean any less."

To those who worry that their mates might find the grass greener on the other side of the fence, Janet is saying, in effect, that the open relationship brings a new kind of bond that is the greenest thing around. In fact, if you analyze that old cliché about greener grass, you'll notice that the crucial part of it is the fence. Of course the grass is going to look greener on the other side to the horse that is fenced in. And if he does jump the fence, then he almost *has* to find that, yes, the grass over there is greener, just because he has dared to escape his confining boundaries and trespass on forbidden territory. If he didn't find it greener, then his longing and his effort at leaping the fence would be made to appear foolish. Likewise, for persons in a closed marriage who feel trapped by its restrictive clauses, the illicit relationship, either social or sexual, seems at first to be very desirable just because it has been forbidden. When the fences are removed, however, one discovers that the grass on the other side is not greener after all, but merely different. We believe, in fact, along with Janet, that the true open relationship creates a kind of bond that makes other grass seem *less* green by comparison.

This is not to say that there are *no* risks in open companionship. This is not to say that extramarital relationships in an open marriage will *never* be sexual. That claim would be just as ill-founded as the claim made by those who defend the exclusivity of the closed marriage that every outside relationship would invariably lead to sex. Neither extreme is true. And it should be remembered that *life* is risky, as Frank said. We believe that the risk of failure in marital relationships is far greater in the closed marriage, with its forced exclusivity that denies individuality and growth, than in the open marriage with its open companionship. Furthermore, there are ways in which the risks inherent in open companionship can be minimized.

Minimizing the Risks

Open companionship works for the husband and wife who have already attained the degree of emotional security, independence and selfhood that we have been discussing throughout this book. Without a strong identity and the assurance of our value both to ourselves and to our mate, open companionship would of course pose a threat and so arouse jealousy. If you are insecure and depend upon your mate to fulfill all your needs, then you will experience a sense of loss when he shares himself with someone else, or even gives over large amounts of his time to a hobby or his career.

When a husband and wife have built for themselves an open relationship based on equality, honest communication, and trust, when their liking for one another, their love and respect for one another is defined by mutual understanding rather than by predetermined role structures or the coercive clauses of the closed contract, then the bond they form between themselves will be the central focus of their lives. Their own marriage will be their primary relationship. Precisely because this bond is so deep, so secure and so central to their lives, they can afford to open it up and let others in.

Frank and Janet, for instance, did not develop their arrangements concerning open companionship overnight. Both had been previously married and divorced. Both had grown children from their previous marriages, and now have a young child of their own. As Janet put it, "Both of us had enjoyable single lives after our divorces, and we sort of knew what we were looking for in one another, but it took time to get to know each other enough to take a chance." Frank added, "We didn't set up any kind of formal agreement at all about open companionship outside our marriage—in fact, for the first two years of our marriage we were involved in settling problems concerning the divorces —but later, when we had a stabilized routine, a home, and had sort of found our groove, then we talked about it, and it happened."

Another couple, who have had an open marriage for several years, suggested certain conditions as being essential to gaining the full rewards of open companionship. The first condition they described as the establishment of priorities. First priority was given, of course, to the relation of each mate to the other both in terms of consideration and the expenditure of time. Devotion, care and respect for the absent mate were fundamental when either one was sharing time with another companion. As the husband, Sam, said in terms of time, "After all, there are only twenty-four hours in each day—and of these twenty-four hours there is only so much extra time that exists. Most of the day is spent in work, in living with Joan, in our productive activity together, our family and responsibilities to each other. Our first responsibility is to ourselves, and we take great care that our subsidiary and complementary relationships do not deprive us of this time—only extra time is used for our outside companionships."

A second condition they found essential was that the third person with whom they had a relationship (whether of the same or opposite sex) must know about their primary relationship. In other words, the openness and honesty existing in the marriage was extended to any companions outside the marriage. Joan had a pertinent comment to make concerning this condition. "It's sometimes ridiculous to think that a man can't believe it when I tell him, yes, I am free to go out with you and my husband knows about it, gives me this freedom and trusts me. But then, if the man reacts that way, it's clear he's not the kind of free and open person with whom I would want to have a friendship, so it sort of levels itself out."

A third consideration was to be concerned for the welfare of the outside companion, to be sure that they were as well off, if not better than, before the relationship. This means, as Sam said, that "you are concerned for and respect any person with whom you have a relationship."

Allied to this third condition is a fourth: that they sought out people who were themselves stable and independent. This condition, Sam explained, meant that they steered clear of initiating relationships with persons who were, for instance, in failing marriages. "Sure we could help them, or advise them," he said, "but it would be impossible as well as detrimental to their welfare to develop a close, sharing relationship with them, because then they might come to depend on our support too much—either as a substitute for their primary one, or as a salve for their injury in their marriage. In other words, we try to find peers, people who are operating on our level of emotional maturity with whom to share companionship. We have found in this way we exercise the responsibility we think we owe to others and that is essential for ourselves. The funny thing is we started out wanting separate friends—I didn't like some of Joan's, and she didn't like some of mine—but now, we find that mostly we all end up being friends—so the pluses of our open companionship are not only twofold but fourfold." Sam and Joan's relationship reflects the expansion possible through open companionship. With such freedom and trust they can build a larger network of mutual friends in addition to having their own individual friends.

Thus open companionship must be an *addition* to your basic relationship with your mate. It must not be an escape from that primary relationship or a substitute for it. If the relationship is new, the partners more than likely do not yet know one another well enough either to need or to be able to benefit from outside companionship. If the relationship is fragile, as in a failing marriage, open companionship would naturally constitute a large risk for the simple reason that an outside relationship might not only seem but may actually be more stimulating than the marital one.

In both the above cases, it is important to fully establish your relationship with your mate before trying outside relationships in any depth. If your marriage is failing, and you want to try to save it, apply the other open marriage guidelines first, putting to use the ones that seem easiest for you to cope with initially. Gradually, if both partners cooperate in the endeavor, you ought to be able to build up the strength of your primary relationship and then move on to open companionship. The same applies to a new relationship. If, as more young couples are doing these days, you begin by making your own contractual agreement to allow outside relationships for one another, you should still allow the primary relationship with your mate to take priority in terms of both time and commitment, in order to develop the intimacy that lies at the heart of the open marriage. As both couples we have quoted in this chapter found, open companionship should offer no risk or threat if the proper openness has been first established between the marriage partners themselves. When the primary relationship is open, it has a strength to which outside companionships become additive rather than competitive.

Because Frank and Janet, for instance, are communicating honestly and openly and carrying on a true dialogue, they have so much living, sharing and trust in their marriage together that no outside relationship can challenge it. The meaning and intensity of their primary relationship is so strong that outside attachments can never catch up to it. Even the *sum* of the ancillary, or outside, relationships can never possibly be great enough to detract from their primary one—for it is growing at a pace so much faster than the outside ones that they can't reach it in terms of growth.

Some Added Benefits

The primary and most important benefit of open companionship is, of course, its stimulus to the growth of the individual marital partners, a growth that is essential, in the opinion of many psychologists, to the long-term stability of any intimate relationship. Frank sums it up beautifully: "If Janet goes out of an evening, I want her to have a good time, to have an interesting time. She shares her experiences with me and I gain enrichment in my life at the same time. And vice versa. If I am involved in something interesting, I share it with her. The richer her life is, the richer mine is."

But there are also other, secondary benefits. For instance, when you have rewarding and meaningful outside relationships, your mate does not have to become the exclusive dumping ground for your problems. We all tend to dump our problems in the laps of those closest to us; sometimes we do it directly, spelling out the problem, at other times, especially in closed marriages, we do it indirectly, by simply being unpleasant or moody without actually saying what it is that bothers us. Either way, we draw upon the energies of our mate, whether by demanding sympathy from them or by taking out our frustrations on them. When partners are constrained by the bonds of exclusivity, the demands they make in this fashion tend to become greater and more intense. In addition, the boredom that often accompanies enforced exclusivity is mitigated by outside companionship and people quite simply have less to complain about. They are too busy responding to new stimuli, too absorbed in growing to harbor the small grievances that accumulate in the tight bond of the closed marriage.

And when we do have problems, new insights into them and new solutions to them may be found by sharing them with others outside the marriage. Another point of view from a caring companion can often be just as valuable as a visit to a therapist, marriage counselor or encounter group. In the closed marriage the couple-front does not allow the existence of such companions, and professional advice becomes the only recourse. The therapeutic benefits of companionship with others have been recognized in various proposals for the establishment of intimate networks of couples and families who can openly share their problems and give support to each other.

An allied benefit of open companionship is the added understanding we gain of the opposite sex and thus of our own mates. Within the closed marriage the wife can have only female friends, the husband only male friends. Such limitations perpetuate our separateness as male and female, emphasize our sexual differences, and prevent us from understanding one another more fully as individual people sharing a common humanity. Sue, by sharing only with women, becomes more involuted into femaleness; John, by sharing only with men, emphasizes those aspects of his nature he shares with other males only. Each grows further away from understanding the other, instead of closer, each becoming more and more entrenched in their separate camps of male and female. Thus do we limit ourselves, in the closed marriage, not only to a single person who must supply all our emotional and other needs, but to a person who as time goes by becomes more limited himself by these very restrictions. Open companionship breaks these bonds as well, and by allowing us relationships with other members of the opposite sex, increases our ability to communicate with our own mates.

The Friendship Genealogy

Finally, there is the simple sense of joy in life that comes from the possibilities inherent in open companionship. You can graphically demonstrate to yourself the importance of friends in your life by drawing up a friendship genealogy, a kind of family tree of the friends you have had over the years. Take somebody who has been important to you, and has had an impact on your life. Ask how you met him or her? Trace back as far as you can the pattern of acquaintanceship that brought you to a given moment of action in your life. If you try plotting the friendship genealogy on a piece of paper you'll discover that it becomes almost impossible to do—the connections appear endless and the significance of even chance acquaintances becomes strikingly evident. You will also very likely find that the incidence of friendships decreases sharply with marriage, that upon acquiring a mate you began to shut the door upon new acquaintances, and thus upon the new experiences that other people lead us to. Stop and reflect a moment on the amount of pleasure, stimulation and growth you have denied yourself by closing the door on such friendships, by presenting the couple-front to all comers. It can be a sobering thought.

Widening Horizons

Modern life is so mobile that the opportunity to meet new people is abundantly present. Why should we have to ignore these opportunities, haul ourselves in and remind

ourselves that we're married, that we "belong" to someone
else? A husband we interviewed expresses the joy of escap-
ing those hang-ups: "Our open marriage, if that's what you
call it, has meant a whole new way of existence for us, a
whole new kind of inner and outer freedom for both of
us. It's a great feeling to walk down the street or be anywhere for that matter, and know that if I meet someone,
male or female that I want to know, I can do it without
feeling guilty—we can have a drink, take advantage of the
spontaneity of the moment—and I don't have to worry
about how I'm going to explain it all when I get home. If
nothing special is planned with Gay I call her up and say
I've met someone who is interesting and she understands.
We are devoted to each other—but that doesn't mean we
own each other. She has her friends, too, and the same
freedom. Another thing I've discovered is that when you
know you *can* have friendships openly with others, and
don't have to lie and deceive, you become much more
selective about the people you choose to spend your extra
time with. You not only have more friends, but better
friends."

Another husband put it this way: "This kind of marriage
has opened up new horizons for both me and my wife—oh,
it's not just the new friends we can make, it's the feeling
you have within yourself. There is a new excitement for
living, because I feel there are no limits to my own self,
no limits on the capacity to be myself, to relate to others,
to feel and respond without having to rein in a bridle, or
use blinders on yourself. Your spontaneity is *always* there,
and it can bubble out, you don't have to worry about which
way it goes, or how much of it is poured out, what you
should say and what you musn't say, how you should or
shouldn't act—I mean you can really be yourself, which
after all is what this whole humanity is supposed to be
about. What is wrong with people, why can't you just be
your natural self and if you see something you like or some-

one you like, let them know it, that's what makes life beautiful and worthwhile."

There is a Spanish saying, *"La Vida es corta, pero ancha,"*
which simply means, "Although life is all too short, it can
be ever so wide." The exclusivity clause of the closed marriage, the need to maintain the couple-front, makes life
not only short but also narrow. That sad narrowness that
limits the lives of so many couples simply is not necessary.
By building for yourself an open marriage, creating between yourself and your mate a relationship based upon
equality and trust, you can forge a bond that not only allows but encourages you to open your lives to other relationships, which will in turn help you both to continue to
grow in your primary relationship with one another. In
this way, although life may still be short, you will find it
is an ever-widening experience.

GUIDELINE VI

13 Equality

Not the Same but Equal

The battle for equal rights for women and men, both in and out of marriage, is a central issue of the contemporary scene. It is a battle because there are those who would deny such equality, consciously or unconsciously. Those who argue explicitly against it often raise the objection that the uniqueness of each individual makes biological or psychological equality between two different human beings impossible. This statement is, of course, perfectly true—but it is not a valid objection to the pursuit of equality, because it misinterprets the nature and meaning of the goal. The basic premise of open marriage is the idea of writing your own contract so as to take into consideration the individual differences between marital partners, and the uniqueness of each mate, instead of submitting to the old, closed contract that requires every couple to be the same. Equality in open marriage does *not* mean sameness or likeness in the least. It takes into full account the fact that no one person can ever be exactly equal to another in terms of capacities, abilities, talents, needs or desires.

But if marital partners are not to be considered equal in terms of likeness or sameness, what then does equality mean in open marriage? Quite simply, it refers to the equality of *personhood* for both wife and husband, the equality of responsibility for the self, and the equality of consideration, concern and care for the other—which also can stand as a description of mature love. To us personhood also means integrity—the integrated *wholeness* of the self. This equality of personhood means that each partner has the right to his own individuality, to the differences that make him unique. The equality of responsibility for self means that each partner has an equal right to pursue the goals, to meet the personal needs and desires that will result in fulfillment and growth. And the equality of concern for the other means that both partners will equally strive to give the other the freedom and respect necessary to the maintenance of personhood and the pursuit of fulfillment.

By granting one another such equality, husband and wife can become peers. They have no fears about their relative status in the marriage because they start out on an equal basis as persons. Having learned to shed the unequal role prescriptions of closed marriage, they can let the love between them flow freely, unrestricted by the false demands of the closed contract. When marital partners are truly peers, truly equals, then they can relate to one another as full persons rather than as embodiments of "husband" and "wife." The creation of equality in open marriage, then, is the creation of a *feeling* between its partners, rather than the setting up of specific rules that can serve only to force an unnatural appearance of "sameness" upon two unique human beings.

This chapter, therefore, is devoted to a discussion of ways in which that *feeling* of equality, which makes a husband and a wife true peers of one another, can be created.

The 50-50 Deal: a False Equation

Many couples searching for equality in marriage have mistakenly assumed that an artificially contrived "sameness" will turn the trick. "All right, all right," says the husband, giving in reluctantly, "so now we're equal." "Absolutely," replies his wife. "Marriage is a fifty-fifty deal—half for you and half for me." Because the marriage equation was unbalanced in the past, with the major authority, rights and resources vested in the husband, marital partners are led into thinking they can now balance the equation by working out equality on a prescription basis. But this is not really sharing at all; it is simply trading. Even those extreme feminine liberationists who suggest that husbands pay wives salaries for housekeeping are playing the trade-off game, though they may not realize it. These partisans of the 50-50 deal think that by dividing their assets, rights and duties down the middle they can correct the old imbalance. But all they are involved in doing is scoring points and then tallying them up to make sure they match. As Virginia Satir, a consultant on family therapy, has pointed out, "The current Western marriage contract has been derived from a chattel economic base, which stresses possessing. This frequently gets translated into duty and becomes emotional and sometimes literal blackmail. The quality of joy is lost in the game of scoreboard."

Under these circumstances, spontaneity and enthusiasm in marriage are sacrificed to gamesmanship. Marital partners are put in the position of saying, "I get as much as you get, and you can't have any more than I get," or, when one partner has done something to put him a few points ahead of the other, "Anything you can have, I can have, too." This kind of relationship operates on the principle of an "eye for an eye." The wife shouts at her husband, "If you can have an affair, so can I—just wait and see what happens when I go down to Miami in January!" If she carries out her intention in the spirit of retribution, not only she and her husband but also the third party might get hurt. That is the hallmark of eye-for-an-eye justice, of course—the hurt is passed back and forth endlessly, affecting all who come within range.

Balancing the equation by retribution isn't limited to only the serious infractions, such as having an affair. The technique is also used in the course of minor domestic squabbles. One couple we interviewed had recently moved from the city to the suburbs. "I've always loved cats," the husband, Barry, told us, "but Jill didn't like them and we lived in apartments, so we long ago decided no pets. Well, what does Jill do but go out and buy a dog as soon as we moved into the new house." Barry was so incensed by Jill's action that he immediately brought a cat home. The dog and cat fought, the baby got scratched, and Jill sulked for days.

This method of balancing the marital equation might be called the "equality of hurt," for all it achieves is to make certain that everyone is equally miserable. The equality of hurt has its roots, of course, deep in the old patriarchal marriage, with its built-in inequality. As the authority of the male gradually waned during the first half of this century, marriage became more and more of a power struggle, with the woman attempting to gain greater status and the man attempting to keep as much of it as he could for himself. Each is forced to wage this struggle with the aid of whatever weapons are available. Ironically, those weapons are often determined by the same role restrictions that have brought about the unequal status of husband and wife in the first place. Thus the wife uses tears while the husband bangs his fist on the table. He withholds money, she withholds sex. Marriage becomes a battlefield, with both sides engaged in a war that neither can win: for the partner who wins the power play inevitably loses the respect and love of his mate.

Many marriage counselors recommend the 50-50 deal as the best way to effect a truce in the war between the spouses. As part of this deal, each partner is expected to meet the other half way, giving up part of what he wants in order to get the other half. On the surface this seems both civilized and realistic. But in fact it is destructive and phony. The 50-50 deal makes no attempt to meet the problem of unequal status directly, but tries instead to dodge the issue. The partners are supposed to end in "compromise," that favorite word of the marriage manuals, and to reach that compromise they are supposed to bargain with one another. Let's take a closer look at what they are actually doing.

To begin with, in order to make this kind of bargain you have to be prepared to give something up. Notice the last word of the previous sentence: up. Give *up*. Not give, but give up. There is a distinct and very important difference between giving and giving up. Closed marriage makes constant demands upon marital partners to give things up. The wife may be asked to give up her career, the husband some of his former friends. The husband will give up skiing if the wife will give up horseback riding. The process of diminishment of both individuals (as we discussed in the chapter on open companionship) begins to take its toll. And the eventual result is that the wife agrees to give up being a person, a growing and unique individual, if the husband will too. That is not the way they look at it themselves, of course, but that is what has happened to them. They have bargained their way into boredom and stagnation.

We call this kind of relationship an equation of diminishment. As with the equality of hurt, it is an entirely negative achievement. Equal they may be, but it is the equality of prisoners in a cell they have constructed themselves. They find themselves indeed in a compromising (to use the word in another of its meanings) situation. Their individual identities, for which they supposedly loved one another in the first place, have been compromised right out of existence.

You cannot have equality, in any positive sense of the word, between non-persons, or even between half persons. And if you attempt to build a 50-50, bargaining relationship with your mate, you will inevitably find that you are less and less of the person you were before marriage. Unfortunately, the idea of bargaining to a compromise dies hard. It was born at the start of the togetherness era, two decades ago. Yet as recently as 1968 a new marriage manual contained the following pronouncement: "We state vigorously and unequivocally that bargaining is an essential part of the workable marriage." It is time such exhortations to self-diminishment were laid to rest.

Equality: the 100-100 Equation

Stemming from the patriarchal marriages of the Victorian era, the contemporary closed marriage is rooted in inequality. Attempts to introduce equality into it by means of a "share and share alike" 50-50 deal will only end in the equality of hurt or the equation of diminishment. You cannot achieve equality in a closed marriage; the restrictive clauses make it impossible. Open marriage, on the other hand, is rooted in equality. You cannot have an open marriage without equality. And because the open marriage, in all its aspects, encourages individuality and growth for both partners, the result is a relationship between two whole people instead of two half-persons.

Mates who must give up 50 percent of themselves in the marital relationship can never achieve full equality; but mates who are full persons to begin with, who retain 100 percent of their personhood, their identity, have the security within themselves to grant to one another openly those freedoms that they would have to bargain for as half persons in a closed marriage. Instead of maintaining their relationship by giving up this or that right, as the 50-50 deal makes necessary, the partners in an open marriage freely give to one another the freedoms that make for a steadily growing relationship.

In a closed marriage, Richard must give up watching football on Sunday television in order to get Gwendolyn to allow him to play golf on Saturday; and Gwendolyn must give up Thursday night bridge in order to persuade Richard to let her work at the local library two days a week. Both, in accepting these "compromises" are giving up part of their personhood, denying themselves not only pleasure but the possibility of growth. Supposedly, the reason that each demands that the other give up watching football or playing bridge is so that neither will be left alone in the house with nothing to do. But that time they gain to spend together by denying one another's natural wishes is only spent in arguing about what they've already given up for one another and searching for new compromises that they can force one another into. In an open marriage, each gives the other the opportunity, the freedom, to pursue those pleasures he wishes to, and the time they do spend together is fruitfully and happily spent in catching up on one another's individual activities.

Equality, then, is based upon personhood, upon the sense of individual identity that is developed when both partners in a marriage grant one another privacy, open companionship, and freedom from stipulated roles. Once again, we must emphasize that the guidelines to open marriage form an interwoven pattern. This means, of course, that the achievement of an open marriage is a gradual, step-by-step process. It is a steadily rewarding process because the interweaving of the guidelines means that progress made in one area inevitably leads to a linked step forward in another area. As each partner's sense of identity is strengthened, therefore, he will find it easier to acknowledge his mate's equality, to leave behind the status-conscious power plays of the closed marriage.

Stature Instead of Status

In a marriage based on the closed contract, status is predetermined: the man is dominant, the woman submissive. As we showed in the chapter on role-flexibility, higher status accrues to the husband's role simply because he carries the heavier financial burden and works outside the home, while the status of the wife is lower because housekeeping has no achievement value in our culture. Stature, on the other hand, is something that is created from the inside between the partners in an open marriage.

Stature can be created in two ways. One can make one's own stature by taking full responsibility for the development of one's selfhood, by becoming a person instead of remaining an actor in a role. If you believe in your own stature as a person, then it exists no matter how other people treat you. When you succumb to the demands of a role, you are declining to take responsibility for yourself, declining to believe in yourself; you are saying, I will be what the role declares me to be. And if you do not accept responsibility for yourself as a person you can't very well expect other people to treat you as an individual instead of as a representative of your role. Self-respect and self-stature thus go hand in hand.

Stature can also be mutually *granted* to one another by marital partners. The way partners make one another feel about themselves is crucial. After all, a person can have status but not stature in his mate's eyes. As one husband said, "I may be her husband, her supporter, the breadwinner, the big magnanimous guy, but I don't amount to much in her eyes, if she doesn't respect me." You cannot demand that your mate grant you stature; it is something that must be given. But it is far less likely to be given unless you believe that you have it and behave accordingly.

Thus equality is an attitude, a state of mind, an understanding between husband and wife, between two peers of equal stature. If it were put into words, this understanding might go something like this: "I am going to consider you, and treat you, and relate to you and with you as an equal. When you complain about something, I am not going to treat you like a child—instead I am going to give you my attention, I am going to listen to you, I will try to provide you with feedback. I am going to give you equal privileges, equal rights, equal access to my time and feelings, giving you what I expect you to give me when the situation is reversed and I need the same. When you are joyful and happy, and want to express it, I will share it with you as enthusiastically as you share my particular joys. I will listen to your opinions and decisions as I expect you to listen to mine. There is no necessity for me to agree, but I will respect your opinions as you respect mine. Perhaps I will try to influence you, but I shall never force you, or take your opinions or feelings for granted. If we split the workload, we do it from choice, not as the result of bargaining. We do it because our goals are mutual. If we want to get ready for a weekend trip, I'll do the breakfast dishes so you can pack the suitcase (not, I'll do the dishes *if* you'll pack the suitcase) in order that we can get off sooner together. There is a mutual joy in making an equal effort to achieve something positive for each other and for the two of us as a unit. However, when we go our separate ways, as we sometimes will, each of us will grant the other the freedom to take that time away as it is individually necessary to us, with no feeling of threat. We will not bargain for specifically equal time apart ("I get to go out Tuesday because you went out Saturday") because it is not the time itself that must be equal but rather the freedom to take it. Without the need to bargain, each of us can make his own decisions, and whether that decision is for joint or separate action, it will be taken with equal consideration, concern and love for each other."

Equality of stature, then, is something that is both granted and earned. You must grant it to yourself, and you must earn it for yourself. Your mate must grant it to you, and you must grant equal stature to your mate. This entire book, in a sense, concerns itself with ways in which you can learn to grant that stature to yourself and to your mate. All the guidelines are designed to help you discover the meaning of stature between two individuals united in an open marriage. Mutual appreciation of one another's stature is the abstract essence of equality for the married couple. But although it is an abstract concept, each application of a guideline to your own particular situation makes a part of that abstraction real. Equal stature is an idea and an ideal, but it is also a way of living.

A Woman's Place

A special problem exists for women in respect to the equality guideline. The closed marriage contract, as we have noted before, specifies that the wife's place is in the home. Her horizons are inevitably limited by her relegation to domestic duties, and it is hardly surprising that she often fails to "keep up" with her husband, that he simply outgrows her. She is merely a wife, but he is more than a husband, having an additional role in the outside world that usually presents him with far greater challenges and wider opportunities for growth than are available to his wife. So long as she accepts this imbalance in opportunity, the chances of establishing herself as her husband's equal will remain minimal: not only is her status less than his, but her development as a person is bound to lag further behind his.

There are, of course, some women who are entirely content with this domestic role, who prefer to be protected, to be taken care of, and to devote themselves exclusively to taking care of others. And there are some husbands who are completely content with such wives, who simply do not care that their wives are not growing as much as they —in fact they might feel threatened if their wives did grow. We doubt that any such wives or husbands, men and women who really like the old closed marriage system, will have continued to read this far into this book if they ever started reading it in the first place. If you have read this far, and you are a wife who professes to be content with a domestic role, or a husband who professes to be content with that kind of wife, we believe it is a sign that you know or suspect that not all is as well with your marriage as it might be, whatever you profess. So we do not hesitate to lay it on the line: no wife in today's world can hope to grow in a manner commensurate with her husband unless she is involved in some kind of activity, beyond homemaking, that makes commensurate demands upon her and that offers her opportunities equal to his for personal growth.

Some wives may *think* of homemaking as a professional career. But nobody else will, because of the status differential we have already discussed. Furthermore, even those demands that homemaking does make upon a woman (and they grow less with every new electrical gadget) have a life-span plugged into the length of time it takes to rear children. With today's longevity, that means that the wife will have thirty long years to share with her husband *after* the children leave. How long will it take, when your only challenge is making new drapes, to become boring to your husband? Not very long at all, a fact to which the rising incidence of divorce after twenty years attests. Finally, the relegation of the wife to the ultra-domestic role (as Philip Slater has termed homemaking) programs her for mediocrity and dulls her brain. With her senses thus dulled she may be able to delude herself into thinking that homemaking and motherhood are sufficient to make her a stimulating companion to her husband, but she won't delude her husband. He will more than likely have already found or be searching for a more exciting companion on the side. This may sound a harsh conclusion, but the divorce courts support it.

Nor can she keep up in terms of growth and earn equality

by dabbling—whether in painting classes, lecture-going, the local drama group, or attending Wednesday matinees of the latest Neil Simon or Harold Pinter play. Such dilettantism may have its pleasures, but none of them makes sufficient demands to bring about real growth. If you want to paint or pursue a creative endeavor at home, fine, but make sure you are serious enough about it so that a mate's or child's whims don't cause you to drop the paintbrush every five minutes. You can dabble at painting, you can dabble at social work. But only if you take it seriously, only if you become fully involved in it, and, unfortunately. only if you are materially rewarded for it is it going to be taken seriously by others. Again, this may sound harsh, but in our culture that is the way things work. "Right or wrong," says Edith de Rham in *The Love Fraud*, "the admired individual is he whose talent has been enfranchised, given the seal of approval in that somebody is willing to pay for it. . . . There is an aura of futility and condescension about dilettantism today, a sense of inadequacy in non-professional talent, because it merits no recognition and has no place in the modern world." If you want to grow in personal dimensions, to develop your capacities, to keep up with your husband's growth, then, you must be willing to accept the same kind of demands that he does. No hobby can ever exercise the kind of demand that work for which you are paid does. Nor do hobbies, important as they can be, fulfill our deep need to be allied to a cause or purpose larger than ourselves.

Thus, women have to seek out meaningful activity that will expand their minds, develop their talents and is productive in the full meaning of the word, contributing to some larger purpose. Motherhood, as a result, may have to be delayed. When a child is born, time should be taken off from work for the infant's first months or years, but that should only be a temporary detour from active productivity. Being productive can mean getting a job, teaching, going back to school for a degree, preparing in some other way for a serious career, becoming immersed in a creative endeavor, forming a company of your own, or even running a shop selling yarn to the wives who are still penned-up at home. There are many possibilities, but one of them must be taken. The move must be made into the outside world where challenge exists, where skills are learned and valued, where growth is possible. With the equality gained by such a move, husband and wife can grow together, in different ways and at different rates, of course, but grow, and so be able to provide one another with the constant stimulation of interesting companionship. Together they can shoulder the responsibility for family support, switching with one another at times, perhaps, to allow new job opportunities to be grasped and new risks to be taken. Growth then is parallel rather than divergent, and equality will naturally exist.

We are well aware that such completely equal sharing of family support is hardly possible for everyone until major societal change is effected in terms of family and child-rearing arrangements and all women are afforded the same opportunities in training and jobs as men.

The ESE Factor

Equality for women, in and out of marriage, is a subject that upsets a great many people, both men and women, whether pro or con. But the matter might as well be faced, for it has become one of those historical and even evolutionary inevitabilities about which there can finally be no argument. Until three separate avenues of freedom were opened to women, they had no chance for equality, but once those avenues were opened there could be no denying them an equal place. As long as the wife was uneducated, financially dependent, and subject to the whims of nature due to random childbirth, she could never escape the role in which our historical tradition of closed marriage cast her. Nor could the husband be released from his unequal share of the burden of full support for her and the family. To keep your wife at home, keep her barefoot and knocked-up, the old joke went—but it reflected a painful truth. Whatever the woman might have wanted (and she was never asked) she had no choice but to remain in the home. She was trapped there.

But twentieth-century technology, as we pointed out in our first chapter, combined to effect social change, giving to women educational, sexual and economic freedom. These three components, taken together, form what we call the ESE factor. And the ESE factor is the single most important force affecting change in today's marriage styles. Education broadens the woman's horizons beyond diapers and gourmet recipes, promotes intellectual growth and prepares her for a career; sexual freedom has been gained through absolute birth control, new knowledge concerning the nature of her sexuality, and a more permissive sexual climate; and economic freedom from dependency is possible through work and a career. Lacking any one of these components, the woman becomes a subsidiary partner in marriage. With all three, she is free to lead a life of fulfillment in all dimensions without even choosing to marry. And if she does marry, the ESE factor not only means that she *can* be her husband's equal, but in a larger sense *demands* that she be his equal. Before the ESE factor came into play, most women were not fully aware of the extent to which they were being deprived of their rights. They accepted the old patriarchal or closed form of marriage because there was no alternative. But any woman who accepts such a marriage today cannot help but be aware that there are other women around her who will not accept such limitations upon their actions, who are seeking growth and fulfillment on the same level as their husbands do.

We have mentioned before what we call the language of

inequality: such phrases used by men as "the little woman," "the wife," and "meet the Mrs." are outward signs of inequality, of the husband's dominance, of the wife's status as a possession. When we refer to "man and wife," (a combination sanctified in our marriage vows by the phrase "I now pronounce you man and wife"), we are slipping automatically into a terminology that reflects the actuality of closed marriage, where the man has identity as a man and the woman has identity only as a wife. To get an indication of how conditioned we are to that inequality, and how deeply imbedded in our thinking such language is, try to imagine the opposite phrase. How many people have ever referred to a married couple as "woman and husband"? Somehow it doesn't ring true, does it? But neither should "man and wife." Hopefully the day will come when that phrase will sound just as strange to us as "woman and husband."

But true equality between men and women will come only gradually. In the meantime, as we pass through the transition period, there is bound to be increased friction, and griping on both sides. Women, having been dominated for so long, have greater reason to complain, and a complete right in demanding change. But as change takes place, women must not carry their cause to the extremes of retribution against men, and the wife who seeks equality in an open marriage must be ready to listen when her husband complains that *he* is being treated unjustly. Inevitably, in a period of transition, he will sometimes have cause to cry "foul."

Some Justified Gripes

As we pointed out in the chapter on role flexibility, the new freedoms of women have created an imbalance in the marriage equation: little girls are now expecting to grow up to be *women* while little boys are expecting those same little girls to grow up to be *wives*. When the boy grows into a man he does so with the same role expectations that governed his father's behavior, but those expectations cannot be fulfilled without the acquiescence of women, and they suddenly are not cooperating. They have developed a whole new set of expectations and the men are finding themselves in the peculiar position of having to adjust to the demands of women. This role confusion creates what Dr. Anne Steinmann, of the Maferr Foundation, has termed the male dilemma and the female quandary. Given the changes that have been brought about by the ESE factor, the woman can't go backward, or even stand still, but finds that every step forward is painful: a quandry indeed. The man's dilemma is how to react to all these changes, how to adapt to the new needs of women without losing all sense of his own masculinity. Women, it must be admitted, do not always give as much help as they might in helping him to adjust.

"Look, honey," complains the young husband, "if we're going to work out this equality routine, don't you think it's time we put *both* our salaries in the same pot, instead of using yours just for your clothes and mine for everything else?" A single young man who would like to get married has doubts about whether he's included in the new equality. He talks about his girl friend: "I'm all for *equality*, but she doesn't stop there. So, okay, she wants everything I've got —a job, money, initiative, aggressiveness. That's fine. But when the sledding gets rough she falls right back on her old female wiles. If she can't win an argument by logic, then she'll turn to old-fashioned bitchery. She wants to be able to ask me for a date, which is great, but when she asks me I have to accept or she goes into a decline for the next two weeks; if I ask *her* for a date, on the other hand, she feels perfectly free to say no. She pays her own way to the movies, but I'm expected to pay for dinner, which is the expensive part of it. That way she gets to show how independent she is without spending much. It just isn't fair.

She can't have what I've got and what she used to have, too."

Griping is justified in such situations. There are women who take advantage of the shifting currents in role determination, reverting to the safety of the old role when it is advantageous, while at the same time they try to accrue to themselves the traditional male prerogatives. But in many cases the woman doesn't really intend to take advantage, it's just that the old patterns, instilled over generations, are hard to eradicate—especially when there remain so many men who would deny a woman's right to full equality in the first place. The real tragedy in these misunderstandings is that it is not the individual person (man or woman) who is to blame, but the cultural imperatives that have shoved them into these positions.

Until major shifts occur in both attitudes and societal planning, to accommodate new and more flexible roles for both men and women, the men can be expected to resent and resist change, and the women can be expected to fluctuate, from situation to situation, between full personhood and dependency. During the transition period, with both men and women scrabbling back and forth on the sexual seesaw trying to find a new point of balance, we believe that good communication between men and women is of the greatest importance. Open marriage in its entirety was conceived as a response to the strains imposed upon marital relationships by the changed expectations of men and women in the 1950s and '60s, and any of the guidelines in this book can, we believe, help husbands and wives to move toward a new point of balance—one based on full equality between them.

The Peer-Bond

The couple who achieve the feelings of equality described in this chapter become partners in the fullest sense of the word: they work, play and grow together as peers. Sharing the responsibilities, rewards and privileges that come with being mature selves, they help each other to pursue their individual identities while at the same time they are brought closer together by the commonality of giving, sharing, trusting and loving.

This commonality of purpose creates a new type of bonding, one that goes far beyond simple pair-bonding. Based primarily on biological affinities and the goal of producing a family, closed marriages are typical pair-bonds held together by the glue of conformity, convention and those restrictive clauses of the traditional contract that turn this form of marriage into what might be called a pair-bondage. On the other hand, peer-bonding, as Dr. James Ramey, a behavioral scientist, has termed it, is the open union of equals who have the freedom to be themselves. As peers they can be friends as well as lovers, people who think as well as feel, who evaluate as well as enjoy. They become persons, in fact, with an unlimited outlook.

When both man and woman are equal in feelings of stature, when they are peers, the strength of the bond between them owes no allegiance to the old clauses—it comes from within. It is a true bonding, not a bondage, and the paradox is that its strength as a union is derived from the freedom each partner has to be himself.

Cathy and Mark are a young couple who have created this kind of peer-bond relationship within their marriage. Listen to their description of what equality means to them:

"Because Cathy is my equal, a person, an adult, I can ask her opinion about something usually considered a man's prerogative—a male decision, about my job for instance, which assignments to accept or refuse. Because I respect her, her opinions mean a great deal to me. She has a different, well, maybe even less prejudiced view. In most things we make decisions collectively. After all what is a *male* decision? A decision is a decision, no matter who makes it. Why not both of us?"

Obviously, Mark and Cathy have erased the old mascu-
line/feminine stereotypes and have moved on to making
decisions by consensus. For with equality comes congruency. When two partners are congruent—or equal in status
and stature—no deference is necessary between them, and
the ideas that are stimulated can flow freely. If someone is
your superior (in a job situation, for instance) you hesitate
to make suggestions, become inhibited, and censor your
spontaneity. The superior person also loses in such cases,
for he can never fully share his thoughts or experiences
with an inferior and remains to a large extent locked up in
himself. With equality, better problem-solving ability naturally follows with discussion based upon mutual respect
rather than upon bargaining. The goal to be achieved, or the
problem to be solved becomes a mutual endeavor rather
than a mutual conflict.

Mark and Cathy both work. He is a professional pho-
tographer and she owns and operates a shop selling foreign
crafts. Both live a high-speed, demanding life, working long
hours in different areas of the city, and are sometimes separated by out-of-city assignments and shopping trips abroad.
Both of them spoke of the dynamic nature of this kind of
life together. Mark said, "I suppose the real reward of an
equal relationship is that a door is opened up to a much
fuller, more fully rewarding life, a more creative existence."
And Cathy added, "But it's really more than one door; it's
two. If a woman has a career, there are two roads, two
possibilities for leadership, depending on the situation. The
man doesn't always have to be the locomotive force with
the woman as caboose."

This couple practice what they preach, and demonstrate
the flexibility many young people exercise today. Mark had
previously worked as a salesman in a very lucrative business
and was able to help Cathy start the shop. When he finally
decided to move into photography, Cathy's work at the shop
supported them during his years of apprenticeship. Now

that both of them have full earning capacity in their careers, they have found that they not only share responsibilities but that new avenues open up to them. Mark put it this way: "We could both theoretically walk out the door together and be able to start a new life together anywhere —not so much because we're both creative as because we're equals, not dependents. There are no boundaries to what we can do together. Since we're open and equal we can create our world together again and again—a total life style of our own—and that gives us not only two doors, but really a thousand doors."

14 Identity

Am I You?

A perplexed husband whose marriage was collapsing around him recently told us what he believed a marriage should be. This belief was summed up in three small phrases: "I am you, you are me, and we are one." His statement is sincere, touching and beautifully expressed. Yet nothing could point more clearly to the root of the problem in his marriage than this cherished concept, which in practice can only have the result of effectively denying personal identity to either partner. This husband, Steve, admitted that for over twenty years of marriage he and his wife had been unable to achieve this oneness. But that did not stop him from continuing to seek the fulfillment of this impossible dream, bringing himself only frustration and driving his wife to the verge of leaving him.

At the beginning of this book we showed how the togetherness syndrome, the unrealistic ideal of "becoming one," led John and Sue to begin conforming to the restrictive clauses of the closed marriage in the first days of their married life, locking themselves into a pattern of inappropriate self-denial and mutual misunderstanding that would last as long as their union. Few couples who strive to "become one" actually succeed in doing so; all they achieve is to deny one another the right to exist as individuals, and to reap the unhappiness that inevitably accompanies that denial. There are, of course, occasional couples who do achieve the "ideal." We have all seen them eating together in a restaurant at one time or another: a gray little old couple who have been "growing together" for so long in their isolated prison of togetherness that they have even begun to look alike. They sit there with mute masks and glazed stares, eating through an entire meal without exchanging more than a few perfunctory words. So perfected is their response to one another that it has become mere habit—a stultifying ritual acted out in no man's land. Through togetherness they have fused their identities to the point of mutual anonymity. They have succeeded in making nobodys of one another.

The importance of identity has been emphasized throughout this book. All the previous guidelines touch upon it in one way or another. We have pointed out the need for privacy in order to seek and discover one's self, for open communication in order to better understand your mate's and your own true selves, for role flexibility in order to separate your identity from the predetermined responses of traditional male/female roles, and for open companionship in order to fulfill those aspects of yourself that do not match up to your mate's individual personality. We have shown that the achievement of equality between husband and wife is intimately linked to the question of identity. Thus, you should already have understood the importance of identity in many of its aspects, and in this chapter we shall concentrate upon some additional facets of the subject that we believe can help you in achieving the full sense of your self that is basic to open marriage.

Appeasement: Salve for the Wounded Identity

Rachel is cleaning and reorganizing the house to make space for her husband Andy's aged mother, who is coming to live with them. In the overstuffed basement storage area, where her mother-in-law's trunk and suitcases will have to be stowed, Rachel comes across Andy's trombone, covered with fifteen years of dust. Now really, she thinks, let's be practical, what are we keeping *this* for? Andy had lugged it along through all their moves, from small apartment to large apartment to their present house. He never played it, hadn't for twenty-five years, but it was *his* and it was the only material thing left from one of the pleasantest, most carefree periods of his life, when he had traveled with a nightclub combo for two and a half years. Rachel decides that the sentimental attachment to his trombone must have faded by now, and so she pitches it out along with a lot of junk that is to be collected later that day.

But, only half-consciously, Rachel feels guilty. In spite of her long day cleaning, she prepares a special candlelight dinner, which surprises and delights Andy. Andy gets romantic and puts on his old Glenn Miller records, which unfortunately remind Rachel of the trombone. They dance for a while, and end up having unusually spontaneous sex; Rachel responds with a warmth and vitality she hasn't shown in months. It isn't until the weekend, when Andy goes down to the basement, that he discovers his trombone is missing. A furious argument ensues, but neither of them ever fully recognizes that Rachel's candlelight dinner and responsive sex were a form of appeasement, in expiation of her guilt at having thrown out the trombone in the first place.

By throwing out the trombone, Rachel has not only violated our cultural rule to respect other people's property (a rule that becomes diluted in marriage due to the togetherness syndrome), but she has also raided her husband's ego-territory. In throwing out his trombone, she has symbolically thrown out his memories, a part of his inner self. This assault on her husband's identity was merely thoughtless, rather than vindictive, but that did not prevent it from being destructive. Such assaults are extremely common in the closed marriage. In thousands of ways, many of them trivial in themselves but collectively damaging, spouses attack one another's identities, undermining them, tearing them down. Sometimes they do so out of personal hurt and deficiency in their own identity, sometimes out of blind thoughtlessness, sometimes in angry retribution. Then feeling sorry or guilty, they proceed to appease one another.

The appeasement game can be played in several different ways, and for a variety of reasons. It can be used to assuage your guilt at having invaded your mate's ego-territory, as in Rachel's case. It can be used to pay your dues for having transgressed against a clause in the closed marriage contract. In such cases, it may be the clause rather than the transgression which is basically "wrong." For instance, if John were to take an old girl friend out to lunch, violating the "ownership" clauses of the closed contract, he might take his wife out to a very expensive restaurant on Saturday night to appease her outrage and to assuage his guilt. In terms of open marriage, of course, it is not *John* who ought to be feeling guilty, but his wife, for denying him the right to open companionship and the fulfillment of his own identity. But within the closed marriage, John would be the one who would feel guilty.

There is a third way of playing the appeasement game that is very common but little noticed. A husband, for instance, might offer his wife a new car if she will turn down a job she is thinking of taking, or a vacation in the islands if she will give up her part-time commitment to some cause of which he disapproves—the county Democratic Club, say, if he happens to be a Republican. This amounts to a kind of appeasement in advance or, to be blunt about it, bribery. It also closely resembles, of course, the kind of bargaining described in the chapter on equality. In the traditional marriage, wives are fully accustomed to appeasement for their loss of identity. It is almost a way of life. A great fuss is made over their roles as mothers, for instance, to appease them for their lack of identity as women. In his book, *Pursuit of Loneliness*, Philip Slater notes that many men "make their wives an island of stability in a sea of change. . . . Men in their jobs must accept change—even welcome it and foster it—however threatening and disruptive it may seem," he writes. The men thus participate in the twentieth century yet assign their wives "the hopeless task of trying to act out a rather pathetic bucolic fantasy oriented toward the nineteenth."

A New York psychoanalyst commented on this kind of appeasement to prevent assertion of identity and the change that naturally goes with it. "I wish I could tell you how many wives tell me their husbands offer them cars, coats and trips if they will only stay *out* of analysis. It is pure *bribery* not to change." Sometimes, of course, it is the wife who is afraid of change, who attempts appeasement in advance to persuade her husband not to give up his job with an advertising firm, say, in order to become a free-lance writer, even though that is what he needs to do for the sake of his identity.

But whichever spouse is doing the appeasing, and for whatever reason he is doing it, whether he has invaded his mate's ego-territory as Rachel did, or transgressed like John against one of the closed contract clauses that produces guilt in those who try to assert their identities, or because he wishes to bribe his mate to remain a static, unchanging person, this method of dealing with your mate is fundamentally an outgrowth of the false and ultimately destructive belief that "I am you, and you are me, and we are one."

The Woman: Programmed for Dependency

As with equality, the question of identity poses special problems for women. Carolyn, who is now divorced but nevertheless looking for another husband, expressed it well to us. "I don't like it," she said, "I don't want it, but there it is. For a woman, marriage is an accomplishment, for a man it isn't. He has a career and so many other things that can fill up his life. But a woman doesn't feel complete unless she is part of a union, she is more needful in all kinds of ways to make up for her incompleteness as a person."

Our society attempts to program women for a dependency status, to persuade them that marriage is an identity in itself. By and large, she achieves identity *through* her marriage and consolidates and merges it with her husband's. Until recently, most women accepted that programming as natural and inevitable. Having very little opportunity to establish an identity of their own prior to marriage, they were not concerned about giving up their own names to become a Mrs. Somebody Else, or relinquishing certain property and other legal rights. (Even today, in some states, single women hold numerous legal rights denied to married women.) But the ESE factor, described in the chapter on equality, is changing all that. These days more and more young women, like Carolyn, are recognizing that they have been programmed for dependency. Some, more independent than Carolyn, are strongly resisting such programming and recognizing that neither being a wife nor a mother can in itself constitute identity. Yet there are still those who tell her otherwise. Listen to the voice of Dr. Theodore Isaac Rubin

in one of his columns for *Ladies' Home Journal*: "The ability
to understand men is much more important than looks, talent or education . . . a woman will consider her man the
most important person in her life. She will value him above
all other people—including herself." Such an injunction
amounts to a denial of identity, and demands the sacrifice
of a women's feeling of self-worth and human dignity.

Despite the amount of attention given to the feminist
movement by the press and other media, the majority of the
big name columnists dispensing advice (on whatever level
of seriousness) echo Dr. Rubin's brand of outdated and
repressive thinking. The woman who tries to live up to this
image of self-abnegation often finds herself feeling quite
simply ill, as well she might. National Institute of Mental
Health statistics show that women have a higher incidence
of psychiatric hospitalization than men, and generally demonstrate that a woman is more "psychologically distressed,"
as one report puts it. Her incidence of symptoms such as
nervousness, headaches, inertia, insomnia, etc., far out-
weighs man's. There is no question that her lack of personal
fulfillment or commitment to her own individual growth
contributes in large part to her ever-increasing assortment of
physical complaints. It is often suggested, of course, that her
depressions and "distress" are due to her feminine nature:
i.e., menstrual cycle, hormonal flow, and menopause. But
this line of reasoning is demolished by the fact that in other
societies around the world where women are *not* solely
confined to homemaking and motherhood, the same feminine
"nature" seldom leads to such problems.

The most important thing about the nature of women,
then, is exactly the same thing that is most important about
the nature of men: in order to be an emotionally healthy,
productive human being, it is necessary to have identity,
and to seek the continuous personal growth that develops
out of identity.

Identity Is an On-going Process

You now know a good deal about what identity is *not*. It is not being a wife or a mother: those may be aspects of your total identity, but then again they may not. At most they can only be a part of the whole. Similarly, for a man, the role of breadwinner is not in itself an identity. Some men make their jobs the equivalent of their identity. You need only think of the number of men you have known who have dropped dead of a heart attack within a year after retiring to recognize that this male tendecy to concentrate all their energies on their job or profession at the expense of nearly all other interests is self-destructive. Identity can never be just one thing. It is not even, in fact, a *thing* at all. It is a process.

Having identity is becoming your own individual, and being able to express it. It means that you know yourself. It means that you are able to fit together into an integrated whole, into a good self-image that is rooted in reality, all the different images of yourself that have accrued to you throughout the years. Within that whole, however, there must be room for future images. Our quest for identity involves both *being* and *becoming*, for we are constantly changing. The man who never changes is not the man who has found his ultimate identity—it is rather a man who is afraid to seek his identity and has instead attached himself to a static role like a barnacle to a rock.

Having identity means that you know who you are and *like* who you are. You are able to be an authentic person in your disclosures to others. You have integrity. You believe in yourself, and are responsible for your actions. You have your own opinions and you let others have theirs. You are confident of your abilities and respect those of others. To be able to make choices for yourself and to function as a sepa-rate individual is a demonstration of your *autonomy*. It is just this vital aspect of identity that is so often absent in the closed marriage, in which dependency, the opposite of autonomy, reigns supreme.

Granting Autonomy

Couples in the closed marrige, dedicated to togetherness, often come to lean on each other like the sides of an A-frame house—together they stand, separated they fall. Each learns to expect the other to fulfill his needs to such a degree that neither knows any longer how to function as a separate and independent person. Do you recognize the wife who can't open a jar lid by herself, or the husband who can't pick out his own ties? You are sure to know the husband who falls apart when his wife gets sick, or the wife who becomes hysterical when the pipes break and the basement floods.

In this kind of relationship, marital partners tend to project parts of themselves on to one another. The mate becomes an extension of yourself. You see his mistakes as your mistakes. When he does something you wouldn't do, you become embarrassed for him. The criticism he receives you interpret as criticism of yourself. You may in one situation leap to defend your mate, as though he were you yourself, but in other situations you are likely to turn around and criticize your mate for acting as he did, because it has made you feel vulnerable or embarrassed. A serious lack of autonomy is evident here. You are failing, because of your own lack of identity, to recognize your mate as a separate person. And by so failing you are, of course, making it more difficult for your mate to *be* a separate person, to establish his own identity. Your ego has become involved with his to the point of mutual confusion.

In closed marriage, in fact, spouses in many ways actively seek to curtail one another's autonomy. Because they are too much together, too dependent on one another, and too ego-involved with one another, they deny one another the opportunity to make decisions for themselves, thus cutting down drastically on the options that each one should have available. Closed marriage decrees that neither partner can make autonomous decisions concerning his self—only *spouse-approved autonomy* is permitted. If Greg likes the last dress you bought, you can keep it. If Maisie approves of your bowling partners, you are free to go. If the possibility of more money or greater prestige is involved, the latitude of spouse-approved autonomy is naturally wider. Phyllis willingly sends Brian off to a week-long convention when it means the possibility of a promotion. But she pouts when he goes on a fishing trip with just friends. Brian, for his part, feels abandoned when Phyllis takes dancing lessons one night a week for her own enjoyment, but he heartily approves of her banging away on the typewriter either to supplement his salary or to help him with a job report. Spouse-approved autonomy, in other words, isn't really autonomy at all. Some husbands and wives become so adept at this game, however, that they are able to con their mates into believing that they have much more freedom than they actually do.

What the partner in the closed marriage does not realize is that by limiting his mate's autonomy, and so undermining his sense of identity, he is also limiting his ability to love. For without the self-esteem that comes with identity it is much more difficult for a human being to reach out and share with others in intimacy and love. As Erik Erikson has pointed out in his studies on the formation of identity, it is only when a man has achieved an identity that he is "ready for intimacy, that is, the capacity to commit himself to concrete affiliations and partnerships. . . ." Thus closed marriage, with its many clauses that restrict autonomous action on the part of either mate, tends to prevent the very intimacy that it seeks in principle to engender.

The Nowness of Self

Having personal identity, whether you possess it before marriage or achieve it through open marriage, means having an affirmative outlook on life—it is an attribute of a healthy person relatively free of the debilitating neuroses that impede growth. No one has described the benefits that flow from having a positive identity better than Dr. Abraham Maslow, who made a life's work of the study of what he called *self-actualizers.* Self-actualizers are creative, original, realistic people absorbed in life and growth, making full use of their talents, capacities, and potentialities, while retaining the ability to "appreciate again and again, freshly and naively, the basic goods of life, with awe, pleasure, wonder and even ecstasy. . . ." Above all, such people are capable of non-possessive love in their intimate relationships.

The self-actualizing person, Maslow tells us, displays in his love relationships "an affirmation of the other's individuality, the eagerness for the growth of the other, the essential respect for his individuality and unique personality . . . Respect for another person acknowledges him as an independent entity and as a separate and autonomous individual. The self-actualizing person will not casually use another or control him or disregard his wishes. He will allow the respected person a fundamental irreducible dignity . . ." This seems to us an excellent description of what the relationship between a man and a woman in open marriage should be.

The open couple can work toward such a relationship, can discover the self-actualizing potential in themselves, by making use of a concept that we call the *nowness of self.* This concept is in part an extension of our first guideline: living for now. Identity cannot be sought in any tomorrow. It partakes of the past, in that it is shaped by the sum of your experiences, but it must be *felt* in the present. The exploration of the self that we described in the privacy guideline is another important aspect of the nowness of self. Without such time to investigate yourself, the achievement of full identity is impossible. But it is not just a matter of introspection. You must seek your self in the midst of activity as well. The new kind of awareness of your surroundings, the fresh pleasure that can be taken in ordinary everyday jobs, will also be of help. The broader perspective and new experiences that come from role flexibility are an invaluable way to shed your merely habitual, reflex reactions to the world around you and gain a more immediate, more intense awareness of the present moment.

At a still more involved level of reaction, you must seek out the nowness of self in your associations with other people. Clearly, open companionship will assist in this endeavor, by giving you the opportunity to express those parts of you, those hook-up points not matched by your mate's. And gradually, as you open yourself more and more completely to the world, and come to know yourself better and better, you will find that it becomes more and more possible to experience the nowness of your self in the intimacy of your relationship with your mate—and that he will find the same thing to be true for himself.

It may seem paradoxical, but as you become more intensely aware of yourself, and as your mate becomes more aware of himself, your union will become richer and more deeply felt. As each of you more completely fulfills his own identity, each will discover that he has more to give the other. As we noted at the beginning of this book, it is supposedly because we love our mate's self that we get married, yet the traditional closed marriage contract contains clause after clause that demands the extinction of self, that restricts the possibilities of growth, so that as the years pass each partner has less and less of the self for which he is loved to give. By opening up and by writing your own unique contract, each partner develops a stronger selfhood, and thus has more rather than less to share. "As he gets to be more purely and singly himself," writes Maslow, "he is more able to fuse with the world . . ."

Open marriage thus prepares the way for increased self-actualization. And self-actualization, in turn, makes it possible for each partner in the marriage to open himself still further to the other. Maslow says that self-actualization can be seen as "an episode, or a spurt in which the powers of the person come together in a particularly efficient and intensely enjoyable way, and in which he is more integrated and less split, more open for experience, more idiosyncratic, more perfectly expressive or spontaneous, or fully functioning, more creative, more humorous, more ego-transcending, more independent of his lower needs."

Two people who can react to life and to one another in this way will inevitably enjoy a far richer relationship than two people who, like Steve at the beginning of this chapter, are striving desperately to pare themselves and one another down to a small enough size so that they can fit together into that restricted space in which, as Steve put it, "I am you, you are me, and we are one." The all but impossible task of "becoming one" can produce only frustration and bitterness along the way, and if it should be achieved would bring only a gray, joyless mutual anonymity. That is a kind of death; if you would have life instead, then you must begin by seeking your nowness of self.

Restoring Identity

Closed marriage stamps out identity; but if you have lived for some years in a closed marriage and are only beginning to move toward an open one, how do you go about restoring identity? Clearly, the various guidelines we have already explored each lead in this direction. Privacy and living for now are essential to establishing nowness of self. Shedding roles, becoming the other through role reversal and exchange will give you a new flexibility and help you to rid yourself of the influence of the old role models that limit your experience and range of emotion. Comunication is the bond and bridge between you and your mate, promoting self-knowledge through self-disclosure; honest feedback prevents misunderstanding and nurtures the equality that underlies mutual respect, which is in turn essential to the development of self-esteem in marriage. All of these lead toward greater freedom for both you and your mate, and the granting of mutual autonomy.

Each one can help you move by natural progression toward a fuller sense of yourself and new stature as a person. But we would like to add here a few further specific suggestions, any one of which can, we believe, help you along the road to identity. Some of these suggestions are refinements, or extensions, of points already made. Others are new. You can pick and choose among them for those that strike your interest or seem most pertinent to your own particular situation.

(1) *Let the Other Be:* Marriage does not give anyone a license to remake his spouse. All of us have habits that are irksome to others, but when it comes to the point that different methods of squeezing the toothpaste tube lead to divorce then something much deeper than any mere habit is at fault. If you must try to change your mate, it should be approached from the point of view of discovering why a particular habit in him bothers you so. The real problem may be in you yourself. The best kind of change, remember, is that which comes from within. Change must be perceived by the person himself as necessary to *him*, as something that will accrue to his own advantage. Carl Rogers, the psychologist, has said, "The more I am open to the realities in me and the other person, the less do I find myself wishing to rush in and 'fix things.'" Your mate's habits, defenses and idiosyncrasies may be the expression

of his individuality, so until both of you are secure in your separate identities, try not to project your ego on to your mate's: try to let him be.

(2) *Don't Put Up with People Who Put You Down:* One young woman we interviewed, Elena, told us of her weekly visits to her mother, a very critical lady. "I'm doing great," said Elena, "making strides with my job, reinforcing my self-confidence all the time, and I go home and say, 'Look, Mom, how great I am doing, no cavities, see?' And Mom says, 'But dear, just look at how wrinkled your dress is!'" Our advice to someone in Elena's position would be to simply stay away from the person who is putting you down. But when the person who's putting you down happens to be your mate, the situation is more difficult. Divorce is always a viable option, and sometimes a necessary one; if it comes down to your marriage or your identity, we think your identity is more important. But there are steps you can take far short of divorce.

One man, through ten years of marriage, eroded his wife's self-esteem to the breaking point. He told her constantly that her eyes were too close together, her face too long, her thighs too big—all being physical qualities she could not possibly change. In more subtle ways, he disapproved of her clothes, her friends, and cut off her avenues toward an acting career. She walked out for a while, finally, but then she decided to take a hard look at what was happening. His put-downs were destructive, but she had allowed him to keep it up for so many years. Because she cared enough for him, for herself, and for them together, she went back and fought. She stood up for herself and learned to build her self-esteem. And because he cared enough, he began to look at why he was constantly tearing her down. It's not a fully successful marriage yet, but each is learning more about himself, and about the dynamics of relating. Their subsequent relationships, whether together or with other partners, will be better for having tried to deal with this problem. So if your mate puts you down, don't accept it, try to make him look at his reasons for doing so.

(3) *Look for the Newness in Yourself:* This relates both to role flexibility and the nowness of self. So many of our ways of doing things, or our likes and dislikes, are second-hand. A woman may wear a certain kind of makeup because her best friend at school (who was very popular) put it on like that. A man may choose a certain style of tie because his father did. So seek out the you that lies buried beneath the accepted role and the hand-me-down habit. Follow the impulse you usually repress. Making changes on a trivial level, buying the wild tie or having your hair done in an entirely different way, can help you along the road to making more profound role changes, and give you a gradually increasing confidence in your own way of doing things.

(4) *Find a Sustaining Theme:* Sustaining themes are threads that run through our lives, ordering our experience and giving us a faith or belief in some larger ideal. All cultures have sustaining themes; an American one would be, "All men are equal in the sight of the law." A sustaining theme may not always be lived up to, but it generally indicates the way a culture, or the people in it, expect a person to behave. What is the thread that has run through your life, your own particular belief that has been sustaining to you in times of trouble, that has been most affirming of *you?* When you find a positive one (negative ones take you nowhere but backward), keep looking for the incidents that reinforce it. In this way you can help yourself to discover the reactions to the world that make you a unique individual.

(5) *Find Yourself a Meaningful Goal:* The goal itself can be many things—a cause, a study, your present work, a new job or interest, but it should be an endeavor which involves *you,* not necessarily your mate, your children or your marriage. It should, above all, be a goal which is larger

than yourself—something to which you bring sufficient commitment and creativity of your own—which will be a vehicle for self-discovery at the same time that it will contribute significantly to the human community. As you achieve one goal, or change and grow to the point where another goal supplants it, you should be able to look back and see how a successive series of goals relate to your sustaining theme.

(6) *Create Your Own Symbols:* A symbol of identity is most important when a person feels least secure. The stronger your identity becomes, the less will outward symbols of its existence matter to you. But at the beginning they can be very important. Women especially may find that such things as a checking account of their own, or stationery with their own name instead of Mr. and Mrs., can be reassuring, and helpful in maintaining a sense of their individuality. If you feel it matters enough, go ahead and use your maiden name, or hyphenate it with your husband's. For those women who are still only housewives and mothers, a single day off during the week can be a symbol of new emergence as an individual, and a means to discover who you are.

The usual symbols of identity, such as personal mail, phone calls, possessions, and even a corner of your own in the house, should be respected by both mates. Private property is a highly respected symbol in our society—except in marriage, where everything tends to get thrown into the same pot. In most societies, however, husband and wife clearly distinguish between their separate properties. No self-respecting Nama Hottentot owns a jointly held his-and-hers cow; each animal belongs to either husband or wife. If it helps you with identity, keep some things separate and designate them as your own—when you have achieved full identity, symbols will diminish in importance.

(7) *Build an Individual Nest:* If women's identities are eroded by giving up their maiden name and careers when they marry, men's are often completely submerged when

it comes to decorating the house or apartment. According to closed marriage, that is the woman's job. The man may pay for it, and help to choose appliances, about which *he* is supposed to know more, but that's often the limit of his participation. Some couples compound the error by choosing "model" living rooms and kitchens, predecorated by the local department store, so that the home in which they live reflects neither the husband's nor the wife's identity. Both husband and wife should contribute to the building of the domestic nest, and if it turns out a bit kooky, what's wrong with that? At least when people come to visit they'll know that two individual *people* live there, and not just a couple of role-robots.

(8) *Try Taking Separate Vacations:* A good way to break out of the "together forever" situation is to take a separate vacation. If nothing else, it will reveal how tightly tied to one another you are. Many couples do take separate trips, to visit the family (that's for the wives) or to a convention (the husband's gambit). But seldom do they contemplate a trip purely for their own pleasure and interest, still less one that provides solitude. We are *not* suggesting here that you eliminate the all-important vacations together, with or without children, but simply that you take an additional one for yourself alone. And if the idea appalls you, we hope you will at least try to discover why it upsets you so. If anxiety is your reaction, or your imagination lights the fires of jealousy, it could be an indication that both strong identity and trust are lacking. Why are you so insecure within yourself that you can't let your mate go off alone? Why do you lack the enthusiasm and initiative to get away by yourself? You could begin, after all, by taking it a day at a time. Next time take two days away, gradually building up to longer periods, moving at your own pace. As you grow more secure in yourself, and your mate sees the benefits in you, you can then think of taking a longer trip. Women will probably find the idea harder to accept than

men, because they have less sense of their own identities within the closed marriage structure than men do, and for any woman who really can't face the prospect, we suggest reading Anne Morrow Lindbergh's sensitive account, in *Gift from the Sea*, of the need to have time alone with one's self in a man-woman relationship.

* * *

Some readers may feel that the emphasis on the individual and on self-development in this chapter approaches an endorsement of selfishness. But nothing could be further from the truth. Selfishness, whether it be in the form of withholding love, sympathy, interest or resources, usually arises out of a fear that if one gives too much one will not have enough left for oneself. The creation of a strong identity, however, combats such fears, and makes it easier to give, as has been clearly established by the studies of Maslow, Erikson and many others. Giving and identity are intimately related to one another. The development of a strong identity leads to increased openness, not increased selfishness.

15 Trust

The Degrees of Trust

Let us take a look at the degree of trust that exists in three marital relationships:

I. Mary and Roger have been married for twenty years. The degree of trust between them is often summed up by Mary. "Why, I wouldn't trust Roger further than I could throw him," she confides to anybody who will listen.

II. Dorothy has been married to Gene for twelve years, and she has a more relaxed attitude. "What do you mean?" she asked, turning to the woman sitting on her right by the golf club pool. "That you're jealous of the women Henry works with? That's just silly. My husband has lots of female friends at work. Why should I object. After all, I'm not a computer analyst—all I know about Gene's job is what he tells me. We trust each other, so what difference does it make if he has lunch with them to talk shop? I can't share that part of his life with him, so why should I keep him from sharing it with a co-worker, even if she is a woman."

"But what if he went to bed with one of them?"

"That would be the end of our marriage," Dorothy answered vehemently, without a moment's hesitation.

"Even if it was just *once?*"

"Absolutely. You know why? Because it wouldn't happen unless something was wrong with our relationship together. If you have to look outside it means it isn't working anymore at home. I know Gene feels the same way I do."

"But what if he were a little high or something and just sort of 'fell' into it—for example when he was at a convention?"

Dorothy shakes her head. "That would be no excuse. If it *did* happen it would mean there was something wrong between us in the first place. He just wouldn't do it if our relationship was what it should be. If I'm not enough, well, then forget it."

III. Robert and Glenda, a young couple who had been married four years, were questioned as to how they established trust in their marriage.

GLENDA: Time, that's all—and work. Like anything else in life, it takes time and work.

ROBERT: That's a hard question. Trust is hard to come by and hard to understand. When you examine it from the back end, a lack of trust is fear—but mostly it's fear of yourself. Once at a party, years ago, I thought Glenda was playing up to another man. She wasn't of course. But I was *interpreting* it that way. I was going through a bad time then; I couldn't decide about whether or not to drop out of night college, I was changing jobs and feeling very insecure—so it was more a matter of dealing with myself and my own feelings than with what she was actually doing. I suppose these fears, jealousy and so on, are usually of your own making and they are in yourself. Trust is the same kind of thing, it's a feeling that you have to work through for yourself first.

GLENDA: Trust is a confidence you have in the other person, a belief in him. I believe in Robert, he believes in me. Sure, it takes time, but we love each other enough to be honest with one another. If we weren't honest with each other, it wouldn't be possible.

ROBERT: You know, trust is freedom—a lack of fear. When you get down to it, trust is really faith. We have a faith in the fact that what we have together is much more than any temporary relationship could ever be. So we aren't afraid of one another's relationships with other people.

Of the three marital relationships outlined above, the last is clearly the most highly developed in terms of trust. The first woman, Mary, had no trust at all. Such a deep *mistrust* could, of course, exist for the good reason that the husband can't be trusted; but often, especially when it is so vocally expressed, this kind of mistrust simply reflects a deep insecurity in the person who is so mistrustful. Mary's nature is just plain suspicious, and she's not going to trust her husband or anybody else no matter how they behave. The second couple, Dorothy and Gene, have some degree of trust in one another, but only in particular areas. They have what we will call *static trust*.

Dorothy's belief that she can be everything to Gene is unrealistic and at the same time reveals her own insecurities. The boundaries of her trust are determined by the expectations of the traditional closed marriage: she is willing to let Gene have lunch with the women he works with because he has convinced her that he could never, ever have any sexual feelings toward another woman. Since both Dorothy and Gene have mutually agreed to this delicately balanced trust, it works for them. But from Dorothy's vehemence on the subject of possible infidelity, it's clear that the balance could be tipped by even the *appearance* of infidelity on Gene's part. Thus Gene is forced to pretend that he never has a single moment of sexual interest or attraction to anyone other than Dorothy. Their trust, then, is based on a fiction rather than on the truth, and there is no room in it for a compassionate acceptance of human nature. Where there are unrealistic demands, there is no room for growth. Dorothy and Gene are stuck right where they are, with their narrow, static trust in one another.

Robert and Glenda, on the other hand, are working toward what we will call *open trust*. The crucial difference between open trust and static trust is honesty. Gene cannot be honest about even a passing sexual interest in another woman for fear of damaging the trust that exists between himself and Dorothy. But Robert can say, "I think Jane has a sexy figure," without harm to the trust he shares with Glenda. In fact, that honest admission will increase the trust between them.

Trust is the most important quality two partners can share in a marriage. It is absolutely essential to a dynamic, growing relationship. Yet it is seldom described in books on modern marriage. Perhaps such silence could be attributed to the complexity of the subject, but more probably it exists because the traditional closed marriage is inimical to the development of trust—and most books on marriage in the postwar era have devoted themselves to the patching up of the closed marriage rather than to offering any viable alternatives. In the context of open marriage, however, trust not only can be discussed, it must be discussed. Without trust, open marriage cannot function. Trust is the pivot upon which the open relationship turns. In a sense, it might well have been the first of our guidelines. But the concept of trust in the open marriage is best understood in terms of the other guidelines, and, indeed, by putting those guidelines into practice you will find that the development of trust naturally flows from them.

It does, of course, take time to develop true open trust between even the most loving of partners—as Robert and Glenda both noted. We learn through painful experience that trust cannot be given indiscriminately in life, that there are people who are not loving and are not honest, people who would take advantage of others through manipulation, aggression and dishonesty. Generally, and unfortunately, a person's trustworthiness must be proven to us.

Thus, in developing trust in our intimate relationships, we are to some degree struggling against our natural, and justifiable, caution. Only you know who you are dealing with. To those who are deeply mistrustful, like Roger's wife, Mary, at the beginning of this chapter, honesty may indeed seem an aggressive act. In marriage, as in life, some spouses must exercise caution with one another because of the neuroticisms, dependencies and psychological problems of one or both. For these people, complete honesty and openness might be unwise, or even destructive. Our proposals for complete trust are not meant to be swallowed whole by such couples, although we do believe that our previous guidelines can help even these people to develop a relationship that will build to a degree of trust.

A completely realized open marriage cannot be quickly achieved, nor can the full trust upon which it depends. But each additional step you take toward openness and trust, by applying at first those guidelines that are easiest for you to cope with, will, we believe, help you to develop a more realistic and at the same time more dynamic marital relationship.

Deception, the Enemy of Trust

Cindy maintains her friendship with Donna, an old schoolmate, in utter secrecy and deception. Her husband has always disliked Donna and has asked his wife not to see her. But that doesn't deter Cindy. "Oh, I find a way," she says. "All he knows is that I'm shopping or having my hair done or running some errand. We have lunch or go to the beauty parlor together. If I told him he would be mad as hell, so I figure what he doesn't know won't hurt him—or me, either."

As she admits, Cindy is defending and protecting herself as well as her husband. Both of them are sabotaging the possibility of trust between them, he by denying her her individuality and making unrealistic demands concerning her friendships, and she by her deliberate deception. In open marriage, where each partner respects the individual choices and desires of the other, there is no need for such subterfuge. Unfortunately, the typical closed marriage is a breeding ground for deception.

Deception prevents us from knowing ourselves and others, and is the direct enemy of trust. Most of the minor prevarications in marriage, and often even the major deceptions, are excused or rationalized in the name of humaneness. Husbands and wives tell themselves that they are "saving" their mates from unpleasantness or worse by deceiving them. We, however, do not believe that either deception by omission or by outright lying will help any marriage to grow, or that in the long run this kind of "humaneness" will result in anything but marriage partners drawing further apart.

Building toward greater honesty, and thus toward increased trust, must be carried out at a slow pace and with great caution in those marriages in which it least exists to begin with. When one spouse is particularly neurotic or dependent, the other must be protective of him in his most sensitive areas, avoiding reprimand, ridicule, or overt criticism. As we pointed out in the chapters on open communication, there is no excuse for disguising cruelty as honesty. Examine your own motivations, first. Are you really concealing your friendships (like Cindy), your secret purchases, or your infidelities to protect your mate? Or is it to protect yourself? And why? By recognizing your own as well as your mate's weaknesses and areas of greatest dependency, you can work toward greater honesty with consideration and judgment.

Spouses can start by being open and honest about small things first. Wives can tell husbands the real price of a purchase, instead of saying, "I bought it at a sale," and trying to falsely uphold her image as the efficient wife. She can stop practicing hypocrisy by pretending to admire her husband's wild ties when she really hates them. Since her husband usually knows all too well that she isn't being truthful, such hypocrisy merely convinces the husband that his wife's word is not to be trusted. On the other hand, there is no need to say, in the name of honesty, "No, I think it's an awful tie, and you have terrible taste." That is simply being destructive, especially if the husband is sensitive about the subject. But she can say, "Well, dear, you know me, my taste is pretty conservative." In this way she is being honest about *her* feelings without directly challenging his right to his feelings.

A husband can deal with his wife's rhinestone-studded eyeglasses in the same way. He can tell his wife that he doesn't really relish the idea of spending another evening at the Joneses, or that he feels silly attending the garden club tea party with her. Thus both mates can start being honest in minor matters where sensitivities are less easily bruised and dependencies less large. Each time that spouses practice telling the truth to one another, they are learning to strengthen their own identities and belief in themselves. As they gradually learn that small honesties hurt less than they thought, they are also building mutual trust in one another, so that they will be able to move on to more sensitive areas.

Among the more sensitive areas, sex is a vital one in which to establish honesty and trust—and it is one in which small deceptions abound. Adherence to the traditional closed marriage view of male dominance almost demands deception in bed. The wife in such a relationship frequently fakes orgasms in order to bolster her husband's male ego and her image of herself as responsive wife. The husband, to reassure himself of his virility, feels he must manage to bring his wife to orgasm every time. So long as the wife continues to say, "Yes, yes, I came," when she didn't, and her husband continues to *wish* to hear these words, neither is building honesty and trust. They are engaged in the attempt to live up to a myth that undermines her self-esteem and falsely inflates his. The built-in demands of the male-dominated closed marriage inevitably create such deceptions.

But any couple willing to follow the guidelines, applying them flexibly to their own individual situations, can move toward a new honesty in their sexual relations as well as in other aspects of their lives together. By breaking out of predetermined roles, sexual and otherwise, by recognizing one another's unique identity, by openly communicating their real needs and desires, they can, in true equality, develop the kind of tender concern for the other's feelings that results in the fullest mutual understanding and pleasure. When predetermined demands and false expectations end, honesty in sex can begin. And that honesty, coupled with a compassionate understanding of one another's vulnerability in sex, can lead to the building of the kind of trust that will not only make sexual deception unnecessary but that can also be channeled back into other areas of their marriage.

Two Kinds of Trust

Avoiding deception helps partners build toward trust, but there are other conditions that are essential, too. Trust in marriage can never be unilateral—it is a two-way street. Each partner must be trustworthy as well as trusting. Trust grows in a marriage because it is mutual, because husband and wife share their experiences and through time prove their trust in one another. Yet, true though all this is, it remains too simplistic. For trust, we have found, comes in different degrees. As we pointed out in discussing the three marriages outlined at the beginning of this chapter, it is not just a matter of trust existing or not existing between a couple. There can be either *static trust* or *open trust*. Let's examine the differences between them in greater detail.

Static trust is based on expectations and reasonably assured predictability. We count on people to keep their promises, to pay their bills and to keep their appointments. Static trust is absolutely necessary for cooperation anywhere, but since it is based solely on the expectable, and predictable, it does not easily accommodate change.

Couples marry, vowing to love, honor and cherish one another, and to forsake all others until death do them part. They make promises only angels could keep. Because they have promised, they expect trust simply to exist, as though decreed by God. They expect each other not only to keep their explicit promises but to live up to all the implicit clauses of the closed marriage contract. Unfortunately, the expectations on which they base their trust are unrealistic. They expect their mates always to be as they were on the day they married. Change comes as a surprise, even a shock. How many spouses have said, "I don't know what's happened to my husband/wife lately, he/she has changed so much," or "Gee, you never used to act like that, honey, what's happened to you?" (What's really being said, of course, is "what's *wrong* with you, you're not acting like I *expected* you to. I'm suspicious.")

Such couples impose rigid, absolute standards of idealized behavior on one another and when they inevitably fail to live up to them, they think that trust has been violated. Remember the attitude expressed by Dorothy at the beginning of this chapter—one transgression against the clause of absolute fidelity and that was the *end* of it. Since each partner also must strain to conduct himself according to these unrealistic standards, denying his identity in the process, any failure on the part of the other takes on an increased significance: "Here I've been sacrificing myself, and you just go and do as you like!" How many times has that cry of furious disappointment been heard between couples? Under such circumstances, with each basing his own conduct and his trust in the other on unrealistic expectations, one slip can bring the whole relationship tumbling down like a house of cards. For, as Erik Erikson puts it, "Every tired human being may regress temporarily to partial mistrust whenever the world of his expectations has been shaken to the core." The more unrealistic those expectations are, the more often they will be shaken, and the harder it will be to establish trust.

Expectations of dependability are all very well in the outside world. But marriage is a personal relationship, not a business transaction. It is a continuous relationship, made up of living people who change through the course of time. If you expect your partner to live up to unrealistic expectations (and try to do so yourself), your static trust will force you into a restrictive relationship in which change becomes traumatic, instead of a creative challenge, as it can be in open marriage. Many couples have in the past managed to build a reasonably happy life based upon static trust; the closed marriage contract in which this kind of restrictive trust is found functioned well enough through a considerable period of history. It may still function for a steadily diminishing number of couples. But in our era of constant change, a more flexible kind of trust, operating within a more flexible kind of marriage, is necessary. Open marriage requires open trust.

Open Trust

Trust in the open marriage must go far beyond simply proving oneself dependable in terms of rigid expectations. Static trust not only inhibits change, it does not even imply honesty or intimacy. One can keep one's promises without being honest about how one feels about doing so. One can break promises, such as the closed contract clause pertaining to absolute fidelity, and never be truthful about it. Static trust, being based merely upon expectations, can be satisfied by mere appearances. So long as the appearances are maintained, whatever the truth may be, static trust is maintained. And since the expectations involved are determined by the prescribed ethical standards associated with specific roles, you cannot become truly intimate with your partner—you know the role, not the person, and intimacy with a role is impossible. Thus the basis of open trust is more than a matter of being trustful and trustworthy, more than a question of responsibility and predictability—it is a matter of being open and honest with one another in your feelings and in your communication with each other.

Open trust implies a degree of intimacy, honesty and openness far beyond what is possible in static trust. To be so open means believing in your mate's ability and willingness to cherish and respect *your* honesty and *your* open communications. A friend defined this kind of trust by saying, "Trust is the feeling that no matter what you do or say you are not going to be criticized—it is an open policy of not having to keep embarrassing secrets, and the willingness to say what is in your mind knowing that the other person isn't going to use it against you later on. This is trusting *in* someone, not just trusting him. We can be naked in the presence of the other not just physically but in a real intimacy of thoughts and feelings. The idea is that we know we are not perfect, but we also know we are not going to be faulted for what we are."

Knowing that you can open up to this degree with your partner, knowing that you can trust in one another in full honesty is creating a climate of *belief* in each other. When such honesty exists you know where you stand with each other. With such open trust between partners, each one can grow to his fullest dimensions. It need not take years to develop—we believe that if partners open up to each other, even if only gradually, they will soon discover that honesty, love and trust are interdependent and mutually reinforce and augment one another.

You can see once again how all the guidelines for open marriage interlock. Everything we had to say about open and honest communication is applicable here to the establishment of open trust. There are, however, a few additional things that should be said about honesty as it relates to open trust.

Honesty and growth are intricately tied up with each other. Honesty of course is not always easy, nor is it ever black and white, for it depends on how you perceive things. Even so, honesty can be approximated gradually in constructive ways. The more we can open up and tell our mate how we honestly feel, without being critical or destructive, the closer we are getting to knowing each other in intimacy. The more we *try*, the closer will be the approximation to honesty and truth between us.

Partners who have related on a level of honesty that has been rather static tend to feel that everything is falling apart when honesty comes in big doses, or when they say things in the heat of argument that they would ordinarily not have revealed even though they do in fact deeply feel them. When facts do come out into the open, it must be understood as a learning experience rather than as an ultimate revelation. It cannot be stated too often: people change. In a closed marriage it may be that people change less (which is also to say that they grow less) but inevitably they do change. And they will go on changing, long after the argument or revelation of the moment has ceased to be of any real importance. When a new fact about your mate comes out into the open, even if it is the unexpected admission of an infidelity, for instance, it is *new informa-*

tion, and when new information becomes available, even though it may be painful to you, the only sensible response is to explore what that information means in as constructive a way as possible.

You may feel that it is impossible to be constructive about the sudden news that your husband or your wife has been involved with someone else. But if you really do love your partner, and care about your relationship with him or her, then it is far more important to discover *why* a deception has occurred, whether large or small, than to avoid the pain or anger this honesty may bring. The only thing that a person like Dorothy proves by saying that any infidelity would be "the end" is that he or she cares more about the image of his partner than about the person himself. Dorothy is saying she would rather be a role and relate to another role than be a person and relate to a person. And, in many cases, the fact that the Dorothys of this world would rather be a role than a person may well be the primary explanation of why their mates are deceiving them in the first place.

Roles remain static. People change. If you wish to be a *person,* then you must be willing to take a new fact about your mate, even if it be a violation of your expectations concerning him, and use it as the basis for a dialogue that can lead to a more realistic, honest and open appraisal of your relationship as people. With such a dialogue, couples can seek a better understanding of one another, one that allows them to reintegrate on a new, more open level of knowledge concerning one another, a level more closely approximating the full honesty and trust that should exist between marital partners. Only then can inevitable change be accommodated, and mutual growth occur. It takes courage to accept responsibility for your own actions in the face of the rigid, role-dominated clauses that too many of us have lived with for too long. For partners who trust and believe in each other, this responsibility is accepted by choice as a part of growth. For those who are still in a closed marriage, however, it may bring pain, in varying degrees. But just as pain in the human body acts as a warning system that something is wrong, and leads us to try to discover the exact nature of the trouble, so psychological or emotional pain is often one of the necessary steps toward finding a cure.

The greater the degree of honesty between a couple, the less pain will result in the long run, for full honesty means that husband and wife can truly relax together, can reveal themselves to one another in all frankness, with no need for pretense or for self-defense. To be fully honest, to achieve open trust, means that change in one partner or another does not come as a surprise. And the couple who can achieve that trust are forging for themselves a far stronger bond than can ever be created through role-conscious, unrealistic static trust.

The Chinese say that you never put your foot in the same river twice, meaning that time, like the water of rivers, is constantly flowing. You can, of course, stop the flow of a river by damming it, which is what static trust attempts to do, but the result is more than likely to be either stagnation or flood, sooner or later. As people, we must flow with life and its changes. Open trust implies forgiveness, in the sense that each partner must allow the other to be human, to make errors, to be imperfect, to grow and to change as life's situations alter. With open trust, partners are honest about the reality of human life, realistic about change, and courageous and truthful in meeting a challenge or a crisis. The open couple knows that neither is perfect and that change often involves taking one step backward to take two steps forward.

The nature of trust in open marriage means that partners can be alone together or alone apart, go out together or out apart, have friends that are mutual or individual. They can respect one another's differences and yet become closer for having done so. They can share their problems, and their temporary dependencies, because they have given one another the mutual knowledge of their inner selves necessary to come to one another's support in time of need.

Trust, then, open trust, has nothing to do with expecting or doing specific, predetermined things in marriage, but rather with sharing the knowledge of your immediate desires and needs with your mate, living for now and not for yesterday or tomorrow, living not the life that somebody else has laid out for you in terms of role expectations, living instead for your own self through shared communication and growth with your mate's self. Trust then is freedom, just as Robert said in his interview with us—the freedom to assume responsibility for your own self first and then to share that human self in love with your partner in a marriage that places no restrictions upon growth, or limits on fulfillment.

16 Love and Sex without Jealousy

The Roots of Jealousy

To most couples, love, sex, and jealousy will seem a perfectly natural, even inevitable threesome, intimately associated with contemporary marriage. We certainly agree that the first two of this trio, love and sex, are basic to marriage, whether closed or open. But anyone who has read the guidelines with care should already know that we do not believe jealousy has any place in open marriage. The fact that it is so prevalent in closed marriage does not mean that love and sex must always be accompanied by this dark shadow.

To begin with, we would like to lay to rest the idea that sexual jealousy is natural, instinctive and inevitable. It is none of these things. Jealousy is primarily a *learned* response, determined by cultural attitudes. In many societies around the world, including the Eskimo, the Marquesans, the Lobi of West Africa, the Siriono of Bolivia and others, jealousy is at a minimum; and in still others, such as the Toda of India, it is almost completely absent. If in other societies it is greatly reduced or hardly exists at all, then it cannot be regarded as "natural" to man's behavior. Why, then, is it so prevalent in our society?

We can begin to answer the question by distinguishing clearly between jealousy and envy. Jealousy is aroused in relation to that which you already possess. Envy develops when you see something you do not have but would like to have. A husband, for instance, may envy another man whose wife showers him with attention, fixes his cocktails and plumps his pillows. But the same man will be jealous of his own wife if she showers such attention on anyone but him. He will be jealous because he thinks that these attentions *belong* to him. The distinction between jealousy and envy, then, is important because of the element of prior possession that creates jealousy. No one person can ever "own" another person, as we have said before, but the closed marriage contract creates the semblance of such ownership or possession, and the clauses of the contract are reinforced by our traditional cultural attitudes toward love and sex.

The idea of sexually exclusive monogamy and possession of another breeds deep-rooted dependencies, infantile and childish emotions, and insecurities. The more insecure you are, the more you will be jealous. Jealousy, says Abraham Maslow, "practically always breeds further rejection and deeper insecurity." And jealousy, like a destructive cancer, breeds more jealousy. It is never, then, a function of love, but of our insecurities and dependencies. It is the fear of a loss of love and it destroys that very love. It is detrimental to and a denial of a loved one's personal identity. Jealousy is a serious impediment, then, to the development of security and identity, and our closed marriage concepts of possession are directly at fault.

In this chapter we want to look at some of the misconceptions that cause jealousy to arise in the closed marriage and make clear how open marriage, by doing away with such misconceptions, will help you to disassociate jealousy from love and sex.

Love Is a Feeling

It may help to understand the complexities of love if you think of it as a *feeling* to which we bring the *energy* of our emotions, or better, to which we bring emotional energy. Thus, we can think of emotion as "energy-in-motion" within the individual, and through the guidelines we can hopefully learn to control, at least in part, the direction and degree of expression of this energy. We invest the feeling of love, for instance, with more or less energy depending on the situation, object, person, fantasy or whatever upon which we are focusing. We bring to the feeling of love the degree of intensity of emotion that the person or thing arouses. We can have a small amount of affection for someone or something, or we can have a lot. Affection comes from the same area of feeling as love; it can become love, can become increased to love, according to the degree of emotion you bring to it. One man may bring a greater amount of emotional energy to his feeling about his ancestral home, for instance, than he ever does to his feeling for any person. But that fact may not be obvious to the casual observer because of the many differing ways in which feelings can be expressed. Sometimes we misdirect our feelings, at other times we apply too much emotion to them.

Possessive love occurs when we invest the feeling of love with too much emotional energy drawn from the wrong sources—energy arising out of feelings of dependency and insecurity. The nature of the excess can perhaps more readily be seen by showing it in relation to hate, the opposite of love. The same principle applies: when the feeling of antipathy for someone or something is small, it is dislike. But when this same feeling is invested with enormous emotional energy, it becomes hate. You dislike spinach, but you may *hate* lobster, especially if it made you deathly ill at one time. When you dislike a person, perhaps because he is simply not your type, the feeling is mild. But you may hate someone if you believe he is responsible for direct harm to you. Of course, that belief may be quite irrational, if you could see both sides of the question. But, and this is the point, possessive love is not rational, either.

Romantic Love: an Irrational Heritage

It is said of romantic lovers that "the heart rules the head." This description is entirely accurate. When a person is in a state of romantic love, an excessive amount of energy is harnessed to his basic feeling of love, making him react like a car in the hands of a thrill-seeker on a curving mountain road. The ride is exhilarating, of course, and most of us go through it at one time or another. But, essentially, it is a distortion of reality and, as we shall see, it combines with other distortions to produce a totally false understanding of the relation between love and sexuality.

The Western concept of romantic love developed out of the courtly tradition of the middle ages, in which the passion of the lover and the beloved was not only extramarital but never intended to be consummated in actual physical fact. Marriage never entered into this kind of love—yet in the modern world we have taken many of the components of courtly love (to which the ideals of romanticism were later added) and applied them to marriage. Troubadours and their ladies (both or one of them always married to someone else) breathed heavily, made trysts, knitted gossamer dreams and lay down in embraces that never ended in the lusty satisfaction of sex at all. At least, they were not supposed to. For courtly love was ideal, not real, a game people played to keep themselves amused. Since the lovely ladies involved had little to do but embroider and throw handkerchiefs from balconies, they devoted their spare time to artificial stimulation of this game of courtly love, even drawing up rules for it, which were codified in the twelfth century "Courts of Love." We would like to quote a few of the rules or "clauses" from one of these documents to make clear how directly our own concepts of love and jealousy are inherited from such gamesmanship:

—a new love makes one quit the old
—real jealousy always increases the worth of love
—suspicion and the jealousy it kindles increase love's worth
—the least presumption compels the lover to suspect evil of the co-lover

Two ideas are intertwined in these examples of the code of courtly love: the idea that love is limited, that you cannot love more than one person at once, and the idea that love is proven by the existence of jealousy. As rules for a courtly game, these ideas serve splendidly to make the whole exercise at once more difficult and more exciting. Taken seriously and applied to modern marriage, they are a prescription for unhappiness, for they are not based on human realities.

Limited Love

Limited love is the ordinary garden variety of love that couples in a closed marriage subsist on after romantic love has run its course. It is the kind of love reflected in one of the primary clauses of closed marriage: you can be truly committed to, in love with and deeply intimate with only one person at a time. This clause, originally derived from the game of courtly love, was given scientific respectability by Freud (that very proper Victorian gentleman) in the doctrine that each individual has only a fixed and limited amount of libido, or general sexual energy. "Freud assumed," writes Abraham Maslow, "that one has only a certain amount of love and that the more of this love was spent on one person, the less was available for others."

The pernicious influence of this idea can most clearly be seen in the relationship of young married couples to a first child. If a person believes that he has only so much love to give, and that his mate has an equally limited amount to give back, then it follows that any affection or love felt by your mate for anyone else diminishes the love that he can feel for you. Naturally, then, you are going to make up rules or clauses that prevent your mate from seeing enough of anyone besides you to appreciably diminish his or her supply of affection. People believe so much in this false concept that they even fear the amount of affection given to their own children by a mate. One marriage text after another takes note of the fact that a first child is a disrupting force in a marriage, with the father frequently becoming jealous of his wife's relationship to the child.

Obviously, if you believe in the concept of limited love, you will guard it carefully, parcelling it out stingily and even bargaining over it. In the process, your actual *ability* to give love will inevitably diminish: you are learning how to withhold it rather than to bestow it. And as your ability to give love shrinks and atrophies, you will become more and more convinced that you do in fact only have so much to give. The concept of limited love is thus a self-fulfilling prophecy for diminishment. And unfortunately, it diminishes not only you and your mate, but your children as well.

Man Is Not Naturally Monogamous

The confusions caused by the distorted view of romantic love and the false concept of limited love we have been discussing are intimately bound up with the very narrow definition of monogamy that prevails in our culture. According to that cultural definition, monogamy means having sex only with your marital partner. In scientific terms, however, monogamy simply means being *married* to one partner at a time. Depending on the society, the partners in a monogamous marriage may have sex only with one another or they may have it with partners other than the mate as well: the word monogamy alone does not indicate whether a society's sexual rules are restrictive or permissive.

In many of the societies around the world that allow only one marriage partner at a time, monogamy does not mean sexual exclusivity at all—other partners in sex are permitted, and even specified by the society. Even in societies that have adopted plural marriage (Polyandry: 1 female + X males; Polygyny: 1 male + X females; or Group Marriage: X males + X females), sex is not always restricted to just those within the marriage. Our society may *tell* us that *sexual* monogamy is the best kind there is, but you should be aware that it is not the only kind that exists.

It should also be understood that man (and we mean both sexes) is not sexually monogamous by nature, evolution or force of habit. In all societies around the world in which he has been enjoined to become sexually monogamous in marriage (and that is in a minority of the world's *cultures*, even though those cultures embrace a majority of the world's people), he has failed to live up to that standard. He may fail gloriously, impudently, nonchalantly, regretfully or guiltily, but always he fails, in numbers large enough to make that failure significant. Even in those societies where sexual restrictions are the most stringent and uncompromising, this human "failing" which we commonly call "infidelity" remains an extremely frequent occurrence. And that leads us to an inevitable question: is it the "unfaithful" human being who is the failure, or is it the standard itself?

We have no intention, of course, of denying that some

people *can* be sexually monogamous for life. Some couples can and do achieve a union in which neither one ever has or even wants extramarital liaisons. But they are rare, and becoming rarer. There is the story about the man who had been married six times, but who boasted that while actually married to any one of them he had never been unfaithful. A paragon of virtue, clearly. The question must be seriously asked whether sexual monogamy provides a realistic or viable standard in a society so diverse and pluralistic as ours, where life styles change, life-span is lengthened and men and women must adapt to constantly new situations. Even though some may accept sexual monogamy as a standard, it should not blind them to a compassionate understanding of man's varying sexual standards. Nor should we forget that in conjunction with distorted culturally determined views of love, it gives rise to some extremely unpleasant side effects. "Monogamy, then," writes Dr. Albert Ellis, "not only directly encourages the development of intense sexual jealousy, but also by falsely assuming that men and women can love only one member of the other sex at a time, and can only be sexually attracted to that one person, indirectly sows the seeds for even more violent displays of jealousy."

Monogamy, as our culture defines it, *is* closed marriage. It implies ownership, demands sexual exclusivity, and denies both equality and identity. It perverts jealousy into a "good": many husbands and wives actually *try* to make their mates at least a "little" jealous, going just far enough to elicit a response that assures them they are really "loved." For them, jealousy is supposed to show you "care." But no matter how little or how much, jealousy is never a good or constructive feeling. It may show you care, but what you are caring for is too much for yourself, and not enough for your mate.

But monogamy does not have to mean any of these things, as we have seen. The guidelines throughout this book are dedicated to redefining monogamy, to creating a kind of monogamy in which equality naturally exists and identity flourishes, in which jealousy and sexual exclusivity become beside the point, in which decisions are made by choice, not coercion, and love grows in a climate of freedom. We have examined thus far a number of false conceptions of love and sexuality. The remainder of this chapter will concern itself with redefining those concepts, in showing how monogamy *can* be equated with *open* marriage.

Liking Is the Key to Loving

A husband and wife can "love" one another without liking one another. Many couples marry while still in the throes of romantic love, never having looked clearly enough at one another through the haze of romance to know whether they like one another or not. Even after the romance fades and they discover that they do not in fact like one another, they may continue to "love," to desire one another in a possessive way, or to need one another because of neurotic dependency. But spouses who lack autonomy and the fulfillment of their individual needs, who lean dependently upon one another, often come to resent that dependency, and if there is not even liking between them love can turn quickly to hate.

Liking, we believe, is the key to loving. It is the element that Rollo May calls friendship, or *philia*, in love: it "is the relaxation in the presence of the beloved, it is simply liking to be with the other . . . Philia requires only that we accept the beloved, be with him, and enjoy him. It is friendship in the simplest, most direct terms." Liking is only one aspect of love, but we believe it is the key to discovering the individual creativity, the mutual esteem, and the erotic fulfillment that make up genuine, mature love, what we call open love.

Romantic love is blind, and often irrational; liking, however, is rational, and based upon respect rather than passion. This is not to say that passion is unimportant, but only to demonstrate that a love that encompasses both liking and passion is far stronger than love that is based solely on passion. Without liking, and the respect that it implies, we believe that true open love cannot be achieved, for mutual respect is essential to the establishment of identity, equality and open communication between mates. In fact, in putting any one of the guidelines to use, respect is essential; but at the beginning that respect need be no more than a mutual willingness to *try*, for the proper exercise of the guidelines naturally reinforces, and builds upon, the respect you start out with.

Open Love Has No Limits

Open love similarly builds upon itself, expands itself. Once you have freed yourself of the false idea that love is limited, once you have begun to give openly of your love, you will find that your capacity to give will grow continually greater. The concept of limited love holds that love is like money; the more you spend the less you have. And so love is hoarded. But the giving of love is not like spending money, it is like investing it. The more you invest, the more you get back. The rich get richer because money creates money. But love also creates love. The more you give, the more you receive and are capable of receiving; the more you have, the more you are capable of giving.

Because open love is based upon the identity and equality of both partners, it is non-possessive love. As you become fulfilled as a person, love becomes, as one analyst put it, "the overflow of your own fulfillment." It rests upon a feeling of belonging *with* rather than *to* another person. Open love is free of the restrictions, injunctions and prohibitions on your behavior that are the hallmark of possessive and limited love. Partners who accept one another openly in this way, who can communicate openly and honestly with one another, are able to relax with one another in a way unknown to those still bound in a closed marriage. Such a climate of relaxation is not only comforting and reassuring, it also nurtures growth. Each helps the other to become more of what he or she could be. Because they are growing and changing, because they are not possessive or limiting, there is a vibrancy to their relationship, an ever-unfolding newness and spontaneity. They are both being and becoming at the same time.

Speaking of this kind of love relationship, which he observed in self-actualizing people, Abraham Maslow says, "What we see . . . is a fusion of great ability to love and at the same time great respect for the other and great respect for oneself. This shows itself in the fact that these people cannot be said in the ordinary sense of the word to *need* each other as do ordinary lovers. They can be extremely close together yet go apart quite easily. They do not cling to each other or have hooks or anchors of any kind . . . Throughout the most intense and ecstatic love affairs, these people remain themselves and remain ultimately masters of themselves as well, living by their own standards even though enjoying each other intensely."

Thus, if two people can open up to the possibilities within them, to the freedom that comes through mutual respect, they can experience the full flowering of a new kind of open love. "The paradox of love," says Rollo May, "is that it is the highest degree of awareness of the self as a person and the highest degree of absorption in the other." This is similar to the paradox we spoke of when discussing identity. Just as by becoming more yourself you can relate more fully to other people, so by loving non-possessively can you become closer than ever before to your mate. And because you are closer than ever to your mate, because the love between you is constantly expanding, so too is it possible for you to include others more easily within the widening circle of your love.

As open love expands, it floods out, encircling and including others. It will include your children, of course, if you have children. But open love expands beyond the boundaries of the immediate family. Despite our tradition of limited love, it is entirely possible to love your marital partner with an intensely rewarding and continually growing love and at the same time to love another or others with a deep and abiding affection. And this extra dimension of love feeds back into the love between the partners. One husband put it this way: "It's incredible, once you loosen the bonds and know that freedom is a part of love—there has been nothing less than a quantum leap in my life, not only with Joan and the things we share, not only in our relationship with the few really close friends we share this love with, but the quantum leap has come in *me*, in my *self* —all of my relationships are different, I look at everything differently, everything opens up—it seems like there is no limit."

Good Sex Grows Out of the Good Relationship

Cultural attitudes toward sex have changed drastically since the Second World War. There are still a few people around who believe that it should be hidden away behind closed doors and under the covers in a darkened room, but they are growing fewer all the time. Most people now recognize sex for what it is: a natural function that should be enjoyed for its own earthy self without hypocrisy. As the world grows continually smaller through the communications revolution, more and more people are becoming aware that sexual mores are scripted for us by the specific culture we live in, that what is taboo in one place is totally acceptable in another. Each culture tells us how males should act and how females should act. The culture of the Victorian age dictated that males could enjoy sex but women could not, and it took nearly a century for the confusions caused by that bit of scripting to begin to dissipate. Today this same dichotomy still persists in the idea that men can enjoy sex without love but that women cannot. The sooner we clear away the myths and superstitions about sex and man and woman's role in it, the sooner we can get on to finding sexual fulfillment and understanding each other better.

There are books and more books, and now even movies, telling us how to improve our sexual enjoyment. Certainly we need to know as much as we can in order to dispel the myths, superstitions and misinformation of the past. The availability of this information is in itself good. But the proliferation of all this material, educational and otherwise, does create problems for a lot of people. The first problem is that, in most of this material, the mechanical and technical aspects of sex tend to be emphasized and the feeling aspects neglected.

The second problem is that these materials, taken all together, tend to create an expectation level for men, women, and couples that is unrealistic. These expectations tend to become new norms. And the idea of imposing a cultural norm on a man-woman or marriage relationship, whether it is yesterday's or today's norm, belongs to closed marriage. In open marriage one should be influenced (in sex as in everything else) primarily by a consideration of each partner's needs, both individual and mutual. If the attractions of the new cultural norms are so great that you feel you need to respond to them, you have that option in open marriage.

Sex, natural though it is, *is* learned; but remember that it is conditioned by cultural scripting and individual variations. Learn as much as you want, but allow for this conditioning, and use your own judgment about what is right for you.

One idea that should be unlearned in our culture is the assumption that a person's sexual expression, his bodily function in coitus, becomes a *possession* of the mate in marriage.

It is a basic assumption in closed marriage. Yet no idea could be more detrimental to a good sexual relationship. Sex is a personal possession, a personal expression, a function of a person's being. The ultimate and intimate joining of psychological and physical processes in sexual expression is as much a part of the person's identity as is the expression of his selfhood in any other sphere of life. And these functions belong to each individual, not to a partner in marriage. Sex, love, affection, care, concern and responsibility are expressions of a person's identity—they are his and his alone to *give* and *share* with another person, not to be owned, demanded or controlled by another person. Thus good sex between partners grows from sharing and giving in the sexual area with the same respect, freedom, autonomy, equality and identity that exist in all other areas of their relationship.

Although good sex grows out of a good relationship, that is not to say that you can't enjoy sex with someone you only recently met. You can, and those who say you can't are still under the influence of those Victorian myths we spoke about. The idea that sex without love is destructive, alienating and unpleasurable is a purely cultural evaluation much akin to the idea that sex is dirty. Anyone knows that sex with love is best, but that doesn't necessarily mean that any other kind or degree of sexual involvement is wrong, debasing, or the result of neuroses. Sex can be, and is, enjoyed with varying amounts of affection, warmth, comradeship. It may not be as rewarding, fulfilling or rich an experience as sex with love but it can still be enjoyable, exciting and generally life-enhancing.

When we are talking about a long-term relationship, however, the quality of the sex the two people share is influenced by that relationship. Having physically good sex is no guarantee that the long-term relationship will be good, nor does it save or patch up a marriage which is failing in other areas. Sex, in other words, is not the single most important factor in marriage. It is fundamental, but it is complexly interwoven with many other aspects of a marriage. Most importantly, it is a *way* through which you express your love. New techniques may freshen up or expand your sexual repertoire, but they cannot in themselves make your feelings any better. On the contrary, your *feelings* can make your sexual expression better, can imbue your sexual repertoire, however enjoyable itself, with another level of meaning. And it is the meaning we attach to things that gives them significance.

The more open and accepting you become in respect to your mate, the more open your relationship becomes, the better your sex should be. Every guideline that you make use of to enhance your relationship, to make it grow, expand and become more vital, will also add to greater enjoyment in sex. Think of each of them in regard to sex: equality, realistic expectations, emphasis on the now, identity, flexibility in roles, honest communication and trust. Through open communication, combined with their respect for and sensitivity to one another's feelings and needs, partners can become more patient and aware in respect to one another's frailties in the area of sex. Equality and flexibility in roles can help to bring new explorations and a greater variety of attitude toward their sex experiences. Their trust in one another can make it possible for them to orchestrate their sex to express the full complement and range of feelings and emotions that they share. When the sexual experience is at its very best, it can bring a total fusion, that paradoxical moment of ultimate togetherness in which each partner simultaneously transcends and most fully experiences himself. At such times, sex becomes the total expression of their personalities, their separate identities, their growth and commitment to one another, and their knowledge of both the self and the other.

Yet sex need not always be a profound experience. There are many other dimensions to sex, and all can be enjoyed.

It can be fun or serious, exploratory or comfortably hum-drum, it can be creative and tender, or casual and teasing; it can be passionate, exotic, erotic or just plain lustfully abandoned. And above all, it can be playful, as Maslow here describes it: "It is quite characteristic of self-actualizing people that they can enjoy themselves in love and sex. Sex very frequently becomes a kind of game in which laughter is quite as common as panting . . . It is not the welfare of the species, or the task of reproduction, or the future de-velopment of mankind that attracts people to each other. The sex life of healthy people, in spite of the fact that it frequently reaches great peaks of ecstasy, is nevertheless also easily compared to the games of children and puppies. It is cheerful, humorous and playful."

Intelligence in Sex

We believe sex is something to which you should bring your full faculties—feeling, emotion, sensitivity, sensuality and, yes, intelligence. Our culture has long taught us to accept things as they are, to turn off our minds in bed. When you climb into bed, you are supposed to shuck off your intelligence along with your clothes. The theme is: if you think, you can't feel; if you think, you'll turn it off. As one analyst writes: "We cannot possess pleasure; pleasure pos-sesses us. It exists in the body as pure sensation in the mo-ment of happening, independent of our will. As soon as the body comes under the conscious control of the mind, plea-sure ends." We believe this emphasis is exaggerated. While it is true that sexual response is a physiological reaction which can be blocked by inhibition, control, anxiety and fear, it is not true that you have to turn off your mind completely to enjoy sex. Many persons do have to learn to let themselves go enough to enjoy and experience sexual pleasure in order to counteract the degree of repression that our past experiences and society has trained into us.

But intelligence and knowledge are surely formidable weapons against repression and inhibition. Contrary to the attitude that pleasure can come only through will-less and thought-less sex, we believe sex improves when you bring to it your mind as well as your body, your intelligence, curiosity, anticipation, knowledge and a sense of discovery, as well as sensuousness and a vital awareness. An open relationship with your mate, in or out of bed, depends on the use of intelligence, on knowing and trusting each other through open and honest communication, on being sensitively aware of each other's needs and preferences.

The importance of an open relationship and the application of knowledge to sex in marriage has been demonstrated in therapy programs designed to help couples with sexual problems. Dr. William H. Masters and Mrs. Virginia Johnson have pioneered in this area, developing a comprehensive and multi-faceted program. They emphasize all aspects of sex, with primary focus on mutual communication, and education to dispel sexual misconceptions and taboos. These types of programs have achieved success in remedying sexual inadequacy in large part because they require the marital partners involved to work *together* on their problem. And working together means mutually developing the *relationship*. The partners learn to communicate honestly and without inhibition on all levels (by touch, gesture and words), to express their needs and become sensitive to the needs of their mates, to give as well as receive pleasure, not to demand or expect too much, and to respect each other's individuality even as they are working on the technical and physical aspects of sex. And it is the newly established, more open relationship, not the mechanics alone, that ultimately brings better sexual adjustment.

Whether your own sex life is already more than adequate or unfortunately less than adequate, we believe that by applying the open marriage guidelines to your relationship with your mate, the improvements in your relationship will bring about an improvement in your sexual experience as well.

Throughout the book we have emphasized that an open relationship depends on applying your intelligence to all aspects of your relationship. This means knowing what your options are. It means examining old myths and superstitions and discarding old ideas of sexual and social determinism so that you can find your own way to fulfillment by choosing what is best for you.

Fidelity Redefined

Sexual fidelity is the false god of closed marriage, a god to whom partners submit (or whom they defy) for all the wrong reasons and often at the cost of the very relationship which that god is supposed to protect. Sex in the closed marriage is envisioned in terms of fidelity, thus becoming the be-all and end-all of love, instead of being seen in its proper perspective as only one facet of the much larger reality of love. Fidelity in the closed marriage is the measure of *limited* love, *diminished* growth and *conditional* trust. This fixation in the end defeats its own purpose, encouraging deception, sowing the seeds of mistrust and limiting the growth of both partners and so of the love between them.

Fidelity, in its root meaning, denotes allegiance and fealty to a duty or obligation. But love and sex should never be seen in terms of duty or obligation, as they are in closed marriage. They should be seen as experiences to be shared and enjoyed together, as they are in open marriage. Fidelity then is redefined in open marriage, as commitment to your own growth, equal commitment to your partner's growth, and a sharing of the self-discovery accomplished through such growth. It is loyalty and faithfulness to growth, to integrity of self and respect for the other, not to a sexual and psychological bondage to each other.

In an open marriage, in which each partner is secure in his own identity and trusts in the other, new possibilities for additional relationships exist, and open (as opposed to limited) love can expand to include others. Fidelity does not have to be interpreted within the narrow context of closed marriage, in which you are suspected of possible infidelity every time you show an interest in someone of the opposite sex other than your mate. In open marriage, you can come to know, enjoy and share comradeship with others of the opposite sex beside your mate. These relationships enhance and augment the marital relationship of the open couple in turn.

These outside relationships may, of course, include sex. That is completely up to the partners involved. If partners in an open marriage do have outside sexual relationships, it is on the basis of their own internal relationship—that is, because they have experienced mature love, have real trust, and are able to expand themselves, to love and enjoy others and to bring that love and pleasure back into their marriage, without jealousy.

We are not recommending outside sex, but we are not saying that it should be avoided, either. The choice is entirely up to you, and can be made only upon your own knowledge of the degree to which you have achieved, within your marriage, the trust, identity, and open communication necessary to the eradication of jealousy. Outside sexual experiences when they are in the context of a meaningful relationship may be rewarding and beneficial to an open marriage. But such relationships are not necessarily an integral part of open marriage. It is another option that you may or may not choose to explore. Open marriage is called open for that very reason: the options are there for you to take or leave according to your individual decision.

To have an extramarital affair without first developing yourself to the point where you are ready, and your mate is ready, for such a step could be detrimental to the possibility of developing a true open marriage. You must do more than simply grasp the idea of fidelity as a commitment to growth; you must put that idea into effect in your marriage. Freedom in open marriage does not mean freedom to "do your thing" without responsibility. It is the freedom to grow to the capacity of your individual potential through love—and one aspect of that love is caring for your partner's growth and welfare as much as your own.

We would go further, in fact. If outside companionships *are* to be more than casual ones, and might involve sex, then those relationships too should be approached with the same fidelity to mutual growth, and with the same measure of respect that you would show your partner in open marriage. You must be honest in your extramarital relationships as well. If you are not, the deception you practice outside your marriage will eventually seep back into the marriage itself.

The considerations developed by Sam and Joan in regard to outside relationships, which we mentioned in our chapter on open companionship, reflect the necessary honesty, concern and consideration for everyone involved. When you have developed a relationship of trust and honesty in your own marriage, and are able to enjoy outside relationships, care and concern for *everyone* involved becomes a primary consideration. Often, although not always, such outside relationships eventually come to involve the other mate (or mates, if two open couples should meet through one partner from each marriage). Sharing then becomes threefold or fourfold—not necessarily sexually, at all, but in terms of friendship and open sharing.

We believe that if you achieve an open marriage, your marital relationship will be more vital, more fulfilling, and that you will be continually growing and discovering. Under those circumstances it would be only natural that you should wish to expand the circle of your love, to develop additional relationships in an open way, with or without sex. And that additional sharing can in turn make your marriage a still deeper, richer, more vital experience. Once you have achieved a true sharing within your marriage, there are no limits on its further development.

17 Synergy: Couple Power through Person Power

A Dynamic Process

Open marriage is not just a matter of a new freedom for marriage partners, for its true goal is the mutual growth that such freedom fosters. If the guidelines are followed, open marriage will become an on-going process, open-ended, and not just a new state of being. The key to putting all the guidelines together, and to understanding open marriage as a dynamic process, is the concept of *synergy*.

Synergy is a word for the dynamic process that occurs when the combined action of two things produces a more beneficial and greater effect or result than the sum of their separate individual actions. It is a process by which the whole becomes more than the sum of the parts, while at the same time those parts retain their individuality. You can move a calf or thigh muscle separately, for instance, but when you move them together you can walk or dance or run. But as you walk, the separateness of the calf and the thigh muscle is retained. This is quite different from what happens when you bake a cake; here, too, you end up with something that is more than the sum of the flour, sugar, eggs, and other ingredients in it—but each element has lost its identity. They have combined, but in a way that has changed the ingredients into something else. In the true synergic process, a new thing is created without any loss of identity for the original elements that have combined together.

Synergy occurs when two organisms, or people, are brought together, or combined, in such a way that the end result is enhanced—that is, when the combination of the two produces a quality or effect that is more intense than what either of the two contributing parts originally had or could independently attain. Thus in synergy one and one makes three, not just two. It is this special effect, this enhancement, that makes it possible in open marriage for husband and wife to exist and grow as two separate individuals, yet at the same time to transcend their duality and achieve a unity on another level, beyond themselves, a unity that develops out of the love for each other and each other's growth. In a synergistic, cooperative way, each one's individual growth enhances and augments the other's growth, pleasure and fulfillment. The more of a whole person each one becomes, the more self-actualized, the more he has to offer his mate. The better he feels within himself, the more he can love; the more he can give freedom, the more he can take pleasure in seeing his mate grow; the more both partners grow, the more stimulating and dynamic each one becomes for the other.

The Development of the Concept

Functional synergy was first delineated by the pioneering anthropologist, Ruth Benedict, in her comparison of low synergy cultures such as the Dobuans of the South Seas, which were hostile, aggressive and, above all, insecure, with high synergy cultures such as the Zuni of the American southwest, which were secure and cooperative. Dr. Abraham Maslow, whose studies of self-actualizing people we have discussed throughout this book, worked with Ruth Benedict while she was developing this theory, and he applied it to interpersonal relationships. In high synergy societies, Dr. Benedict had found that what was good for the individual in a society was also good for the society as a whole. According to Dr. Benedict, a high synergy society is one ". . . where any act or skill that advantages the individual at the same time advantages the group . . ." Maslow explained his extension of this idea as follows:

". . . if I get more pleasure out of feeding my strawberries into the mouth of my little beloved child, who loves strawberries, and who smacks her lips over them, and I thereby have a wonderful time and enjoy myself watching her eat the strawberries, which would certainly give me pleasure if I myself ate them, then what shall I say about the selfishness or the unselfishness of this act . . . My action is neither selfish exclusively nor unselfish exclusively, or it can be said to be both selfish and unselfish simultaneously . . . That is, what is good for my child is good for me, what is good for me is good for the child, what gives the child pleasure gives me pleasure, what gives me pleasure gives the child pleasure."

It is easy to see how this principle operates between husband and wife: each one enjoys giving the other pleasure in the same way as the parent enjoys his child's pleasure in Maslow's example. It can be understood in a very concrete sense: if the husband gets a raise in salary or achieves an increment in status, his wife and family will benefit. The same result would follow from the wife winning a lottery. But this kind of "what is good for you is good for me" can operate in closed marriage as well as in open marriage. Open marriage, we believe, carries the concept of synergy to an entirely new level of interaction.

Synergic Enhancement

We take the concept of synergy a step further and concentrate on the aspect of mutual enhancement implicit in the definition and meaning of the term synergy. Through the process of augmenting feedback and build-up, in open marriage what is good for you is not only good for me but *better for both of us.*

For husband and wife, all the myriad aspects of their growth become synergic and mutually enhancing. If John enjoys fishing but Sue doesn't, in an open marriage he can nevertheless go out and experience that pleasure in fishing and then return. His pleasure makes him happier, more content, and his wife benefits from his attitude, from his happiness. Happiness breeds happiness through positive feedback—that is the essence of synergy. Sue is happy in seeing John enjoy himself, and thus benefits from his enjoyment of himself. If Sue enjoys reading a particular book, or taking a course of some kind, and gains insight from these activities, she shares her insight with John, and he too benefits, not only from her pleasure or excitement, but perhaps through learning something new as well. She becomes more stimulating, he enjoys her pleasure and becomes in turn stimulated by her excitement—their growth becomes mutually augmenting. We can even see this enhancement effect as a series of steps:

(1) It makes me happy to see you happy.
(2) When I see you happy because I have done something to make you happy (given you a gift, perhaps the gift of freedom), or have done something for us together, I become happier with your happiness.
(3) Through open love and open trust, I am able to take that same pleasure in your happiness even when it is someone or something else that has made you happy.

(4) Your happiness is *further increased* by seeing and knowing that my happiness is augmented and increased by your happiness.

(5) This mutual enhancement effect gives us synergic build-up.

This enhancement theory can be applied at any level of growth, and at any point in the development of your usage of any of the open marriage guidelines. It can take effect in relation to every aspect of your life together, from careers, to sex, to watching a sunset together. Here is a simple model for synergic enhancement:

Transcendence

Synergic interaction → Enhancement → Elation

The elation can come from anticipation, from pure enjoyment, from validation through the partner or another, or from meeting a challenge. This principle of enhancement is exactly the same as the feeling that prompted Frank, whom we quoted in the chapter on Open Companionship, to say that his life was enriched by Janet's outside interests, and that her enjoyment increased his own enjoyment. When couples have eliminated jealousy and competition, when they have achieved identity and equality and have open love and trust in each other, all their actions—both separately and together—become synergic. Each one's experiences build up the other's. This is in direct contrast to the diminished attitude of partners in a closed marriage, the attitude which proclaims "you shouldn't have fun if I can't have just as much fun at the same time"—which is negative diminishing feedback.

A person who uses negative diminishing feedback is a "diminisher"—one who is constantly "putting down" his mate or others. This is a dampening effect, which blots out a mate's enthusiasm, self-esteem and creativity, eventually leading to zero feedback and a static state.

On the other hand, a person who responds to, and relates to others with positive feedback is an "augmenter"—
one who shares and inspires enthusiasm and zest for living
in his mate and others. An "augmenter" is turned on to
himself, and thus turns others on.

Synergic Build-up

Like a chain reaction, synergy once begun builds upon
itself, intensifying and expanding, and as it expands it feeds
back new meaning, new discoveries, new explorations of
self and mate into a self-reinforcing regenerative and growth-
enhancing system that has no limits except those that you
yourself set upon it.

Synergy is the process that allows open marriage to expand. It is more than just positive feedback between partners—it is the utilization of *positive augmenting feedback as
a system for generating further growth*. Each one's growth
augments and builds upon the other's. As a system, augmenting feedback works in all areas: love generates more
love, growth more growth, and knowledge more knowledge.
The more you know, the more you can know. The more information you have, the more easily you are able to understand and absorb still more information—to integrate and
make associations with new information. The more you
know about yourself and about your mate, and the more
you explore your mutual knowledge together, the greater
will be the intimacy into which you can grow. Open and
honest communication thus enhances further communication.

Closed marriage, with its boundaries and restrictions,
operates on a closed energy system. Since love is seen as
limited, so too must growth be limited. Closed marriage
is a matter of linear development, along a predetermined
line on only one level of experience. Open marriage, however, develops like an expanding spiral (see diagram). Closed

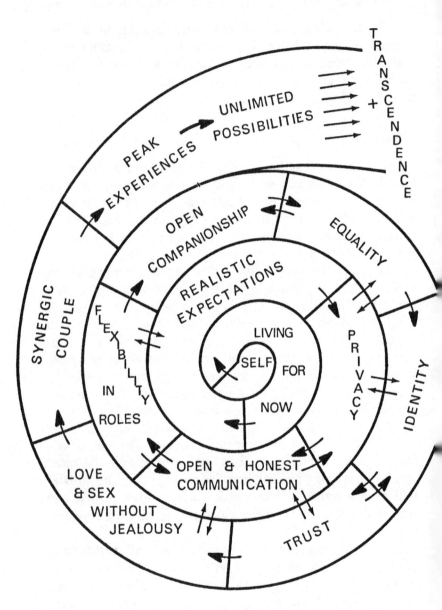

Expanding Spiral of Open Marriage

marriage reduces, bringing diminishment to both husbands and wives. Open marriage is an open energy system, for not only does each partner add to and increase the other's growth, creating new energy, but the partners' individual autonomy allows them to absorb additional energy from outside stimuli which can then be brought back into the marriage.

Open marriage transcends mere togetherness, mere freedom for individual development. It becomes the ultimate in cooperation, a dynamic system that creates, through expanding feedback and growth, a *synergic couple*.

Let us look once more at the contrasts between open and closed marriage:

OPEN MARRIAGE	CLOSED MARRIAGE
dynamic framework	static framework
open to the world	shuts out the world
open to each other	locked together, closed in on one another
spontaneous	calculating
additive	subtractive
creative, expanding	inhibiting, degenerative
infinite potential	limited potential
honesty and truth	deception and game-playing
living in the now	living in the future, or with hang-ups from the past
privacy for self-growth	smothering togetherness
flexibility in roles	rigid role prescriptions
adaptable to change	threatened by change
individual autonomy	possession of the other
personal identity	selfhood subjugated to couplehood
incorporates others—grows through companionship with others	shuts others out—exclusivity limits growth

OPEN MARRIAGE (Cont.)	CLOSED MARRIAGE (Cont.)
equality of stature	unequal status
open trust	conditional and static trust
open love	limited love
an open, expanding energy system	a closed, self-limiting energy system
freedom	bondage

A comparison of the two kinds of marriage points up the matter of choice: closed marriage offers no options, while open marriage is full of them. Closed marriage may offer a phantom security, a measure of static and stable contentment, but it will inevitably stunt growth. Open marriage offers to all of us, to the degree that we want to use it, in whatever way we want to use it, the ability to continually expand our horizons. Knowing and fulfilling yourself along *with* your partner in open marriage instead of *through* your partner, as in closed marriage, becomes a voyage of discovery. Not only is it challenging, but it prepares us to flow with change. It offers you the possibility of elation as opposed to mere contentment.

The kind of elation of which we speak corresponds to what Abraham Maslow has defined as peak experiences—bursts of insight, discovery, the creative moment—unique, intense moments in which a person experiences total absorption in the moment in a state of selflessness, a transcendence of self. Though peak experiences occur only occasionally, they are the high points, the always remembered super-moments of our lives—the moments in which we are most purely and completely ourselves.

When the peak experiences come more frequently, as they can in open marriage, when the synergy that a couple generates is high, then the partners have the capacity to achieve transcendence, to share, to grow, to exist on a new intellectual, emotional and spiritual level.

The peaks are there—you and your mate can ignore

them, can huddle in the narrow valleys, or you can seek them out. You as a couple can be the creators of a new life style for yourself and your mate, you alone can create the possibilities for transcendence.

Notes

Full identification of sources mentioned in the text and in the following notes will be found in the Bibliography.

Chapter 1   Why Save Marriage at All?

PAGE

15: Bierce, p. 86.
17: *alternatives to traditional marriage:* Rimmer, Stoller, Mead (1966). Term contracts were proposed over fifty years ago, Baber, p. 577.
19: The quotation from a *film star* is in an article, "Conversation with Catherine Deneuve," by Edward R. F. Sheehan, *Holiday*, August 1969.
23: *the pair-bond:* Morris (1969).
24: Malinowski's argument appears in Briffault and Malinowski, pp. 40–44.

PAGE

28: The quotation is from "An Answer to the Critics of Companionate Marriage," Lindsey and Evans, p. viii.

31–32: Lawton, pp. 74–75.

33: Montagu (1970).

34: Deutsch; Lundberg and Farnham, p. 142.

35: On the influence of Freud's background and cultural heritage, see McClelland, and Gilman. Robinson, p. 170.

36: Robinson, pp. 157–158.

43–44: Ellis (1965), pp. 53–54.

Chapter 2   Who Has the Open Contract?

50: *"I don't believe in a complementary"*: paraphrased from a statement in an article by Alice Lake, entitled "Two-Career Marriages: How 4 Young Couples Make Theirs Work," in *Glamour*, February 1971.

Chapter 3   Rewriting the Contract

54: Dr. Guze's statement appears in a paper presented at a symposium on the topic: "Marriage—a Death of a Relationship."

Chapter 4   Open vs. Closed Marriage: The Guidelines

72–73: For the survey on marital happiness and children, see Hicks and Platt; quotation appears on p. 569.

Chapter 6   Privacy

91–92: The ethnographic survey mentioned is Murdock.

92: Stephens, pp. 270–278, contains a short comparative survey of cross-cultural differences in togetherness and separateness.

93: *"Some kinds of self-discovery"*: Moustakas (1968), pp. 199–200. For an exploration of the experience of loneliness, its benefits and therapeutic values, see Moustakas (1961).

Chapter 7 Open and Honest Communication: Verbal and Non-verbal

102: Non-verbal communication, and the importance it plays in human interaction, has only recently come into the limelight. Research in this field (today called *kinesics*, or "communication through body motion") has been pioneered by anthropologists, most notable among them, Dr. Ray Birdwhistell. An interesting overview of kinesics, "The Way We Speak 'Body Language,'" by Flora Davis, appeared in *The New York Times Magazine*, May 31, 1970.

106: Sensitivity and encounter groups are not, of course, limited to physical contacts but include a whole spectrum of encounter techniques. See Schutz, Howard, Rogers (1969), or the article, "Human Potential: the Revolution in Feeling," in *Time*, November 9, 1970. For the importance of touch, mothering and love to the healthy development of the human being, see Montagu (1962), pp. 99–112, and (1971), and Bowlby.

Chapter 8 Communication: Self-Disclosure and Feedback

109: The data from the sentence completion test was part of an unpublished pilot study conducted by Dr. David F. Kahn and Dr. Robert Harper at the Merrill-Palmer Institute of Human Development and Family Life. *Mutual analysis:* The kind we are suggesting here is based on disclosures such as those described by Jourard (1968), pp. 93–96, 152–165; and (1964), pp. 59–65 rather than analysis in a psychoanalytic sense or even the "ego-therapy" mentioned by Blood and Wolfe, pp. 175–220.

113: Jourard (1964), pp. 27, 10, 153.

115: We first heard the story of the three umpires in a lecture by Dr. David Kahn at the Human Relations Center of the New School for Social Research.

123: For a description of men's problems in communication, see the chapter entitled, "Some Lethal Aspects of the Male Role," Jourard (1964), pp. 46–55. *duo-.*

logue: taken from a description of Dr. Kaplan's work presented in *Time*, January 24, 1969.

125:   For the application of feedback phenomena and cybernetics to communication theory and networks in human relations see Smith. *completing the communication:* an exercise described by Lederer and Jackson, pp. 277–280.

Chapter 9   Communication: Productive Fighting and Fantasy Sharing

130:   Both quotations are found in Bach and Wyden, pp. 50, 53.

Chapter 10   Role Flexibility: Masculine and Feminine— Which Is What?

138:   On traditional roles see de Beauvoir, Roszak and Roszak and Janeway. For a discussion of crisis rites in the life cycle see Harris, pp. 545–561 and Honigmann, pp. 512–514.

142:   See Vivian Gornick's comments on the fact that "no man is raised to be a husband."

143:   A study of leisure time carried out in fourteen nations concluded that working mothers are "overburdened with work" and that *both* working and non-working mothers have less leisure time than their husbands. "Study Finds Men Freer Than Wives," by Will Lissner, *The New York Times*, March 5, 1967.

143–144: On the relationship of status to role, see Linton, pp. 113–131.

144:   Rossi (1970), p. 271.

145:   For a review of biochemical research and its import for reproduction, see Rosenfeld, pp. 103–186.

147–148: The information on the three groups is from Mead (1968); the quotations, p. 259.

149:   *A recent research report:* Vogel, *et al.*

Chapter 11   Role Flexibility: Role Reversal and Role
Exchange

154: Simple role reversal is a technique used by many
therapists, marriage counselors and others. The full-
scale use of role-playing is found in *psychodrama*, a
therapeutic technique and system developed by Dr.
J. Moreno and described in his book.

156: The article mentioned is entitled "I Am a Househus-
band (But Call Me Mister)," *Redbook*, May 1971.
Quotations on pp. 156 and 157 are from this article.
Another excellent account of switching occupational
roles appears in "Mother Went to Work . . . and
Father Stayed Home," by Jorie Lueloff in *Woman's
Day*, August 1971.

157: "*I like to play with children*": quoted from an article
entitled "From Sweden and Denmark: Experiments
in Marriage," *Life*, August 15, 1969.

157–158: Stress occurs in both the husband's and wife's traditional roles today, but for each role it stems from
different sources. For woman's biological adaptations
to stress see Montagu (1970) and "Man: the Weaker
Sex," by Dr. Estelle Ramey in *McCall's*, January
1971. See also McGrath for factors to be considered
in stress.

158: *broader bases than the nuclear family*: all kinds of
proposals have been made, from state-run nurseries,
day care centers, communal and extended family living, supportive community arrangements and spe-
cially planned housing to replanning the work week
by having husbands and wives work on alternate
days, or each work for only half a day. Suggestions
for change in this area come from such various
sources as Sussman, Mead (1969) and (1971), Toffler, Rimmer, and Rossi (1970). Numerous articles on
change in marriage and family structure appear in
Otto (1970), Farson, *et al.*, and Skolnick and Skolnick.

161–162: Morris (1970), p. 226.

162: Morris (1970), p. 227. Berne summarized his philos-

ophy as follows: "Losers say 'But' and 'If only.' 'Yes'
and 'No' are all a winner needs, along with 'Wow' to
express the healthy childlike wonder in all of us," in
an article by Jack Fincher, "Psychiatrist in the Chips,"
Life, August 12, 1966.

163–164: Gibb, p. 160.

Chapter 12   Open Companionship

166: *"fantastic notion"*: Birdwhistell, p. 212.

169: Maslow (1968a), p. 205.

171: The data on the Babchuk study is from an article by
Norman M. Lobenz on the topic of marital friend-
ships entitled, "The Unexpected Conflict That Upsets
New Marriages," *Redbook*, May 1968.

172: *"central paranoia"*: Pearce and Newton, *passim*. In a
paper delivered at the New School for Social Research
on March 4, 1968, Dr. Pearce elaborated on this
concept and its relationship to validation in the
years beyond infancy.

172–173: *"It is the natural and constructive"*: Pearce and Newton, p. 220.

173: On the consequences of continuing in exclusivity,
Philip Slater (1968), pp. 89–90 comments: ". . . one
would anticipate that the greater burden placed on
the marital bond by the reduction of alternative intimate and enduring relationships would increase marital discord . . . As emotional alternatives are removed,
its [the relationship's] limitations become less and less
tolerable."

181: On proposals for intimate networks of families, see
Stoller.

Chapter 13   Equality

187: Satir, p. 63.

190: Lederer and Jackson, p. 272. These authors, whose
book is so excellent in many other ways, have applied
the systems concept (and a closed one, at that) too
vigorously to marriage, which leads to an overempha-

sis on the "something for something" (*quid pro quo*) process.

195: Slater (1970), p. 76.

196: de Rham, pp. 116–117.

197: Although over 40 percent of married women and "a record 43% of all U.S. women—32 million strong—are in the nation's labor force," (see *Time*, July 26, 1971) they do not receive commensurate pay with men occupying the same jobs.

198: Many women are *still* not aware of the legal rights they lose in marriage. For some suggestions on how to make them aware, see an article by Enid Nemy, "Almost All Agree—Women Marrying Should Know Their Rights," *The New York Times*, August 10, 1970.

198–199: On the language of inequality see Richard Gilman's comment in "Where Did It All Go Wrong?" *Life*, August 13, 1971, and an amusing account of solutions and problems in equalizing it in "Is It Possible for a Women to Manhandle the King's English?" by Israel Shenker, *The New York Times*, August 29, 1971.

200: Dr. Steinmann's extensive research points out significant discrepancies between men's and women's perceptions of their own and each other's roles. Her book on this research, *The Male Dilemma*, co-authored with Dr. David J. Fox, is soon to be published.

202: *peer-bonding:* Dr. James Ramey, personal communication. See Turney-High, p. 291, on the equality possible in a dyadic relationship.

203: For a discussion of status congruency and its effects see Homans, p. 264, and Secord and Backman, pp. 383–386.

Chapter 14 Identity

209: Slater (1970), p. 74.

210–211: Dr. Rubin's quote appeared in his article, "What Makes a Woman Lovable?" in the *Ladies' Home Journal*, June 1969.

211: *NIMH statistics:* From 1950 through 1968, 223.268 more women than men were hospitalized in state and county mental hospitals. From 1964 through 1968:

125,351 more women than men were treated on an out-patient basis. This data is drawn from an article by Dr. Phyllis Chesler. *the same feminine "nature":* see Rossi (1971) for a short review of Mead and Newton's and Niles Newton's important cross-cultural and experimental research on childbirth.

212: On identity formation see Erikson (1963), and identity as an on-going process, Rogers (1961).

214: Erikson (1963), p. 263.

215: Maslow (1954), p. 214. For a full description of the self-actualized person, see Maslow (1954), pp. 199–260; (1968a); and (1970a), pp. 119–136. *"an affirmation of":* Maslow (1954), pp. 252–253.

217: Maslow (1968a), pp. 105, 97.

218: *Change must be perceived:* for an excellent treatment of this topic, see Wheelis. Rogers (1961), p. 21. His italics are omitted here.

220: The idea of sustaining themes is partially adapted from Gerald Sykes's use of "sustaining myths" in his course at The New School for Social Research. We feel that "themes" is a more practical term and closer to reality than "myths."

Chapter 15 Trust

227: Lederer and Jackson, pp. 106–113, *do* discuss trust in their book. The authors state that "the word 'trust' originally came from the Scandinavian language and meant 'to comfort,' 'to console,' 'to confide in.'" They conclude that their conception of trust in marriage, based on this Scandinavian meaning, "supplies the best definition we know for a workable marriage."

233: Erikson (1968), pp. 82–83.

234: The quoted definition of trust is from a conversation with Robert C. Snyder, consultant on human development and effective learning management, and former president of Language Laboratories.

Chapter 16 Love and Sex without Jealousy

239–240: *In many societies:* see Linton, pp. 136–137 and Stephens, pp. 44–49, 206–207. Additional sources and an analysis of jealousy in relation to American marriage in Ellis (1962), pp. 138–162.

241: The distinction between feeling and emotion and the concept of "energy in motion" are based on discussions with Dr. Harry A. Royson.

242: On the irrationality and "abnormalities" of romantic love in our culture, see Linton, p. 175; Putney and Putney, pp. 106–125. For a comprehensive treatment of love in the Western world, see Hunt.

243: Courts of Love rules: Langdon–Davies, pp. 266–267.

244: Maslow (1965), p. 92. In this same source, pp. 88–107, Maslow develops the idea of synergic unlimited good versus antisynergic limited good. *One marriage text after another:* Udry, pp. 485–493; Blood, pp. 415–424. Also, see Hicks and Platt.

245: *Other partners in sex:* see Stephens, pp. 251–256; Marshall and Suggs; Spencer; Ford and Beach, pp. 106–124; and Neubeck, pp. 108–128. *Plural marriage:* see Ford and Beach, p. 107; Murdock, p. 686, found in his survey of 554 societies that 415 favored polygyny, 135 monogamy, and 4, polyandry. *sexually monogamous:* see Fox.

246: Ellis (1962), p. 148. For changing viewpoints on the sexual exclusivity of monogamy see Neubeck, Roy, Mazur, Kirkendall and Whitehurst, and Otto (1970).

247: May (1969b), p. 63.

249: Maslow (1954), p. 257. May (1969a), p. 311.

250: For a sociological analysis of how our sexual behavior is scripted (and one which flatly rejects Freudian sex drive theory), see Simon and Gagnon.

254: Maslow (1954), pp. 251–252. *"We cannot possess pleasure":* from an article entitled "What Sex Means in a Happy Marriage," by Dr. Alexander M. Lowen and Robert J. Levin in *Redbook,* June 1968.

255: *therapy program:* Masters and Johnson (1970).

Chapter 17 Synergy

261–262: *Functional synergy:* Although Benedict's original manuscript on synergy, written in 1941, was lost, portions of it were previously recorded by John Honigmann, and have since been edited by him and Maslow and published in two sources: see Benedict, and Maslow and Honigmann.

262:   For Maslow's application of synergy to interpersonal relations, see Maslow (1968b) and (1965). Benedict's quotation appears in Maslow and Honigmann, p. 325. Maslow (1965) pp. 88–89.

265:   *positive augmenting feedback:* this concept is analogous to *resonance* in physics—when two sound waves, alternating currents, or other vibrating energy systems attain the same frequency (timing of vibrations), the magnitude of the resulting vibration or release of energy greatly exceeds the sum of their individual forces.

268:   For a description of peak experiences see Maslow (1968a), pp. 71–114, and (1970b). In the new preface, Maslow (1970b) alludes to the differences between peak experiences and high plateau experiences where "one can *stay* 'turned on.'"

Bibliography

Baber, Ray E. *Marriage and the Family.* New York: McGraw-Hill Book Company, Inc., 1953.

Bach, George R., and Peter Wyden. *The Intimate Enemy.* New York: William Morrow and Company, Inc., 1969.

Benedict, Ruth. "Patterns of the Good Culture." *Psychology Today,* June 1970.

Berne, Eric. *Games People Play.* New York: Grove Press, 1964.

Bierce, Ambrose. *The Devil's Dictionary.* New York: Dover Publications, Inc., 1958.

Birdwhistell, Ray L. "The American Family: Some Perspectives." *Psychiatry,* August 1966 (vol. 29).

Blood, Robert O., Jr. *Marriage.* New York: The Free Press of Glencoe, 1962.

Blood, Robert O., Jr., and Donald M. Wolfe. *Husbands and Wives.* New York: The Free Press, 1965.

Bowlby, John. *Attachment.* New York: Basic Books, Inc., 1969.

Brecher, Ruth and Edward, eds. *An Analysis of Human Sexual Response*. New York: The New American Library, 1966.

Briffault, Robert, and Bronislaw Malinowski. *Marriage: Past and Present*. Edited with an Intro. by M. F. Ashley Montagu. Boston: Porter Sargent, 1956.

Bugental, James F. T., ed. *Challenges of Humanistic Psychology*. New York: McGraw-Hill Book Company, Inc., 1967.

Chesler, Phyllis. "Men Drive Women Crazy." *Psychology Today*, July 1971.

Cuber, John F., with Peggy B. Harroff. *Sex and the Significant Americans*. Baltimore: Penguin Books, 1966.

de Beauvoir, Simone. *The Second Sex*. New York: Bantam Books, 1961.

de Rham, Edith. *The Love Fraud*. New York: Pegasus, 1965.

Deutsch, Helene. *The Psychology of Women*. 2 vols. New York: Grune and Stratton, 1944.

Ellis (1962), Albert. *The American Sexual Tragedy*. New York: Grove Press, Inc., 1962.

Ellis (1965), Albert. *The Art and Science of Love*. New York: Lyle Stuart, 1965.

Erikson (1963), Erik H. *Childhood and Society*, 2nd ed. New York: W. W. Norton & Company, Inc., 1963.

Erikson (1968), Erik H. *Identity, Youth and Crisis*. New York: W. W. Norton & Company, Inc., 1968.

Farson, Richard E., Philip M. Hauser, Herbert Stroup and Anthony J. Wiener. *The Future of the Family*. New York: Family Service Association of America, 1969.

Ford, Clellan S., and Frank A. Beach. *Patterns of Sexual Behavior*. New York: Harper & Brothers, 1951.

Fox, Robin. "The Evolution of Human Sexual Behavior." *The New York Times Magazine*, March 24, 1968.

Friedan, Betty. *The Feminine Mystique*. New York: Dell Publishing Co., Inc., 1964.

Gibb, Jack R. "Group Experiences and Human Possibilities." In Otto (1968).

Gilman, Richard. "The FemLib Case Against Sigmund Freud." *The New York Times Magazine*, January 31, 1971.

Ginott, Haim G. *Between Parent and Child*. New York: The Macmillan Company, 1965.

Gornick, Vivian. "The Next Great Moment in History Is Theirs." *The Village Voice,* November 27, 1969.

Graves, Clare. "Levels of Existence: an Open System Theory of Values." *Journal of Humanistic Psychology,* Fall 1970 (vol. 10).

Guze, Henry. "Marriage—The Death of a Relationship." Mimeographed outline. Summary of presentation at March 1970 joint meeting of the New Jersey Psychological Association and the New Jersey Neuropsychiatric Association, East Orange, New Jersey.

Harris, Marvin. *Culture, Man, and Nature.* New York: Thomas Y. Crowell, 1971.

Hicks, Mary W., and Marilyn Platt, "Marital Happiness and Stability: A Review of the Research in the 60's." *Journal of Marriage and the Family,* November 1970.

Homans, George C. *Social Behavior: Its Elementary Forms.* New York: Harcourt, Brace & World, 1961.

Honigman, John. *The World of Man.* New York: Harper & Brothers, 1959.

Howard, Jane. *Please Touch.* New York: McGraw-Hill, 1970.

Hunt, Morton M. *The Natural History of Love.* New York: Alfred A. Knopf, 1959.

Janeway, Elizabeth. *Man's World, Woman's Place.* New York: William Morrow and Company, Inc., 1971.

Jourard (1964), Sidney M. *The Transparent Self.* Princeton, N.J.: D. Van Nostrand Company, Inc., 1964.

Jourard (1968), Sidney M. *Disclosing Man to Himself.* Princeton, N.J.: D. Van Nostrand Company, Inc., 1968.

Kinsey (1948), Alfred C., Wardell B. Pomeroy, and Clyde E. Martin. *Sexual Behavior in the Human Male.* Philadelphia: W. B. Saunders Company, 1948.

Kinsey (1953), Alfred C., Wardell B. Pomeroy, Clyde E. Martin, and Paul H. Gebhard. *Sexual Behavior in the Human Female.* Philadelphia: W. B. Saunders Company, 1953.

Kirkendall, Lester A., and Robert N. Whitehurst, eds. *The New Sexual Revolution.* New York: Donald W. Brown, Inc., 1971.

Langdon-Davies, John. *A Short History of Women.* New York: Literary Guild of America, 1927.

Lawton, George. "Emotional Maturity in Wives." In Fairchild,

Johnson E., ed. *Women, Society and Sex.* New York: Fawcett Publications, Inc., 1962.

Lederer, William J., and Don D. Jackson. *The Mirages of Marriage.* New York: W. W. Norton & Company, Inc., 1968.

Lindbergh, Anne Morrow. *Gift From the Sea.* New York: The New American Library, 1957.

Lindsey, Judge Ben B., and Wainwright Evans. *The Companionate Marriage.* Garden City, N.Y.: Garden City Publishing Co., Inc., 1929.

Linton, Ralph. *The Study of Man.* New York: D. Appleton-Century Company, Inc., 1936.

Lundberg, Ferdinand, and Marynia Farnham. *Modern Woman: The Lost Sex.* New York: Grosset & Dunlap, 1947.

Marshall, Donald S., and Robert C. Suggs, *Human Sexual Behavior.* New York: Basic Books, Inc., 1971.

Maslow (1954), A. H. *Motivation and Personality.* New York: Harper & Row, 1954.

Maslow (1965), Abraham H. *Eupsychian Management.* Homewood, Illinois: Richard D. Irwin, Inc., 1965.

Maslow (1968a), Abraham H. *Toward a Psychology of Being.* 2nd ed. Princeton, N.J.: D. Van Nostrand Company, Inc., 1968.

Maslow (1968b), Abraham H. "Human Potentialities and the Healthy Society." In Otto (1968).

Maslow (1970a), Abraham H. "Psychological Data and Value Theory." In Maslow, Abraham H., ed. *New Knowledge in Human Values.* Chicago: Henry Regnery Company, 1970.

Maslow (1970b), Abraham H. *Religion, Values and Peak Experiences.* New York: The Viking Press, 1970.

Maslow, Abraham H., and John J. Honigmann, eds. "Synergy: Some Notes of Ruth Benedict." *American Anthropologist,* April 1970 (vol. 72).

Masters (1966), William H., and Virginia E. Johnson. *Human Sexual Response.* Boston: Little, Brown and Company, 1966.

Masters (1970), William H., and Virginia E. Johnson. *Human Sexual Inadequacy.* Boston: Little, Brown and Company, 1970.

May (1969a), Rollo. *Love and Will.* New York: W. W. Norton & Company, Inc., 1969.

May (1969b), Rollo. "Love and Will." *Psychology Today*, August 1969.

Mazur, Ronald Michael. *Commonsense Sex*. Boston: Beacon Press, 1968.

McClelland, David. "Psychoanalysis and Religious Mysticism." In McClelland, David, *The Roots of Consciousness*. Princeton, N.J.: D. Van Nostrand Company, Inc., 1964.

McGrath, Joseph E., ed. *Social and Psychological Factors in Stress*. New York: Holt, Rinehart and Winston, Inc., 1970.

Mead (1966), Margaret. "Marriage in Two Steps," *Redbook*, July 1966.

Mead (1968), Margaret. *Sex and Temperament in Three Primitive Societies*. New York: Dell Publishing Company, Inc., 1968.

Mead (1969), Margaret. "The Life Cycle and Its Variations: the Division of Roles." In Bell, Daniel, ed. *Toward the Year 2000: Work in Progress*. Boston: Beacon Press, 1969.

Mead (1971), Margaret. "The Future of the Family." *Barnard Alumnae Magazine*, Winter 1971.

Montagu (1962), Ashley. *The Humanization of Man*. New York: Grove Press, 1962.

Montagu (1970), Ashley. *The Natural Superiority of Women*. rev. ed. New York: Collier Books, 1970.

Montagu (1971), Ashley. *Touch: The Human Significance of the Skin*. New York: Columbia University Press, 1971.

Moreno, J. *Psychodrama*. New York: Beacon House, 1946.

Morris (1969), Desmond. *The Naked Ape*. New York: Dell Publishing Co., Inc., 1969.

Morris (1970), Desmond. *The Human Zoo*. New York: Dell Publishing Co., Inc., 1970.

Moustakas (1961), Clark. *Loneliness*. New York: Prentice-Hall, Inc., 1961.

Moustakas (1968), Clark. "The Challenge of Growth: Loneliness or Encounter?" In Otto (1968).

Murdock George P., "World Ethnographic Sample." *American Anthropologist*, 1957 (vol. 59).

Neubeck, Gerhard, ed. *Extramarital Relations*. Englewood Cliffs, N.J.: Prentice-Hall, Inc., 1969.

Otto (1968), Herbert A., ed. *Human Potentialities*. St. Louis, Missouri: Warren H. Green, Inc., 1968.

Otto (1970), Herbert A., ed. *The Family in Search of a Future.* New York: Appleton-Century-Crofts, 1970.

Pearce, Jane, and Saul Newton. *The Conditions of Human Growth.* New York: Citadel Press, 1969.

Perls, Frederick S. *Gestalt Therapy Verbatim.* Lafayette, California: Real People Press, 1969.

Putney, Snell, and Gail J. Putney. *The Adjusted American: Normal Neuroses in the Individual and Society.* New York: Harper & Row, 1966.

Rimmer, Robert H. *Proposition 31.* New York: The New American Library, 1969.

Robinson, Marie N. *The Power of Sexual Surrender.* New York: New American Library, 1962.

Rogers (1961), Carl R. *On Becoming a Person.* Boston: Houghton Mifflin Company, 1961.

Rogers (1969), Carl R. "The Group Comes of Age." *Psychology Today,* December 1969.

Rosenfeld, Albert. *The Second Genesis.* Englewood Cliffs, N.J.: Prentice-Hall, Inc., 1969.

Rossi (1970), Alice. "Equality Between the Sexes: an Immodest Proposal." In Baresh, Mayer, and Alice Scourby, eds. *Marriage and the Family.* New York: Random House, 1970.

Rossi (1971), Alice. "Maternalism, Sexuality and the New Feminism." Mimeographed. Delivered at February 1971 meeting of The American Psychopathological Association in New York.

Roszak, Theodore, and Betty Roszak, eds. *Masculine/Feminine.* New York: Harper & Row, 1969.

Roy, Rustum and Della. *Honest Sex.* New York: The New American Library, 1969.

Satir, Virginia. "Marriage as a Human-actualizing Contract." In Otto (1970).

Schutz, William C. *Joy.* New York: Grove Press, 1967.

Secord, Paul F., and Carl W. Backman. *Social Psychology.* New York: McGraw-Hill Book Company, 1964.

Shostrom, Everett, and James Kavanaugh. *Between Man and Woman.* Los Angeles: Nash Publishing, 1971.

Simon, William, and John Gagnon, "Psychosexual Development." *Trans-action,* March 1969.

Skolnick, Arlene S., and Jerome H. Skolnick, eds. *Family in Transition*. Boston: Little, Brown and Company, 1971.

Slater (1968), Philip E. "Some Social Consequences of Temporary Systems." In Bennis, Warren G., and Philip E. Slater. *The Temporary Society*. New York: Harper & Row, 1968.

Slater (1970), Philip E. *The Pursuit of Loneliness: American Culture at the Breaking Point*. Boston: Beacon Press, 1970.

Smith, Alfred G., ed. *Communication and Culture*. New York: Holt, Rinehart and Winston, 1966.

Spencer, Robert F. "Spouse-exchange Among the North Alaskan Eskimo." In Bohannan, Paul, and John Middleton, eds. *Marriage, Family and Residence*. Garden City, N.Y.: The Natural History Press, 1968.

Stephens, William N. *The Family in Cross-cultural Perspective*. New York: Holt, Rinehart and Winston, Inc., 1963.

Stoller, Frederick H. "The Intimate Network of Families as a New Structure." In Otto (1970).

Sussman, Marvin B. "The Experimental Creation of Family Environments." Paper delivered at The Groves Conference on Marriage and the Family, May 8, 1971, in Puerto Rico.

Toffler, Alvin. *Future Shock*. New York: Bantam Books, Inc., 1971.

Turney-High, Harry Holbert. *Man and System*. New York: Appleton-Century-Crofts, 1968.

Udry, J. Richard. *The Social Context of Marriage*. Philadelphia: J. B. Lippincott Co., 1966.

Susan Vogel, Inga K. Broverman, Donald M. Broverman, Frank E. Clarkson, and Paul S. Rosenkrantz, "Maternal Employment and Perception of Sex Roles Among College Students." *Developmental Psychology*, November 1970 (vol. 3).

Wheelis, Allen. "How People Change." *Commentary*, May 1969.

Research and Related Works on Open Marriage: A Selected List Since Publication

Adams, J. R., and Rubin, A. M. "Outcomes of Sexually Open Marriage: A Five-Year Follow-up." Unpublished manuscript. Department of Home Economics, Brooklyn College, Brooklyn, N.Y., 1983.

Blumstein, P., and Schwartz, P. *American Couples*. New York: William Morrow and Co., 1983. See chapter on nonmonogamy and pages 582–87.

Buunk, B. "Sexually Open Marriages: Ground Rules for Countering Potential Threats to Marriage." *Alternative Life-Styles* 3 (1980): 312–28.

Clanton, G., and Smith, L. G., eds. *Jealousy*. Englewood Cliffs, N.J.: Prentice-Hall, 1977.

Felton, J. "A Psychoanalytic Perspective on Sexually Open Marriage." *The Psychoanalytic Review*, in press (1984).

Hymer, S. M., and Rubin, A. M. "Alternative Life-Style Clients:

Therapists' Attitudes and Clinical Experiences." *Small Group Behavior* 13 (1982): 532–41.

Knapp, J. J. (1975). "Some Non-Monogamous Marriage Styles and Related Family Attitudes and Practices of Marriage Counselors." *The Family Coordinator* 24 (1975): 505–14.

Knapp, J. J. (1976). "An Exploratory Study of Seventeen Open Marriages." *Journal of Sex Research* 12 (1976): 206–19.

Knapp, J. J. (1977), and Whitehurst, R. N. "Sexually Open Marriage and Relationships: Issues and Prospects." In *Marriage and Alternatives: Exploring Intimate Relationships*, edited by R. W. Libby and R. N. Whitehurst. Glenview, Ill.: Scott, Foresman, 1977, 147–60.

Libby, R. W., and Whitehurst, R. N., eds. *Marriage and Alternatives: Exploring Intimate Relationships*. Glenview, Ill.: Scott, Foresman, 1977.

Lobell, J., and Lobell, M. *John and Mimi: A Free Marriage*. New York: St. Martin's Press, 1972.

Maklin, E. "Nontraditional Family Forms: A Decade of Research." *Journal of Marriage and the Family* 42 (1980): 906–22.

Mazur, R. *The New Intimacy: Open-Ended Marriage and Alternative Life-Styles*. Boston: Beacon Press, 1973.

Neubeck, G. "Maintenance of Open Marriage." Pilot study. Department of Family Social Science, University of Minnesota, Saint Paul, Minn., 1978.

O'Neill, N., and O'Neill, G. (1972). "Open Marriage: A Synergic Model." *The Family Coordinator* 21 (1972): 403–9.

O'Neill, N., and O'Neill, G. (1973). "Open Marriage: Implications for Human Service Systems." *The Family Coordinator* 22 (1973): 449–56.

Ramey, J. W. (1972). "Emerging Patterns of Innovative Behavior in Marriage." *The Family Coordinator* 21 (1972): 435–56.

Ramey, J. W. (1975). "Intimate Groups and Networks: Frequent Consequences of Sexually Open Marriage." *The Family Coordinator* 24 (1975): 515–30.

Ramey, J. W. (1976). *Intimate Friendships*. Englewood Cliffs, N.J.: Prentice-Hall, 1976.

Rejals, K., and Foster, D. "Open Marriage: A Question of Ego Development and Marriage Counseling." *The Family Coordinator* 25 (1976) 297–302.

Rubin, A. "Sexually Open Versus Sexually Exclusive Marriage: A Comparison of Dyadic Adjustment." *Alternative Life-Styles* 5 (1982): 101–9.

Smith, J. R., and Smith, L. G., eds. *Beyond Monogamy*, Baltimore: Johns Hopkins Press, 1974.

Vaughn, J., and Vaughn, P. *Beyond Affairs*. New York: Bantam, 1981.

Wachowiak, F., and Bragg, H. "Open Marriage and Marital Adjustment." *Journal of Marriage and the Family* 42 (1980): 57–62.

Watson, M. A. "Sexually Open Marriage: Three Perspectives." *Alternative Life-Styles* 4 (1981): 3–21.

Watson, M. A., and Whitlock, F. *Breaking the Bonds: The Realities of Sexually Open Relationships*. Denver, Colo.: Tudor House Press, 1982.

Weis, D. L. "Open Marriage and Multilateral Relationships: The Emergence of Non-Exclusive Models of the Marital Relationship." Paper presented at the Annual Meeting of the Groves Conference on Marriage and the Family, May 28–29, 1981.

ABOUT THE AUTHORS

Nena O'Neill is an anthropologist and is well known as a lecturer and social commentator on television and radio. She is the author of *The Marriage Premise* and numerous articles, and co-author of *Shifting Gears*. She received her B.A. from Barnard College and has done extensive graduate work and research. Her late husband, George O'Neill, received his Ph.D. from Columbia University and was a professor of anthropology at the City College of New York for eighteen years. The O'Neills were married for thirty-five years and lived and worked together until George's death. Nena O'Neill continues her writing and research.